A VILLAGE in ASTURIAS

Printed by   Hobbs the Printers Ltd.,
                 Brunel Road,
                 Totton,
                 Hants SO40 3WX

ISBN   0 902 793 40 3

Front cover illustration: A pair of oxen. © Donald Tayler.

Back cover illustration: A village thoroughfare. © Donald Tayler.

A VILLAGE in ASTURIAS

DONALD TAYLER

PITT RIVERS MUSEUM, UNIVERSITY OF OXFORD
Monograph No. 8

I have nothing to say against the Asturians ... and though we must have our wits about us in their country, I have heard we may travel from one end of it to the other without the slightest fear of being robbed or ill-treated (a Galician's comment).

Well, I had curiosity, so I sat myself down at the table too, without asking leave. Why should I? I was in my own house, and an Asturian is fit company for a king, and is often of better blood (an inn-keeper).

George Borrow *The Bible in Spain* (1843)

For Laura and Emmy

Contents

Illustrations

Plates

(All photographs © Donald Tayler)

Preface

Como dato las palabras de liciendo Herrera, Profesor de Alcalá que encarece la necesidad de lanzarse a predicar por la 'montana fragosa' donde las gentes están tan llenas de ignorancia y superstición que 'dan ganas de llorar los errores que tienen' y prosigue: 'No hay Indias donde vuestras mercedes van por tantos peligros de agua y otras miserias que tengan mas necesidad de entender la palabra de Diós que estas Asturias' (José Arduengo Caso: La Religión de los Asturianos).

At that time (the seventeenth century) the words of licenciate Herrera, Professor of Alcalá, stressed the need to undertake to preach to the 'craggy mountains' where the people are so full of ignorance and superstition that their mistakes make one want to weep and he continued: 'There are no Indies where your worships go through such dangerous waters and other misfortunes where it is more necessary to understand the word of God than in this Asturias'.

It was in the early summer of 1957, whilst journeying southwards, that I first caught sight of Celtic Cantabria. Returning some six years later on my way to an Americanist conference in Seville, I was again reminded of this green and forested land of rugged mountains, bears and wolves and my earlier desire to one day live for a while among these most unusual people. And so it was that I spent several weeks in the summer of 1977 walking and busing around western Asturias, visiting villages, helping with the hay harvest, drinking cider and trying to grasp an almost incomprehensible dialect. It was in a bookshop in Oviedo that I came across Arduengo's book and the passage I have quoted. It seemed that, like the Amerindians I had been working with over past years, the Asturians too stood accused of some crime and I found their independence of spirit and proud defiance, even after the passing of centuries, strangely familiar and compatible. Thus it was that the following year I brought my family with me, we found Alcedo and the rest is written here.

I would like to take this opportunity to thank the Faculty Board of Anthropology and Geography here in Oxford for granting me sabbatical leave in 1978-79 for my fieldwork in Asturias; again in 1988-89 to enable me to make a return visit to the village and to write up this text as it now stands; and for a further term this past Michaelmas to finalise the book. I would also like to thank the former Director of the Pitt Rivers Museum, Dr Schuyler Jones, and the Administrator, Julia Cousins, for their continued support; the Publications Committee of the Museum for allowing me to publish in the Monograph Series; and also Malcolm Osman for producing such excellent prints for the plates.

I wish to acknowledge the kindness of Professor Carmelo Lisón Tolosana in Madrid for furnishing me with letters of credence and for his advice prior to fieldwork. I am also grateful to the following institutions in Oviedo: Archivo de Ayuntamiento, Archivo Historia de la Provincia, Delegación de Hacienda, Servicio de Agricultura de la Deputación Provincial and the Instituto de Estudios Asturianos, for their generous assistance at various times. I would also like to thank Padre Julián of Belmonte for his support and interest and especially our hosts and neighbours in the village—among whom I would like to mention everyone but cannot—for their friendship. They in one way or another made our life in Alcedo a time never to be forgotten.

I would like to thank Linda Mowat, who has done far more than any editor should ever be expected to do. She has rectified my faulty syntax and idiosyncratic Spanish, made many helpful textual comments and produced camera ready copy and cover design in record time. To her I owe a great debt, as I do to my wife Ione who has read the text through numerous times, made so many helpful suggestions and reminded me of incidents which time has eroded from my mind and which my diaries failed to record. She also staunchly worked with me in the village, coping with the bitter cold of winter and making friends wherever she went, as indeed did my two daughters, aged three and six at the time. Without them I do not think our hosts would have tolerated our presence for long. As it was they made a wonderful contribution to our lives and won the hearts of villagers young and old.

As for Alcedans, I could not do other than call them by their proper village name, a name of which they are justly proud, though I have changed the names of individuals within the community. I can only hope they will not mind this transgression on my part. I have not consulted them about the final draft of the book. At the time of my research I indicated that my interests lay in their technology, their farming practices and village life; as things have transpired these interests have become history in the intervening time, for what is recorded here happened twenty or more years ago. Many of the older generation who were so generous with their time and reminiscences have now passed on, while the younger generation have seen many changes which were already being implemented ten years ago when we were last in the village. However, I hope this account, should it be translated one day into Spanish, will not be too unfamiliar to them and I can only hope that by what I have written I have caused no one offence, as this was the last thing I wished to do. My admiration and affection for these remarkable people must be all too apparent in the pages which follow.

February 1998

Plate 1 The village and *tierras*

Introduction

Si no fuera la neblina y las espinas
Era mejor tierra Asturias que Castilla.

If it were not for the mists and the prickles
Asturias would be a better country than Castile.

Whether this saying is heard beyond the confines of Asturias I do not know, but it is certainly apt and well known to the villagers of Alcedo, who regard their green and mountainous country as infinitely more beautiful than the dry flatlands of Castile. Gorse and thorn (*espinas*) are a significant part of the moorland scene; while the village itself lies below the vast Sierra Manteca, equally prickly with its craggy peaks and outcrops. As for the *neblina* (mist), whether rolling up the deep valleys from the north and the Atlantic or as piling high cumulus from the south and the plains of Castile, it frequently envelops the little village with mist and deluges it with rain, or heralds days of unabated gales from the west. In winter deep snow and bitter cold winds drive the wolves down from the heights to scavenge around the houses in search of food; while in summer, when the sun breaks through the cloud in time for the harvest, it is with that penetrating heat peculiar to a clear atmosphere at high altitude. It was on just such a day of brilliant sunshine, in mid-July 1978, that we first climbed up the narrow winding road through the thick chestnut woods and came upon Alcedo.

Later, seen from the lower slopes of Manteca, the village appeared to stretch like a speckled red, white and grey ribbon along the spine of a southward rising ridge, and from various viewpoints it always presented different conformations, so that it scarcely seemed recognisable as the same place.

Viewed from the sharply rising ground to the south, all the houses with their barns and granaries appeared to be literally piled on top of one another, as if every bit of space on the narrow ridge had been utilised except for a grassy knoll to the north of the village 'centre' where four cart-tracks converged. On this knoll a *capilla* or tiny chapel seemed to be set apart, and yet to dominate its surroundings. With its raised bell arch and stark exterior, windowless except for three high slits in the masonry to allow some dim light to penetrate, it proved to be a key redoubt for alternating factions in a village wracked by civil war some forty years earlier.

It was the economy of available space, the close proximity, with each farmstead's buildings juxtaposed with the next and all clustered close to the spine of the ridge which narrowed to a few metres at the centre of the village, that gave Alcedo its peculiar character. Lying to the east like a vast curved theatre and sweeping down to the valley some 200 m below were tiers of tiny cultivated *tierras* or small banked garden plots. To the west of the ridge enclosed fields and meadows plunge precipitously down some 300 m to a deep wooded valley.

Precariously perched, vulnerable to the elements, it seemed a strange situation for a village. Conversely, it was perfectly placed to make maximum use of all the available agricultural land in the area, both arable and meadow. Above the village was a natural spring which provided water to a fountain and communal washhouse at the southern end; and although water from its tank had been piped to each house some years previously, the fountain still acted as a meeting place for the older generation of women. There they could gossip while washing clothes, or pass the time while fetching water when the inadequate domestic plumbing failed during the drier summer months.

In a sense the chapel and the fountain were not just at opposite ends of the village physically; they also acted as metaphors for religious and social sensibilities: towards the Catholic church on the one hand and the natural world on the other. Around these two physical representations were seventeen farmstead units, with two more half a kilometre away at Tabla along the ridge to the north, as well as a forge, a school house, and a small shop. The shop consisted of the front room of a farm dwelling, itself originally converted from the upper part of a hay barn, and adapted for its present use with a bar-counter and some tables and chairs. The enterprising owner of the farmhouse had opened this shop to coincide with the surfacing of the former earth road to the village, completed some three weeks prior to our arrival. Some ten years earlier this road had replaced a cart-track, now disused, which had been the only means of access to the village and wound its precipitous way down the western side of the ridge to the main valley lying to the north.

There was one car in the village purchased prior to the road improvements, belonging to a young man named Juan. It was considered enterprising and innovative to own a car and to keep it in the village, and so the villagers henceforth rather proudly referred to him as Luís *con coche* or 'Luís with the car'. After the road improvements, two other villagers purchased vehicles and the shopkeeper obtained a pickup van. A decade later when we returned to the village, the number of car owners had multiplied to six.

The new road transformed the village in many ways, some of which were considered more beneficial by the younger inhabitants than the older generation. Outwardly, it was a cause for celebration, but inevitably the advantages it brought were balanced by a gradual decline of village autonomy and traditional customs which even the civil war had not greatly diminished.

In 1978 however, three years after Franco's death, the village was still caught in something of a time warp. We sensed this immediately as, leaving the freshly-laid tarmac, we entered the main village thoroughfare with its earthen surface underlain by stone cobbles. After the first impression of a plethora of red tiled roofs, grey stone walls and whitewash, two things struck us most forcibly. Firstly, there were the huge double gateways, standing some 3 m high and made out of solid oak or chestnut, each with its tiled stone portico above it. These gateways were the only means of access to most of the farmsteads. Secondly, there were the *graneros* and *hoyos* (granaries) placed within or on top of the walled enclosure of each steading. These elegant wooden structures, with their tiled roofs overhanging verandas, were balanced on four, six or eight mushroom-shaped supporting posts of stone and wood, designed to discourage small scavengers. These buildings were traditionally used for storing grain, salted and dried meat and various other farm comestibles and were once typically found in most western Asturian villages. It was, however, the number of these structures, everywhere we looked, that was impressive: they were not merely relics or symbols of an old tradition, but were obviously still being fully utilised for the purpose for which they were designed. Some of these, I later learned, were hundreds of years old.

Moving on towards the centre of the village, all seemed quite silent and deserted until we came upon three elderly men seated in front of a large stone barn just below the shop. They were all dressed in much the same manner with black waist-coats over open-necked shirts, baggy black woollen trousers and wooden clogs. Two of them wore black berets or *gorros*; the third, a slightly younger man in his early seventies, wore a peaked cap.

They all turned to stare at us quizzically. It was obvious that strangers were not an everyday occurrence in Alcedo. After exchanging greetings I commented on the prevailing silence.

'Everyone is up in the hayfields—everyone—even the children', was the comment of one of the three. Then as an afterthought, the man with the peaked cap, rather elegant and distinguished-looking, added in a jocular manner,

'Everyone, yes—except us! We are all too old to do that sort of work now!'

Lisario was his name. He was a man of immense energy and charm. He still kept a few sheep and herded them to the pasture himself with his huge mastiff, its spiked collar a protection against wolves. Sadly, some three months later, whilst grazing his small flock one hot afternoon, Lisario collapsed. He died shortly afterwards. When we returned a decade later, one of the remaining two we saw on that first day had also passed away, at the advanced age of eighty-five. Pablo however was still there, with his big frame and rock-like jaw, contemplating the *tierras* below and the mass of Manteca beyond, from his stone seat in front of the barn. But now he had been joined by three other villagers who had themselves become elders.

Some while later, as the sun passed behind the high ridge to the south-west, casting a shadow over the village, we heard the distant sound of creaking oxcarts, their axles making a strange characteristic whining noise. Then we heard the putt-putt of diesel engines: recently imported tractor-carts from Italy which, for a minority of villagers, had proved to be more practical then their traditional ox-drawn carts. There followed the hubbub of many voices drifting down from the southern ridge above.

Within minutes the village erupted into activity, with cows being herded along the cobbled cart tracks and the loaded haycarts rumbling towards their respective steadings. The sun-bronzed village haymakers, their rakes, scythes, and empty picnic panniers over their shoulders, were swelled in numbers by the ranks of visiting relatives who, as was customary at this time of year, had come to help with the hay harvest. Their gaily coloured kerchiefs and dresses contrasted with the more sober blues and greys of the village women. As dusk descended greetings and salutations were still being passed as people hurried to and fro and, despite tiredness, their conviviality suffused and transformed the quiet village: transformations to which we became accustomed as work in the village and the fields alternated throughout the seasons of the following year.

Plate 2 Late afternoon haymaking

Plate 3 The village and *tierras* from the east

Chapter 1

The village

The history of Alcedo can for the most part only be reconstructed from material evidence on the ground and from the recall of the more elderly villagers. The stories which have been passed down from earlier generations and individual recollection of more recent events constitute a collective memory: a history based mainly on oral tradition. There remains very little information from official sources, for instance on population figures. Local church archives, usually a reliable source on demography, do not reveal any consistent information on the village prior to 1936. At that time most of the parish books and registers were burnt by Republican sympathisers and records were not re-established until the 1950s.

The district archives are equally silent on Alcedo history. Such records as may have been preserved by the church authorities seem to have suffered the same fate as the parish ones when the church in Belmonte, the district capital, was burnt to the ground during the civil war. The regional archives in the provincial capital Oviedo are also without any specific records on the village.

Taxation

On matters less particular to Alcedo itself there is more information. For instance the once great, now derelict, monastery of Lapedo just below Belmonte was first established in AD 1052. The lands in the area of the present village and its parish, which lie to the west of Belmonte, would have come under this monastery's jurisdiction. It is likely that the origins of Alcedo and its system of enclosures date from about the fourteenth century and would have been developed, possibly with the assistance of monks, from that time, while the villagers would have paid their tithes, known as *decimas*, to the monastery. This meant that one tenth part of whatever the villagers produced, such as livestock, grain or vegetables, would go to the monastery, the villagers themselves being tenants of church lands.

A second form of taxation, known as *foros*, was levied from the eighteenth century onwards by those who retained manorial rights over the tenantry, some of whom had still not become freeholders up until the time of the civil war. Even after the war attempts were made to reinstitute these taxes at a local level. There were several manors, known as *palacios*, in the general region of Alcedo. The village was most affected by one some 7 km to the north and another, owned by the Cien Fuegos family, in the Pigueño Valley south of Belmonte. Whether the smaller manor nearby collected taxes on behalf of the latter, or whether both collected at different times over the years, was never clearly defined by the elderly villagers who still recollected these tax exactions. Nor is it clear whether *decimas* and *foros* existed simultaneously, although it is likely that they did, subjecting some people to a form of double taxation. As one elderly villager laconically summarised, 'In the old days we paid *decimas* and *foros*—now we have to pay taxes and insurance!'

At the time of the dissolution of Lapedo in the nineteenth century, church lands came into the hands of influential local landowners. Whether *decimas* continued after the dissolution is not clear. A second form of church taxation, *bula*, has however continued in part until the present. This was a payment frequently enforced by local priests for performing baptismal, marriage, funeral and other services and until recently on goods sold or exchanged during local saints' day festivals, as well as for the right to eat meat during Lent.

Population

Several villagers in Alcedo owned title to their land towards the end of the nineteenth century, though one or two families may have gained tenure much earlier. The question of tenure in the village is however problematic and to some extent depends on whether a villager came from native Asturian stock or was descended from the migratory pastoralists known as *vaqueiros*. There are still *vaqueiro* communities in the area of Alcedo who at one time used to migrate southwards to the Castilian *mesa* during the summer months, returning to their permanent villages in winter. Of a swarthier complexion than their Asturian neighbours and probably stemming from southern Mediterranean and, according to villagers, Moorish antecedants, they began to form settled communities in this region by the nineteenth century. Since that time they have largely integrated with the settled mixed horticultural-pastoralist farming communities in the Belmonte area, adapting to their mode of living with its dominant agricultural economy.

In the nineteenth century and even in the early decades of the twentieth there was, according to the villagers, a clear distinction between these people and their settled neighbours. Often still referred to as *moriscos*, they were obliged to wear distinctive apparel and to sit at the back of the congregation when attending church. It was mainly these people who still had to pay *foros* to the *palacios* even after the civil war.

With the exception of the *bula* however, all forms of tax paying and labour obligation towards both church and manor had virtually ceased by the end of the civil war. Taxes levied on harvested crops and slaughtered animals were always difficult to enforce. Contemporary taxes levied on ownership of land based on cadastral surveys and aerial photographs probably represent an easier and fairer system.

A general decline in the population of the village since the nineteenth century has come about due to a number of causes.[1] Pressure on available land, and an inheritance system that favoured passing a farm and its possessions intact to either a son or a daughter, meant that in families with upwards of ten children there was little chance for other male siblings to remain in the village. The only alternatives for a man who did not inherit were to marry into another house or remain in his family home as a confirmed bachelor.

At the beginning of the twentieth century emigration abroad, especially to Cuba and Argentina, was particularly prevalent. It became a necessity for any young man unless he was farming, otherwise he would be enlisted by the army to fight in the Spanish-Moroccan war. Villagers dreaded being called up for service, hence the increased exodus of young men from the village at that time.

The second major factor in village decline was during the civil war when the young men enlisted mainly in the Republican army, though subsequently many were obliged to fight for the Nationalists. Those who survived the cessation of hostilities often did not return until many years later. Nor did the villagers who remained escape the ravages of war. Because of Alcedo's location close to the Sierra de Manteca, a major observation position for the Republicans, and its usefulness as a channel for supplies, it was fought over first by one side and then by the other until it was finally taken by Franco's Moorish troops. This caused untold hardship and terror among the villagers who ultimately fled in 1937, leaving Alcedo totally abandoned for nearly a year. In the decades following the war many villagers left to live in nearby towns while others emigrated, the majority to Australia and various European countries.

The ongoing depopulation of the village over recent decades may be attributed to the attractions of city life and its tangible economic rewards; to a greater emphasis on education for the young, involving long absences from the village; and to the reluctance of the younger women to take on the responsibilities of being village wives.

The present move away from subsistence farming towards more economically advantageous forms of production, and the introduction of modern farming equipment and household aids, are making hill farming a marginally more attractive occupation for the young. This may be a factor in slowing down the exodus, for on our return to the village after ten years in 1988, there had been only a marginal decrease in population: perhaps a reflection on the government's efforts to encourage the younger generation to continue hill farming.

Contrary to what would be expected from the foregoing comments on the decline of a village community, there was no immediate evidence of old ruins or abandoned houses in Alcedo. The first impression was one of an active and stable village, with some indications of expansion: several houses were clearly very recently built or reconstructed and modernised from earlier structures, with cement and whitewashed exteriors, brightly painted doors and windows and new industrialised tiles on their roofs. The majority of houses however were constructed from uncut grey stone and looked much older. Some of the houses and outbuildings in the oldest part of the village, although appearing to be substantial structures and externally plastered, were in fact made of mud and wattle, the mud reinforced with maize cobs. In a region with so much stone available this was a surprising feature: the more so in that some of these structures were apparently centuries old.

Initially I sought frequent confirmation of accounts of a more populous past, thinking that villagers might perhaps have exaggerated or romanticised the situation. I found, however, not only affirmation from all the older members of the community, but also confirmation in the form of the frequently reiterated figures for the numbers of *mozos* or eligible young bachelors and spinsters in earlier decades. This was particularly important in the memory of the elderly women, who could cite figures for different periods going back to the nineteenth century in the time of their mothers' and grandmothers' youth. It was something which clearly represented former village pride and self-esteem, and gave Alcedo a certain prestige in the eyes of other communities in the region, not only for the quick wit, intelligence, skills and looks of these young people, but also for the sheer number the village could boast as its own: an affirmation of the vitality of the community.[2]

Settlement pattern

About three months into my fieldwork, while walking down the old cart track on the west side of the ridge which led to the lower valley, I came across an abandoned farmstead about a kilometre distant from the village. This was a very different structure from the customary barns found in or near hayfields and was the only extant example of a dwelling separated from the village complex that I ever encountered. The characteristic features of village farmsteads were there, although the massive solid wood gateways were off their hinges and had fallen to either side of the stone stanchions previously supporting them, but the overhead portico, complete with its red tiles, was still standing. Inside was the courtyard, once cobbled but now grown over with grass and weeds. Across the yard was what remained of the old *granero*, still standing on its squared conical hewn chestnut supports with the typical mushroom-like flat stone capping beneath the wooden floor to prevent access to rodents. On the right was was what remained of a high stone wall. On the left, partially built into the rock face forming the side of the steep hillside and completing the enclosed area, was what at first appeared to be a house with a small veranda built over a large basement. On closer inspection, however, this 'house' was actually a long and commodious barn, only one end of which had initially been in view. The basement of this barn was in fact an old sheep steading of generous proportions with a low roof forming the floor above: sufficient to take at least 50 sheep comfortably.

Mounting a fixed ladder from the byre, I climbed up to the vast hay loft, providing sufficient space for hay to feed the animals through the long winter months. Walking back to the part overlooking the courtyard, I found the old living quarters of the family, who now lived in the village. There was no partition between hay-loft and house. The only additions or luxuries were a small porch and a partially partitioned room on one side with a small window. On the other side of the central porch was the kitchen-living room, in the centre of which was the old stone hearth,

Plate 4 The village in winter

the smoke being allowed to filter out beneath the eaves. The iron cooking hooks still hung from a roof beam. Any furniture that the apartment might have contained had been removed to the house in the village. Otherwise, everything was exactly as it had been left some twenty-five years earlier.

Some months later, I was shown an area in another barn where a family had lived in the village. It had the same flat stone hearth and pot hooks, only in this case it was just one corner of a hay barn and there were no luxuries: no porch with elegant balustrade or wooden partition or indeed window. Winters are exceedingly cold in the mountains of Asturias, and it is hard to think of a better adaptation than being placed over the sheep and cow byre for underfloor heating, nor a more practical use of available space.

The villagers' former reticence about this mode of living—some felt it was a social stigma—quickly changed. I heard numerous accounts of life before the time of the separate house: the hay barns were later converted into dwellings, the open hearths being replaced by the ubiquitous Bilbao iron wood-burning oven. They used to sit around the open fire on winter nights, 'hot in front and cold behind' as one villager quipped, and in a circle of low wooden benches they would roast chestnuts or partake in a meal and recount stories or cap each other's refrains or proverbs in a form of quick-witted discourse in which these mountain people delight.

Some villagers had converted their upper barns into separate rooms surrounding a central dining-room which, like the old hearth, is a symbol of hospitality and feasting for any occasion. But this gradual evolution of the old hay barn meant that the hay had to be placed elsewhere, usually in an outbuilding acquired from a departing neighbour, while vacated *graneros* would also be put to use for other storage. Sometimes a new structure was built with a cow barn beneath and house above, while the hay barn remained, the lower part being converted to take ox-carts or tractor-carts underneath. These adaptations absorbed farmsteads which had been vacated by departing families so that, in effect, very few buildings were wasted or allowed to fall into disuse or ruin. Some families, however, held on to their property despite their absence and hence its later decay. Most of these departing families perhaps esteemed their land more than the farm buildings. This accounts for the system of renting land from those who have left by present villagers, and for the large number of old *tierras* and meadows which have not been rented for various reasons and have become overgrown through disuse. Asturians will, if possible, hold on to their land even if they are living in another country for, as villagers say, 'they never know when they may need it again'.

Although the farmstead buildings have evolved, and the lack of any obvious signs of depopulation in the village may be accounted for by this changing pattern of living, it still does not explain the characteristic layout of these farm units. The central courtyard is predictable, as is the arrangement of the buildings, with the *graneros* placed well away from damp and shaded areas to gain proper ventilation for the preservation of grain and smoked meats, their balconies used for drying various herbs, maize and clothes. The relative compactness of each farmstead may be accounted for by the lack of space for expansion along the village's exposed ridge-top situation. What remains unexplained is the closed nature of each farmstead with its high stone walls and only the vast double doorway allowing access to to the courtyard, house and barns. Perhaps the experience of civil strife and its aftermath of wandering vagrants, or heavy winter snowfalls and bitter winds, or even marauding wolves, may have some bearing on these medieval features.

Although I shall be referring to various aspects of the history and changing way of life and traditions throughout the following chapters, the foregoing brief historical comment will I hope offset any overly timeless presentation of the personality of this remote village community. In many respects it is a custom-bound community and many of its concepts and modes of working stem from centuries of pastoral, horticultural and agricultural tradition. Nevertheless, in other respects the villagers share a commonality with hundreds of other small mountain communities of similar origin and tradition in western Asturias. It is however not possible to describe an ongoing and changing village tradition without reference to the historical influences of the church and the manor, or indeed war. It is perhaps this last experience which, if by no means unique, was unusual and remained a constant preoccupation in the recollections of the more elderly villagers. And although such matters are of relative unimportance to the younger generation, who may view the old ways as something of an anachronism in modern Spain, for the older people, whose fathers and grandfathers were all too aware of feudal and church power in their lives, and who themselves went through the trauma of war, village life is still steeped in the past. For the most part, theirs is a generation which views the present trends and changes with a certain degree of scepticism.

Plate 5 Ploughing the *tierras*

Chapter 2

The land

Unlike much of Spain with its pastoralist tradition, in Asturias the land, indeed the soil itself, takes on an aura of associations and meanings. Pride in possessing land and in caring for it is something very close to the heart of these mountain villagers. One of the first things an outsider notices is not so much the beauty of the natural landscape, but the compact and neat appearance of fields and enclosures, whether perched on the side of some dramatic mountainside or partially hidden in a forested valley.

The land is not only highly esteemed but is something to which a man attaches his closest sentiments, particularly his small arable plots or *tierras*, his hayfields and his pastures. For a woman her kitchen garden is important, but in her case it is the house, family, close kin and neighbourly relations which are uppermost in her daily life, while pride in her breadmaking skills, the preparation of 'feasts' and the quality of the meat products from the *matanza* or Martinmas winter culling of animals is almost as important. Women also relate to the livestock in a way men tend not to, though a man will lavish care and attention on his oxen. Oxen were until the 1980s his main means of working the land, along with his plough, scythes, bill-hooks and hay-rakes, all made by himself. He will also take pride in the upkeep of his chestnut trees, and the sleekness of the *terneros* (calves) which he takes to market.

Among some of the village women in Alcedo orthodox Catholic belief is perhaps an important factor: tempered by ancient customs and folk traditions which frequently surface in unexpected ways. The majority of men however seem to attach little importance to religion although they have a high regard for traditional customs and the 'old beliefs'. Sometimes it is family origins which dictate belief. Although the majority of villagers have been cultivating the land for many generations, former *vaqueiro* pastoralists assimilated into the community have brought different customs associated with their former mode of life, while the demise of sheep pastoralism and an emphasis on cattle rearing for market have also occasioned changing attitudes.

Apart from the kitchen garden next to the house, the open moorland and mountain grazing, and the deep ploughing of an area of upland for cooperative village use in 1978, the tripartite field system of *tierra*, enclosed hayfield and pasture has remained until very recently the core of farming practice.

A feature of all these small mountain communities in western Asturias is the scattered nature of the enclosed fields belonging to different households within each village. Attempts have been made towards agrarian reform by the provincial government in Oviedo in order to rationalise individual holdings so that each household has a more compact or 'parcelled' field system. Such a change would reduce the time spent in visiting scattered possessions, which in purely economic terms would be labour saving. This change however has been staunchly blocked by the farming communities themselves.

The reasons for this objection are numerous and in part rest on time-honoured inheritance practices and on sentiment, because particular fields are those which one's father or forefathers cared for: perfectly understandable attachments. There are also, however, very real practical reasons for this attitude to change, which will become apparent in the following discussion on hayfields. The authorities shrug their shoulders in perplexity and resignation and put their lack of success down to the proverbial stubbornness and innate conservatism of these hill and mountain farming communities.

Individual holdings by villagers may range from as few as 20 or 30 units of land, in the form of garden, *tierra*, meadow or hayfield, to over 100, and in most cases would include stands of chestnut woods. Since the 1950s all these possessions have been accredited to the owner and carefully listed for tax purposes. Before that time taxes were levied on animals—pigs, sheep and goats or cattle—which were slaughtered throughout the year, but mainly during the period of the winter *matanza*. It was the use of aerial photography which enabled the authorities to ascertain these possessions reasonably accurately, each unit being accredited and numbered according to its rightful owner.[3]

On the basis of an average of 30 units per household, a village such as Alcedo with 19 houses in the 1980s would have 570 fields of various dimensions. In fact the number is complicated by other factors, some of which will be discussed below, as no simple estimate can be made.

According to the cadastral survey undertaken in the early 1960s, the holdings of the village number in the region of 240 *tierras* and some 400 meadows and hayfields, these being indistinguishable from the air. In addition there are some 20 or more kitchen gardens and an undifferentiated number of chestnut and other woodland stands and possessions. It is of course misleading to assume that the holdings of each village are neatly packaged within its 'boundary,' for some of the fields may be owned by houses from adjoining villages who have married in, while Alcedo villagers' possessions may equally extend beyond the village confines for a similar reason. Nevertheless, these figures serve as an approximate guide.

As previously indicated, since the nineteenth century village population seems to have consistently contracted: from approximately 50 houses averaging ten members each, to 20 houses in 1978, down to 19 averaging five members each in 1988. This indicates far fewer land holdings per household in the nineteenth century than now; approximately ten pastures, hayfields and *tierras* in all per family; unless some villagers had fewer or no holdings at all and worked for others with more than the average number of possessions.

A large part of the expansion in property holdings can be accounted for by acquisition of fields through inheritance or purchase from families who have left the village. Conservative views on retaining land by families no longer living in the village result in many fields being rented by absentees to still resident villagers, while unrented ones revert to scrubland and are no longer practical for grazing unless restored. There is also a recent tendency for the owner of two adjoining fields to remove the separating stone wall. This particularly relates to hayfields since the purchase of motor-mowers, which can only really be used on the flatter fields. As the majority of hayfields are steeply inclined most of the harvesting was still undertaken with the scythe in 1978.

The recent development of a central farmers' cooperative in the municipal centre of Belmonte and easier access to the village by the new road have tended to change the orientations of a formerly rather inward-looking village community. With more time being spent on cattle-raising because of better returns resulting from easier transportation to markets, and the concomitant increase in wealth allowing for the purchase of certain materials and foodstuffs from non-village sources, there has been a drastic decline in the use of kitchen gardens and particularly the *tierras*. The figure of 240 strip fields recorded by the cadastral survey in the early 1960s was only marginally reduced by 1978. By 1988 only about 30 of these fields still appeared to be maintained. Deep ploughing of former rough moorland pasture had also been undertaken by villagers for improved grazing and crop raising for cattle feed for the increasing stock requirements. A series of broad strips of half a hectare or so each were divided among those who shared the rental of the heavy ploughing machinery needed for this cooperative effort.

The tierras[4]

Villagers say rather wryly that 'earth, like water, always goes downhill'. This is fundamental to the continuing upkeep of these strip fields which are almost invariably found grouped together on an incline. The largest concentration of these *tierras* in Alcedo faces towards the south and east in a concave arc of gently sloping ground directly beneath the village.

These strips, unlike the hand-hoed garden plots, are designed to allow access to and ploughing of the plot using oxen. They are usually rectangular in shape and vary in width from about 3 m up to 20 m or more, and may be up to 50 m in length. There are grassed or earth pathways running down the slope between the strips, just wide enough to allow oxen or mules to pass without having to walk over a neighbour's strip. Often there are upright stone markers or *mohan* placed in the ground to mark the end of a strip. Thus it is possible to see immediately by observing the edge of the grass verge or any repositioning of the *mohan* whether someone has ploughed beyond his allotted area. In the past, when these *tierras* were fully utilised, any increase in strip size or movement of the marker, even by a few inches, through carelessness or deliberation could cause recrimination between neighbours, as the *tierras* were scattered and only very rarely did one villager own two adjoining strips.

These strips are not terraced, although from a distance they may appear to be so. Some however do have low retaining walls which raise the strip lengthwise on its lower side. The majority have only a narrow grassy bank which forms a division between the strips and prevents earth from moving down on to the field below. They therefore tend to follow the contours of the slope and, due to the friability of the earth from constant ploughing and erosion caused by periods of gale force winds and heavy rainfall, the soil on each strip tends to accumulate at its lower edge.

This downward movement of the soil in the *tierras* means that villagers have to replace the earth on the upper part of each strip by digging and transporting it back up the slope. This is done in early spring or autumn, when the soil is drier and lighter, using a large wooden box-like container which is secured to a pair of sled runners and dragged up the slope by oxen (Plate 6). It is a task which villagers find onerous, even more so than the annual mulching of each strip with cattle manure. It is however easier with oxen, as villagers point out, than it was after the civil war when there were no animals left alive. Then they had to carry the soil and manure on their backs in large panniers.

In 1978, although one man owned a steel coulter plough which he sometimes loaned for use on areas of flat land, for all other purposes, including working the *tierras*, villagers still preferred to use their Roman ards. These simple wooden ploughs, though metal-tipped and furnished with wooden mould boards, had no coulter to break up or turn the soil. Made by the villagers themselves, they were ideal for *tierra* use, ploughing to a sufficient depth (about 25 cm) to be effective with minimum disturbance to the soil.

Traditionally the *tierras* were weeded two or three times during the summer months and manured in the spring prior to seeding. The main crops cultivated were potatoes, maize, beets, *escanda* or spelt wheat for bread-making, and lucerne and rye grass for cattle feed. They thus provided for both human and animal consumption, though the latter may have been a recent development.

In the late 1970s villagers still took great pride in their *tierras* and could often be seen ploughing, seeding, weeding and harvesting them. Any villager knew the various strips of his neighbours and would comment on their relative fertility, depth of soil and stoniness, or what crops had been cultivated in them previously on a rotational basis. Everyone knew everyone else's business as all the *tierras* were in full view from the village centre. It was like working in a huge theatre under the scrutiny of one's fellow villagers. By 1988, however, the change was apparent. Many of the *tierras* which had been under cultivation ten years earlier were now abandoned, and because they were overgrown with grass and weeds it was difficult to differentiate one strip from another.

A villager named Rafael had seeded two of his *tierras* with maize and *escanda* respectively. This was in 1988 and the latter was no longer being grown for bread but for cattle feed. A neighbour, Mateo, drove his new tractor-cart, laden with manure, down the narrow pathway between the *tierras*, now mainly disused and overgrown. Mateo had been ill and had fallen behind with his work schedule. He was inadvertently passing his tractor's wheel over the edge of Rafael's *tierra* on the

Plate 6 Earth moving in the *tierras*

way down to his own. Rafael saw this from where he was working and rushed down to remonstrate. A furious argument broke out.

'Why did you run your tractor over the edge of my *tierra*?' shouted Rafael, 'I have only just planted it'.

Mateo explained that he could not reach his own *tierra* without doing so.

'Why are you bringing your tractor down here anyway?' asked Rafael.

Mateo protested that he had got behind in his work and had had to use it. Rafael was adamant and told him he could not pass that way. Their mutual recriminations and raised voices could be clearly heard from the village above.

This unfortunate incident could not have happened a decade earlier, when no-one would have driven a motor vehicle into the *tierras*. Even oxen would be led down in single file along the narrow pathways, the plough being carried on the shoulder and only hitched up when on the owner's *tierra*. Manure would be carried down in panniers on the side of a mule. Any produce from the *tierras* was carried either on the back of a mule, or by a villager. No one would think of walking on another man's *tierra*, let alone drive a tractor over it.

The increasing use of modern technology and the rapid abandonment of most of the *tierras* has allowed one or two villagers to disregard the time-honoured customs of *tierra* cultivation. These included mutual respect for one another's strips and an unstated propriety for the rhythms of the agicultural cycle. Thus all villagers would be working virtually simultaneously at the same tasks, whether manuring, plough-ing, harrowing, or seeding, weeding and harvesting. All crops cannot be planted simultaneously and they were rotated each year, but the acceptance of a proper time to carry out these tasks engendered respect and cooperation. Villagers in the past did walk on others' strip fields and animals did wander on to them. Some failed to cultivate their *tierras* properly and others even tried to expand their prop-erty at the cost of a neighbour, but these were the exceptions.

In the past, if someone was incapacitated by illness or other work, then another member of his household would take on the work in the *tierra*. For Mateo this was not possible. One of his grown-up daughters had left the village and the other had died tragically two years earlier. His wife had work elsewhere and his mother-in-law was old and infirm. He had invested in a tractor-cart some years previously and unlike many he still wished to maintain his *tierras*. Conversely, Rafael was an elderly villager with a large family who still maintained traditional ways. It was inevitable that an argument would erupt between one man who still retained his customary habits and another whose circumstances had changed. Mateo had no alternative but to use his tractor and ignore ancient custom and a fracture in neigh-bourly relations was the result. As far as most villagers were concerned, however, the traditions surrounding *tierra* cultivation had become a memory of the past, an irrelevance, even in the space of a decade.

The meadows

Meadows, known as *prados*, may be characterised as predominantly enclosures for grazing cattle. They, like the hayfields, are all stone walled. Unlike the hayfields however they are used throughout the year, except in the winter months, as grass fields. Occasionally, if the incline is not too steep and a plough can be used, they may be turned temporarily into arable land for cropping. The surrounding stone walls are usually topped with earth sods on which saplings form hedgerows. Each meadow has at least one gate for access. Traditionally made from chestnut, these gates formerly swivelled on pivots set into slabs of stone projecting from the wall. Nowadays these finely crafted gates are being replaced either by wooden shuttles or barbed wire.

The field systems of Alcedo, at the time of the cadastral survey in the early 1960s, numbered in excess of 400 walled enclosures. Some of the stone walling had already been removed before the survey was undertaken, to allow for larger hayfields. Although there may have been more recent additions in upland areas the bulk of these walls, and particularly the enclosures closer to the village, may date back to the time of the expansion of church lands in the fourteenth century, some three centuries after the establishment of the Lapedo monastery.

The majority of these enclosures are small, some no more then one-tenth of a hectare. Hayfields, by contrast, are sometimes two or more hectares in extent. The whole landscape around these sub-montaine villages, with their characteristic patchwork patterning of *tierras* close by, is covered by a plethora of stone-walled enclosures, all carefully nurtured and maintained except for those with absent owners, and it is apparent that villagers spend much time in their upkeep. Like the household *tierras*, each hayfield has its own name, usually taken from some characteristic of the field: *prado de ojo* for one shaped like an eye, or *prado de fuente* for one with a spring in it, or *tierra de la solana* literally meaning 'cultivated ground in a sunny spot'. Each *tierra*, meadow or hayfield is measured in *varas*, a distance slightly short of a metre. A fairly large field may be 350 *varas* around its circumference.

In the mid-nineteenth century I estimate that an average household in Alcedo would have possessed, either as owner or tenant, a kitchen garden, two to three *tierras*, one or two hayfields, and perhaps four or five meadows. There would not have been as much need for meadowland as now, both sheep and goats being difficult to confine, and except when being fattened or during severe winter weather they were grazed on open common moorland and the slopes of Manteca. Households would have maintained two or three cows, sufficient for milk, butter and cheese making. Although goats also provided milk for cheese, sheep's milk was not used. Their wool however provided for most of the villagers' clothing and their meat, together with pig meat, was the mainstay of the winter *matanza*. Thus, compared with today's cattle rearing, the smaller number of meadows would have been sufficient.

As I have described it, the village is built on the spine of a rising ridge and on either side lie deep valleys. This terrain means that meadows fall into roughly three types. Those on a flatter part of the ridge lying to the north of the village are most frequently used for arable. The most numerous type are situated on the precipitous sides of the valleys. Then there are the valley bottom meadows, known as *regeros*, many of which have leats or water channels, providing good pasturage during the summer months.

> *El veintidós de febrero*
> *Da sol por todos los regeros.*

'On the twenty-second of February the sun reaches all the irrigated fields,' goes the refrain recited by an old lady in the village. On being asked if this was an old saying, she replied that it was from *los antepasados* (the ancestors). According to her the saying referred to a specific group of water meadows which had belonged to her family for generations. I went down on that day to check its authenticity, but the sun went behind clouds before I reached the meadows.

Many of the meadows facing northwards, particularly the steepest ones with high hedgerows, may never see the sun all year round. They will, nevertheless, provide good grazing for cattle because of spring water from the hillside and because the shade discourages midges and horseflies which aggravate cattle. In their agitation from bites cattle may bolt, lose their footing on the precipitous slopes and roll, sometimes to the bottom of the field, causing fractures to leg, neck or back. Some cows and most oxen are shod with iron shoes by the village farrier to help prevent such accidents happening.

The older generation of villagers know not only their own fields but those of just about everyone else in the village. They are like a vast patchwork map in the mind. Whether next to the village or three kilometres away at the bottom of a valley, each is known for its good and bad points: its size, inclination and accessibility, the quality of grass, available water, shade and rocky outcrops. Meadows are rotated with others for better grazing and are carefully nurtured, their walls and gates repaired, their hedgerows trimmed, leats cleared, bracken cut and trees polled to provide shade, the young ash cuttings being fed to the cattle.

The hayfields

> Hay is fundamental. Without hay we could not have any cows. That is
> why we work so hard during the summer months.

An elderly woman villager was more succinct than the young man quoted. She just called haymaking *la catastrofe de la hierba*: the tragedy of the hay. Both comments were made on our 1988 return visit, by which time villagers had adopted a more intensive cattle rearing programme, to the detriment of their traditional farming practices.

In the late 1970s haymaking, though hard work, was still considered an enjoy-able activity. It was a time when relatives who had left the village returned to lend a hand. There was an air of expectancy and festivity epitomised by gargantuan bucol-ic picnics of meats and breads, *empanadas* (a sort of meat pie) and sweet cakes, red wine and cider in the midday shade of some distant hayfield. The rhythmic swish of the scything teams and the creaking of laden oxcarts had been largely replaced by the motor-mower and the tractor cart when we returned a decade later. There seemed to be a greater sense of anxiety with occasional outbursts of irritation, alien to the good-humoured weariness we remembered after a long day in the hot sun.

Realities, even in this short space of time, had changed in the new era of hill farming. Farming, and especially haymaking, had become serious business. To feed the expanding stock of cattle more hay was needed as winter feed. Without that the animals would deteriorate before the spring market sales. That would threaten eco-nomic survival and hasten the exodus from the village.

For most of the year hayfields are indistinguishable from the meadows, except that they are almost all of much larger dimensions. Cattle may be found grazing in them, but only after the hay has been harvested and before April when the young hay starts to grow. Unlike meadows, however, which may be converted to arable on occasion, hayfields are not put to any other use.

A hayfield belonging to one villager is known to all the others. Most of the fields will have been passed down over generations within families and their various attributes and shortcomings are well known to everyone. At one time or another older villagers will have scythed, spread, stooked, respread, restooked and carried hay from most of their neighbours' fields, for it was customary to help others com-plete their haymaking as well as completing one's own. It was not uncommon to see six or eight villagers working in *cuadrillas*, scything rhythmically in union, creat-ing echelon patterns across a landscape aesthetically pleasing to the worker and to the distant observer alike.

Some villagers own only one large hayfield, while others use several which may be scattered and far from the village. Some are near natural springs or watercourses which may be diverted in dry weather to moisten the growing hay grass. All are close to trackways or lanes to enable easy access for the hay carts. Most have large tiled and stone-walled barns within the field or close by, where hay not taken to the village can be stored and placed in byres for cattle still grazing in mild winter weather.

In haymaking, distance from the village is often a key factor. A field close to the village has advantages over one three kilometres away. The reason stated for one household's departure from the village in 1978 was the great distance of its scat-tered hayfields from the village. With the increasing emphasis on cattle farming it became impracticable for the two men in the family to keep pace with others whose holdings were closer to the village, even with tractor-carts replacing their oxen. One farmer from a nearby village referred to his haymaking as an *infierno* or hell. He could only manage to take two cartloads of hay a day—one in the morning and one in the afternoon—down to his barn in the valley, some 8-900 m below his fields. With 30 to 40 cartloads to carry each year for winter feed and no-one to help him, it seemed a perfectly understandable complaint. Conversely, the villages lying in the valley to the north of Alcedo have an easier time, as although their fields are no nearer to their villages, the difference in altitude means less snow and cold weather, and therefore less hay is required for byred animals which can remain grazing out of doors most of the winter.

The direction in which a hayfield faces is considered critical. If it lies in an easterly direction it receives the early morning sun and the overnight dew is quickly dissipated, producing a better quality hay. If it lies in a westerly direction the sun will not reach it till later and the dew remains, producing inferior hay. It also means that the whole haymaking process has to be delayed to later in each day, while the likelihood in summer of convectional rainfall after midday is a further disadvantage.

Both quality and quantity of hay are dependant on soil and moisture and amount of manuring undertaken, and the admixture of different grasses including rye, alfafa and clover, the last being most esteemed as cattle feed. The timing of haymaking is important as some grasses have light stems and are leafier when allowed to mature, while others, especially when cut late in summer, develop thick straw-like stems which affect the quality. One or two villagers, encouraged by government grants, constructed silos in the late 1970s, but the heavier stemmed grasses retained air in the stalk and spoilt the silage. Despite the advantages of silos in the inclement climate where continuous mist and rain and lack of sunshine can oblige villagers to stook and spread their hay half a dozen times before they manage to gather it in, there still was no further silo expansion on our return in 1988.

Depending on the prevailing weather between late June and August or early September, there are periods when the village is virtually deserted, as if daily social life is suspended and transferred to the hayfields. At no other time of year, except for during the *matanza*, is there such a concentration on one activity. On fine days all except the very elderly, including young children and babies and visiting relatives, vacate the village: the men to cut, stack and carry, the women to spread and stook the hay.

In 1978 it was still customary to place a large leafy ash branch on the front of the last load of hay made by each household. Known as *hacer ramo*, 'to make the branch' the practice was accompanied by much merriment by those walking with the cart. I never learned why this was done.

Woodland and orchard

> The trees are sad when the leaves fall because they are like us—they live, grow old and die, like people. They have spirit like all plants.

Asturias, perhaps more than any other region of the Iberian peninsula, is endowed with great natural forests. Beech, walnut, oak, ash, pine and holly abound, as well as many other species. Pride of place with mountain villagers, however, is held by the chestnut. It is esteemed for its durability even more than the Spanish oak, which seems to lack the resilience of its British counterpart. Its nut is also extremely nutritious and still contributed to the villagers' winter diet in 1978. Social prejudice has now however largely confined it to the category of pig food. As one elderly lady commented, using the slightly derogative term *mas señoras*: 'They don't eat chestnuts now as we did, because they think of themselves as ladies'.

Situated on the east and west sides of the village are the two northward debouching valley systems where several hundred acres of chestnut woods lie within the village boundary. These woodlands are, like the field systems, mainly enclosed within old stone walls. Each villager owns an enclosed area or areas within these woods. Individual trees, however, may be owned in areas where others own one or several trees. A man may also inherit a tree on land belonging to another person, although the tree itself and its nuts belongs to him. Most villagers own an average of 200 trees.

Villagers show great respect for and attachment to their chestnut trees. I was shown trees thought to be at least 200 years old and others much older. The trees were spaced up to 20 m or more apart, their upper branches forming a canopy over the forest floor, which is cleared of any growth and is covered with mosses and short grasses as if carefully mown. In contrast to the cacophony of village sounds and the cattle and sheep bells in the meadows and uplands, here in these groves, except for the occasional plop of a falling chestnut, there is a heavy silence.

This ambience, like walking through the precincts of some natural cathedral, is however a controlled form of nature. Arboriculture is an important aspect of village tradition. All the trees are carefully polled, usually about 20 m above the ground. This enables the lower branches to thicken and grow outwards, which facilitates the collection of the nuts. Young villagers would climb the trees and pick them off with 6 m willow hoops, allowing them to drop to the ground to be collected by women and children beneath. The agility of these young men as they moved from tree to tree without descending was greatly admired, but accidental broken bones and even occasional deaths put an end to this practice.

Scattered about these chestnut woods are well constructed stone enclosures of up to 8 m in circumference and some 1.5 m in height. Like stone igloos in shape they have a projecting entrance way and at first glance appear to be roofless dwellings. Some stand in open ground, others back on to the base of a tree. Known as *corros* or 'circles,' they are used for the temporary storage of nuts. When full they are covered with branches weighed down with heavy stones, to prevent wild pigs from eating the nuts. Later when the shell of the nut has dried the *corros* are uncovered and the nuts broken open. The smaller nuts are discarded but the larger ones are then sacked and taken by mule or oxcart up to the village to be stored in the *graneros*. An average sack weighs about 80 kg. In past years upwards of fifty sackloads would be collected by each house for both human and animal consumption. By the late 1970s ten sackloads per household would be exceptional. A decade later few houses were even collecting the nuts.

Arboriculture did not end with the polling. In early spring individual trees were grafted with cuttings from branches bearing the heaviest load of nuts. These grafts might be made into the trunk of the tree or on to the branches. At other times of year villagers would come down to the woods to clear away any undergrowth. They would also gather nuts from walnut and hazel trees lining the hedgerows. Neatness and order is indicative of the landscape of these Asturian mountain villages, and care of trees is but one aspect of this. Hedging, trimming, polling and grafting were all part of a day's work and an expression of pride in the care of a householder's property. Arboriculture is however an ongoing process and damage to trees is not just caused by high winds or age. A carefully trimmed cherry tree in the middle of a field may have its branches twisted and broken by a bear partaking of the fruit.

Every village has its orchards and Alcedo is no exception. Despite the altitude and the vagaries of weather, particularly the prevailing northerly winds and late frosts, apple and pear trees are cultivated in sheltered situations. Most of the apples are pressed to make cider, which is the favoured drink in much of Asturias and although there are a few vineyards in low-lying areas, most wine comes from the south. Villagers tend to be a little disparaging about anything that is not locally grown, and wine from the south, unlike cider, is thought to have additives. Drawing a comparison with the apple orchards all around the region, one villager commented, 'Yes, they have plenty of wine here in the bars—but where are the vineyards?'

With the increasing trend away from subsistence farming and self reliance, orchards now tend to be neglected and some of the woodland areas in the region were being exploited by timber concessionaries in the late 1980s. A householder from the next village to Alcedo had just sold off all his chestnut trees. He no longer lived in the village and apparently needed the money. There was a palpable sense of disquiet in Alcedo as timber lorries passed through the village to the wooded valley above and the sound of power saws went on for several days. Such a thing just could not have happened a decade earlier.

Apart from the cutting down of trees another factor is affecting the woodlands and particularly the chestnut trees: the fumes from a coal-fired generating station in the nearby Soto valley. This station, which provides electricity for much of the region, emits large quantities of noxious smoke which is having a detrimental effect on the surrounding woodland. Many of the chestnut trees are defoliating in the summer and are no longer yielding nuts. Fortunately, Alcedo is too distant and high up to be directly affected, but villagers feel that, depending on prevailing winds, their own woodland could be vulnerable, and they express some apprehension about this possibility.

Plate 7 Using a mechanical seed drill

Plate 8 The San Blas mid-winter fair in Tuña

Chapter 3

The fair

> Fairs are for men—not for women. They [men] like to bargain, to haggle over prices. This is not for women!

There is much truth in this verdict by an elderly village lady. Of course women haggle over prices, just as men do, but not at the traditional fairs. Although women do participate by preparing and sometimes bringing and sharing the customary *meriendas* or picnics, the fairs are essentially in the male domain, the main object being to buy or sell animals at a good price. If a countryman fails to do this then he may temporarily lose face and be thought to have let down his house and the village. There is a strong competitive element: among houses, among villages, and between all villagers and the outside traders. In the end these are all matters which have to be resolved amicably, but the tensions and excitement that build up for days prior to the main fairs are palpable.

There are numerous local fairs throughout the year which villagers may attend, in nearby Tuña, Belmonte, Tineo and Cangas de Narcea, as well as more distant ones at Somiedo, Oviedo and further afield. There are however three which generate most anticipation and excitement among Alcedans. These represent something more than mere business negotiations over animals. They are major social events, specific markers in the yearly calendar of village life, with undoubted historical precedence and in which village women do participate.

These three are the August fair in Tuña, the late summer fair at Somiedo and the San Blas winter fair in Tuña. Each represents and exemplifies different aspects of past and present animal husbandry. The first concentrates on the sale of *jeguas*, the semi-wild horses owned by villagers, which roam the upland moorlands. The second at Somiedo, beautifully situated on the edge of the Castilian plateau, centres more on sheep and goats. Economically it is impractical for villagers as they no longer husband many sheep or goats, but its traditional *vaqueiro* link is still important to them. As one villager commented, 'San Blas is a very big fair—everyone goes to it—but Somiedo is now just to look at'. The third tends to centre on cattle: the sale and purchase of *terneros* or calves.

The August fair of Tuña

The setting of this fair is an attractive valley with wooded hillsides and fields surrounding the small town of Tuña and its derelict *palacio*. The market itself, which lies opposite the town on the other side of the river Narcea, has a long open shed with many small stalls inside, opening on to a courtyard of concrete and cobbles around which are hitching rails for animals. Until the road was built everyone either rode or walked to the fair, but in 1978 some cars and about ten cattle trucks from Belmonte, Tineo and further afield lined both sides of the roadway beside the market and over the bridge into the town.

Of the several hundred animals brought to the fair on that day only about 200 were actually sold. These included about 30 cows with young calves, 50 or so well grown calves, five bulls sold for breeding purposes, two pairs of oxen for work, several donkeys and mules and one sheep. Most of the attention however centred on the horses and foals and approximately 60 were sold during the course of the day. Most of these were brought to the market from the area around Tuña itself, or from nearby villages. They had either been driven in on the hoof, or brought in small tractor-trailers or trucks. Ramirez, the shopowner in Alcedo, brought down two foals in his new pick-up van. Many of the foals had come with their dams which had been ridden down by their owners from nearby villages.

The traders, who are mostly abbatoir buyers, usually arrived by truck in threes, two of them being handlers and one a driver who might also be the owner of the business. A few buyers wore a sort of coat-overall; others were in ordinary clothes which might include check trousers, sunglasses and a cigar: a little more ostentatious than the sombre dark clothes of the country people. There were no prior negotiations: the sellers approached the buyers, showed them their animals and suggested a price. Sometimes the buyers would just wander around the market looking at various animals with a rather studied air of nonchalance.

A farmer standing beside his mare, which he had just ridden in to the market with its rather small and frail-looking colt, spoke to a buyer as he passed by. 'I have a good strong colt here—I'll take 12,000 pesetas [about £60] for it.' 'It's rather small and skinny isn't it? I can offer you 10,000,' was the buyer's response.

This figure was in fact down by a third on the current price of 15,000 pesetas for a sturdy colt, and in spite of its obviously slender build the farmer replied in the negative, saying that he would not accept less than his named price. The buyer just shrugged and moved away a few paces, but kept looking at the colt while puffing his cigar, occasionally glancing at its owner who by then was talking to someone else. That man did not buy the animal, but another buyer from Oviedo did. I did not hear the price,[5] but it was likely to have been close to the asking figure as the farmer was very willing to load the unfortunate animal on to the buyer's truck.

Unlike when appraising cattle the abattoir buyers do not run their hands over colts or foals, but judge them from a distance. As soon as they are purchased the animals are marked with the initial letter of the purchaser's first name by cutting the hair on the hindquarters with scissors.

In order to load them on the trucks two methods are employed. One is to lead the mare into the truck first in the hope that the colt will follow. This seems a gentle, humane way, the mare being led out again once the colt is inside. However it will not work if the mare is frightened and baulks at entering the vehicle, or if the colt refuses to follow her, as may happen with high-sided cattle trucks with their steep ramps.

The alternative method is much more dramatic and usually involves many onlookers who may vie with each other to show off their skill and strength in horse-handling, although in most cases the 'horse' is barely a yearling. This involves bringing the mare alongside the ramp, then separating the foal from her and driving it up the ramp, sometimes with sticks applied to its rump. This method almost invariably fails. The animal, already agitated, often terrified by all the hubbub of cajoling and shouting and being separated from its mother, understandably baulks. The buyer or one of his assistants may approach the frightened animal and grip it by one ear; aided by the shoving and pushing of the bystanders and their wagging of sticks, the foal may be cajoled inside. Alternatively the former owner or someone in the crowd may grip it by the nose and fleshy part above the mouth in one hand and, with an ear gripped firmly in the other, literally drag the animal up the ramp with its tail pulled up between its legs, again assisted by others with sticks. Occasionally a foal will escape these attentions and run off for a while, creating a diversion for all. Invariably, however, it will seek its dam and is caught and the operation is repeated. Several foals, long since weaned, try to take milk from their dams just before this separation and once they are inside the truck the clattering of their hooves on the boards and their pathetic whinnyings add to the general din and excitement of the occasion.

Cattle do not react in this way, a fact which perhaps makes the August fair and the sale of *jeguas* in particular such an attraction. As it takes place at the time of the hay harvest many villagers have relatives or visitors staying and their attendance at the fair swells the numbers considerably.

The technique of nose-pulling is obviously admired for it requires considerable strength. An Alcedan household's visiting son-in-law from Madrid, who had been watching the proceedings from a nearby stone wall, suddenly jumped down and, to the great interest of all the onlookers, performed this task on a recalcitrant foal. Dressed in an immaculate white airtex shirt, flared and tailored trousers and well-polished brown shoes, he was obviously a city man. In the process of wrestling the terrified animal towards the ramp it trod several times on his foot, badly damaging his immaculate shoes. He however showed no sign of pain and completed his bravura performance with a flourish, though quite out of breath. He had proved to himself and others that despite being now a town-dweller, he could still master a *jegua*, but he did not try it again. Instead another young man, an affine from another house in Alcedo, stepped up and proceeded to perform the task on several foals in succession.

The horses were mainly tied up to hedgerows while the heifers took pride of place, tethered within the market forecourt. Hundreds of countrymen milled around this area inspecting individual cattle or gathering in small groups to discuss the quality and quantity of animals compared to last year. They discussed the weather and how successive dull and wet days were affecting the harvesting of the hay. Today had proved an exception as the sun broke though the valley mist early in the morning, allowing the coats of the animals to dry. They had all previously been carefully groomed and most had a sheen which made them more attractive to the buyers.

There were varying opinions as to why prices were rather low. 'Money is not easy at the moment—it isn't moving—not very fluid,' was the opinion of one villager, to which the others in the group nodded agreement. Another view was that there were too many animals about for sale and therefore buyers could pick and choose more freely. Others felt the depression in market prices was because buyers were being cautious due to the current political climate.[6]

Soberly dressed, the majority of these countrymen wore dark grey or black trousers and coats or waistcoats over open-necked white shirts. Some wore black berets; others had dark felt hats or caps. Everyone held in his right hand the ubiquitous hazel stick: the badge of the countryman.

'That is a very fine *ternero*,' said one farmer, touching its broad back with his hazel stick. Another *ternero* close by, with an equally broad back, would not fetch such a good price because of its bowed legs. In fact, the potential buyers' main point of interest, apart from an animal's general appearance, was its back and shoulders. These cattle were not the typical Asturian highland breed, but a cross-breed, sired by a *colono* bull to produce calves with a heavy body and a long broad back. Generally light brown to fawn in colour they were specially bred for the beef market.

When purchasing mules, donkeys or brood mares, which may not necessarily be bound for the abattoirs, a buyer will look at the teeth of an animal to gauge its age. He will feel its withers and back and run his hand down to its legs, checking very carefully around the hocks for sprains or bone fractures. With a young heifer a buyer will view it from the back rather than from the side or front. He will then reach over and feel the back, grasping a roll of flesh to test its thickness and resilience. Feeling the back of one fine young animal with evident admiration a villager wryly muttered, '*muy buen filetes*' implying that it would make very good fillet steak. It was no longer an animal which had, after great care and solicitude from birth, been brought to the market with considerable pride. It had become a piece of tasty meat. Countrymen do not mince their words. There is little or no false sentiment among the menfolk. As one villager bluntly remarked, 'I nurtured the animal and have lavished care on it. It is my right to dispose of it how I wish.'

In one sense man's predatory inclinations are very much in evidence at these fairs. Cattle are by nature docile and do not appear to register any symptoms of distress. It is perhaps easier to be objective about their imminent demise. For the equine species different sentiments are involved and it is perhaps a reflection on human nature that it is the horse fair of August in Tuña which seems to generate the big crowds, the excitement and the element of *machismo*.

The autumn fair at Somiedo

'We used to ride all the way to Somiedo on muleback,' said one villager. We had just covered 55 km by road: by the mountain paths it would have been less. 'It took two days to go and one to return; we used to go every year.' The old villager said he knew all the pathways and short cuts and villages en route. It is very mountainous country in the upper Pigueño valley, with many rock escarpments and cliffs and huge tracts of forest and open moorland.

'Once, some years ago now, a villager from near Alcedo, while returning from the fair, fell from the pathway over a precipice with his mule. He was never seen again—they didn't find his body or the mule's.'

Villagers maintained that they had never known the sun not to shine on the day of Somiedo fair. This is perhaps not so remarkable, as Somiedo lies on the northern edge of the dry Castilian plateau. The day we visited the fair was no exception: the sky was cloudless.

We had climbed 1500 m, passing two *vaqueiro* villages perched high above the road with their characteristic high thatched roofs. Passing between two pinkish rocky outcrops, the last of the Cantabrian range which now lay behind us, we emerged on to the plain of León. The treeless plateau was criss-crossed with stone walls and green fields stretching as far as the eye could see. This was fine grazing country for transhumant flocks of sheep and goats during the summer months; in winter it had a near Arctic climate.

'Do you see the chapel down there?' asked one of my village companions, pointing towards a cluster of grey stone houses, barns and a small church surrounded by walled enclosures. 'The snow will cover the top of the bell tower in three months' time. No one lives here in winter.'

One of the very large stone-walled fields next to the village formed the centre of the fair. There all the horses and cattle were tethered to makeshift rails. In adjoining fields were large groups of sheep and goats, tethered close to their owners' vehicles, or contained within temporary wooden hurdle enclosures. Most of these animals, and there were hundreds of them, had recently been herded overland to the fair by their owners.

Most of the commercial buyers had come from Oviedo or León and their cattle trucks lined the roadside. Most of the countrymen had brought their animals from the nearby Pigueño valley, or from the plains to the south. Others came from near León and at least one group had come all the way from Estremadura.

By late morning a huge crowd had assembled, including several villagers from Alcedo. Ramirez had come with his new pick-up, while other villagers had managed to obtain lifts from relatives or neighbours who owned cars in nearby Quintana, Boinas and La Vega. In their view the prices were very high, they had really only come to look. As one villager commented wryly, 'We're walking around a lot, but not buying anything.' Although a lot of bargaining went on, no one from Alcedo had brought any animals to sell, nor in the event did they buy any.

Leonardo had every intention, it seemed, of buying a goat or a sheep, if he could get it at his price of 4,000 pesetas. There were some long-wooled sheep, but most were close-wooled merinos. Some of the goats varied in colour from pure black or white to mottled variations, but the majority were an attractive reddish-fawn. As we moved from from one group to the next, Leonardo would study the animals in each enclosure from a distance. Most of the shepherds had crooks with which they would secure a goat or sheep by the neck, but Leonardo would grab an animal by a rear leg and secure both back legs with one hand. He would then run his other hand over its sides, back and hindquarters: a deep chest was the sign of a good goat, he maintained. He would open its mouth to check its age from its teeth.

Formerly, before they moved to a cattle-dominated husbandry, Alcedans sold many goats at the Somiedo fair and it was noticeable that the older villagers were more interested in these animals than the young were in the cattle. Leonardo never managed to get anyone to drop their price below 5,000 pesetas. He asked one farmer from León whether he had sold anything, implying that his price was far too high. 'No,' he replied, 'but there are many fairs!'

After midday, more and more people arrived. Cars were now parked for a kilometre in each direction along the road, many of them with Madrid number plates. The sombre clothes of the villagers were now less obvious in the sea of bright colours worn by the new arrivals. The villagers seemed in a very jovial mood as we sat down on the shady side of a stone wall to partake of our *meriendas*. Soon we were joined by other villagers who, despite the fact that nothing was within their price range, were enjoying themselves. 'We don't do this sort of thing very often you know,' commented one of them, 'for us it is a *fiesta*!' Later we joined the crowd around the cattle sales again. One fine bull was sold to a butcher from León for 130,000 pesetas. 'That will be worth half a million to him,' commented one villager.

As the afternoon drew on we made our way back down the Pigueño valley where, whenever a bar came into view, we would stop and Leonardo would insist on buying drinks. He had soon paid out the difference of 1,000 pesetas for the goat for which he had been bargaining. Another villager then told him that the sheep whose owner had refused his offer of 4,000 had later been sold for 3,500. Leonardo did not seem unduly distressed by the news.

It was after dark by the time we arrived back in the village. No one was the richer by acquiring an animal, nor for that matter the poorer, except perhaps Leonardo. It was a day, as they had said, on which they would just look at the animals and meet old acquaintances from distant villages. In short, it was a holiday. Alcedans do not often get an excuse for that.

The mid-winter fair of San Blas in Tuña

> All the men go quite crazy about San Blas. For days before the fair they talk about nothing else, nothing but the *terneros* they will sell and what prices they will fetch. The *mozos* however talk about nothing but the dance after the fair. They still have their *ilusiones*.

This rather sardonic comment on male behaviour by an elderly village lady conveys some of the intense anticipation generated among villagers by the San Blas fair. They sense that it is a celebration of the end of winter, premature of course, as late snowfalls have often blighted the event in the past. It also conveys the sense that all the careful nurturing of their livestock through the winter, their flair for good husbandry, will be rewarded. It may indicate their superiority in the village in expectation of better prices for their stock than their neighbours, a factor which generates not a little respect and some envy.

The San Blas fair is however a major social event involving all the village. The women of each house have to prepare the *meriendas* for the day, which some will take themselves to the fair and eat with the menfolk. It is an occasion when former neighbours and distant relatives from other villages can meet and converse on neutral ground, and when the young may meet their compatriots at the dance in the evening.

The market place and the negotiations which take place there are still considered a preserve for the senior male members of each household. Even if a widow is regarded as head of the house, she will still find a male relative or neighbour to transact her fair negotiations for her should she wish to buy or sell animals. Although Alcedans maintain that a man does not demean himself by doing women's work, and women are frequently seen undertaking what might be regarded as men's work, there still remain certain implicit conventions which all respect.

Felipe had discussed with his wife on numerous occasions the possibility of selling their donkey. They were an elderly couple whose children had all left the village. He was still active as an expert butcher and had frequent calls on his time during the winter *matanza*. Apart from the haymaking in summer and keeping up their two *tierras* and kitchen garden, the couple were now able to rely on their pension for most of their needs. They kept a milking cow and a mule which carried manure for the *tierras* and wood for the kitchen stove. They had no further need for the donkey, to which they had over the years become very attached. They did not wish to part with it, but it did require feeding in winter and there was not much hay that year so they decided to sell it. They agreed on a price: it was still young enough to have many years of active work and donkeys are usually quite long-lived. Felipe took it to the San Blas fair, but no one came to bid for it. So he returned with it to the village to await another occasion.

Similar discussions go on in every house at the time of fairs, or when animals are considered for sale. With the possible exception of calves, it could be said that any decision to sell is a joint one between husband and wife, particularly so if the animal is part of her inheritance. Equally, a son old enough to inherit would also be consulted, or indeed a daughter of marriageable age who might inherit the animal as part of her dowry. Thus women participate in any decisions and may advise against a sale, although the sale itself is negotiated by the menfolk.

For the 1978 San Blas fair the village was up early, many of the houses having their lights on by 5 am, well before dawn. Villagers who had not left with their animals the previous afternoon to stay with relatives near Tuña, had all departed by 7 am. It was a wet and rainy day with a bitter north wind and they knew that they had to secure 'good positions' before others got there. This was a much larger fair than the August one, and there were different dispositions for the animals. There were well demarcated areas for *chatos* (male calves) and elderly cattle which were mainly for sale to the *carneceros* (butchers). These were placed in the market itself. Other animals destined for other purposes such as milk cows, bulls, oxen and horses—there being no foals at this time of year—were all placed on the west side of the river, in the main square and side streets of Tuña. Numerous stalls were set up close by to sell various products ranging from kitchenware, clothing and bed linen to luxury items like radios and refrigerators. Most of the stalls were however selling farm items such as baskets, ropes, ironware, harness and saddlery, spiked dog collars and bells for sheep and cows.[7] There was also various mechanical and motorised equipment on sale in the town centre and nearby alleyways. There were tools and iron ploughs, power chain saws, motor-mowers for the hay, and various types of small Italian-manufactured tractor-carts, with attachments for ploughing, seeding and harrowing.

By midday cattle trucks, vans, pick-ups and cars lined the roads leading to Tuña, while the town itself and the market across the river were crowded with thousands of people from outlying villages and towns such as Tineo, Cangas de Narcea and Belmonte and merchants from the cities of Aviles and Oviedo. Unlike the summer fairs however there were few onlookers who had come just to enjoy themselves. All seemed intent on serious business. Later in the afternoon younger villagers started gathering for the evening's jollities of drinking and dancing.

After his early start Rafael, like several other villagers from Alcedo, had his two *terneros* tethered in a good position in the market an hour or so after dawn. Soon the market was full of tethered animals. The villagers dressed for the occasion wore gaberdines or held umbrellas against the rain. They had dispensed with their clogs in preference for smart black shoes or boots which were soon covered in mud, and each carried his hazel stick. The buyers had already started making offers.

Two weeks earlier Rafael had turned down an offer of 95,000 pesetas for one of his two *terneros* from a buyer who had come up to the village. With some pride he had therefore set his figure at 100,000 pesetas for each calf: a price that would be a first for the village. But the buyers just shook their heads, offering him 95,000. 'When I have been offered that price in the village,' he rejoined, in some frustration for he was very proud of his *terneros*, 'why should I accept the same price when I have brought them all the way to the fair?' Perhaps there was something about the 100,000 peseta price which frightened off the buyers. Perhaps paying six figures for a calf would create a bad precedent.

The weather however was not advantageous to the sellers. It was overcast and there was a continuous drizzle. Unlike Somiedo where the animals' coats literally shone in the sunlight, here after an hour the calves were looking a little listless and bedraggled. The villagers, fully aware of this, became tentative and defensive, tending to lower their prices, while the buyers, sensing this mood, became more combative. There were hundreds of *terneros* packed into the market area, providing a seemingly endless choice.

'I didn't bring my *terneros* here today,' remarked one old villager from Alcedo, observing what was happening. 'I thought there would be far too many animals for sale.' Then with a slightly deprecating smile he continued: 'It reminds me of the woman who goes shopping and sees a pretty dress—just the one she wants to buy. Then she sees a lot more—all equally pretty, and then in the end she can't make her mind up. No! Rafael is asking too much for his animals. He should lower his price!' Rafael's son José, however, made him stick to it. After all, he pointed out to his father, they would be the first calves in the village to reach such a price.

Later in the day the rain abated, the clouds lifted and the sun shone. The animals' coats dried out and things looked better. It had got around to many of the buyers that Rafael was asking too much and it was not until nearly five in the afternoon when they returned: first one, then another, until there were four of them surrounding his calves, but still he held out for his price. Two of Rafael's neighbours from the village came over and attempted to intercede for a figure between the two prices. Sometimes villagers will do this, partly from a genuine desire to help, and partly because if they manage to clinch the deal they may get something from both buyer and seller. Rafael however was getting rather tired of standing around. He was no longer a young man and the day had been a long one. So he let his son do the bargaining, indicating that José had come of age, a symbolic relinquishing of Rafael's duty as head of the house. There were not many calves left unsold in the market and clearly the buyers liked the look of these, which were among the best they had seen all day. However, after further exchanges on prices two of the buyers moved off. Then the third one moved away, shrugging his shoulders. As he disappeared into the growing throng of onlookers he shouted back, 'I want to be a rich man too!' In a gesture of continuing defiance José indicated to the remaining buyer that his father would not lower his price. 'Anyway,' he added, 'we can't sell now so late in the afternoon.'

Then after a brief exchange José suddenly shook hands with the buyer. It seemed his price had been accepted: that the mythical six figure number had at last been attained! But this is not what had happened. The buyer had offered to purchase the calves from the village. He would come and collect them for the same price as had been offered two weeks earlier. It was a compromise, but it worked. It was a face-saver for both parties and Rafael and José were satisfied. Their day had not been entirely in vain.

Elsewhere that day of the San Blas fair Juan, whose family was about to leave the village to settle in Oviedo, had brought two good milk cows for sale. They were the last of his herd. All his other animals had either been sold to neighbours or to a buyer who had come to the village with his truck some weeks previously. Juan had secured a position in a side street just off the square leading to the church. There were about twenty other milk cows for sale all in a row. Juan had put rugs on his cows' backs to keep them dry. He, unlike Rafael, was anxious to sell. A man approached to inspect his cows and some vigorous bargaining followed during which characteristically, as a means of emphasising the particular virtues of his animals, Juan gesticulated rapidly with his hands. When his right clenched fist finally smacked downwards into the open palm of his left, an observer would know a deal had been struck. It was a villager from near Tuña who had accepted his price and they shook hands.

In another street nearby, another elderly villager from Alcedo had brought a pair of trained oxen for sale. After much bargaining with various potential buyers and patiently waiting for most of the day, he finally clinched a deal. Reflecting somewhat ruefully on the rather low price and the long wait, he said, 'In the old days we never had any problems in selling our oxen. They were considered to be the best. You could almost ask any price for them that you wanted. But now'—at this point he waved his hand in the direction of the rows of new tractors nearby—'that is what people want now—oxen have had their day.' The old man was not exaggerating. The oxen of western Asturias were renowned not only for their strength but also for their docility and intelligence and buyers would come from great distances, even as far away as the Basque country, to purchase them.

'A few months ago,' another villager from Alcedo commented, 'old Alerio sold his pair of oxen beyond Oviedo, at a fair in Infiesto. They fetched 117,000 pesetas for the pair. That was a good price then. A Basque from near Pamplona in Navarre bought them. He told Alerio that he wanted them for dragging timber as well as other work. My father and I,' the villager continued, 'sold a second pair of *bueys* we had at the time last year at Cangas de Narcea. They were also bought by a Basque farmer with his big beret. He lived near San Sebastián. Our oxen, you know, are greatly sought after, particularly in the Basque provinces, because they are well-trained, large and strong, and are castrated of course.' He then went on to explain how this must be done when they are young or there is a risk of infection. In Alcedo there is a man who castrates all the *bueys* by cutting the cord with his hands. 'It makes all the difference,' the villager continued, 'as then they are very docile and no trouble. If you don't do it then in five or six years' time they can become very aggressive—like the bulls you see in bullfights!'

In another side street, off the main square, there were a number of bulls which had been brought for sale. As a precaution most of these animals had their faces covered with cloth or sacking. 'If you don't do this,' commented Rafael, 'they can go for people. They will also try to mount any nearby cow, or even young *chatos*. Last year, here in Tuña, a bull got loose and managed to dent several cars and break the wing mirrors; it frightened a lot of people as it ran everywhere before it was caught. That is one of the reasons we discourage children coming to the fair. It can be very dangerous.'

Nearby were several large groups of horses. Few were tethered. As one was being secured with a rope it backed into other horses around it and started kicking

Plate 9 Negotiating a sale at Tuña fair

out. Only the quick action of some men nearby prevented a stampede. There was a lot of shouting and recrimination, but tempers soon abated.

Compared to the well-ordered and rather placid marketplace across the river, the centre of Tuña presented a singular contrast. The pungent smell of urine and manure and sweating animals, the milling people and the raised voices of excited bargaining, the imminent risk of animals kicking or breaking free and creating chaos: all made for the highly charged and dramatic atmosphere so characteristic of these fairs.

Fairs and conviviality

If the evening *fiesta* with bands and disco music in the bars of Tuña is for the young, then the midday *merienda* is the main social event for older people. During the summer fairs this takes place in fields adjoining the town, but in winter groups of villagers congregate in the upper rooms of these same bars. Wives, sisters, grown-up daughters and mothers-in-law start arriving about midday. They may come in shared taxis or relatives' cars, but more often in the customary manner on mule-back, with the picnics placed in leather panniers on either side of the saddle.

The town and city buyers tend to congregate in the bars downstairs, while upstairs all the available space is taken up with tables, chairs and benches. All afternoon these upper rooms are filled with villagers, their families and friends. This is when people scattered over this region of western Asturias have a chance to meet in convivial surroundings. It is a time to discuss market prices, politics, the weather, family and village events and just gossip. Their only obligation to the bar owner is to buy their drinks from him, mainly beer and wine, which they like to mix together, and local cider.

The women go to great trouble over the *meriendas* for the fairs, just as they do for the summer hay harvest picnics, preparing huge quantities of food not just for their immediate family but for others who might join them. This is their part of the day and they hold court, proffering food to all. No matter what their guests have already eaten they are expected to eat more, and with gusto. Any hesitation or polite refusal might imply that the *merienda* was not quite up to scratch. This participation and giving of food is of great importance in villagers' lives and occurs whenever there is occasion throughout the year. Husbands take credit for their wives' prowess and the latter take pride in their accomplishment.

The *meriendas* usually include several *empanadas*, each of vast proportions and several centimetres thick. These are made from dough, meat, peppers, various spices and condiments. There are also legs of salted pork, thick slices of beef in batter, *chorizos* and numerous other types of spiced sausages, loaves of baked *escanda* bread, sweet cakes made with sugar and hazelnuts and many other delicacies, all cured, baked and prepared in the household kitchens. No wife should return to the village with food uneaten. No one should ever admit to being gorged. Generosity in this respect is reciprocal and mandatory and a reflection of social worth.

María's husband had set off an hour before dawn, as the mule journey over old paths and tracks took three to four hours. Two villagers had loaded their calves on to the shopkeeper's small truck, but that cost money and Julio, like others, had decided to herd his animals to market and ensure a good position by arriving early. Some four hours later María had set off, her mule's panniers bulging with the carefully packed *merienda* inside. When she arrived the town square was a seething mass of people and animals, while inside the upstairs bar-room, where her husband and father-in-law Miguel had already secured a table, it seemed even more crowded. Perhaps the continuing rain had prompted an early *merienda*, for there were upwards of a hundred people already squeezed into the modest room, mainly male villagers in their dark clothes, lightened by the women's bright headscarves and kerchiefs used as food wrappings and now transformed into tablecloths. María's mother-in-law Severa was also at the table, having just arrived from Boinas in a car with some neighbours.

Julio and Miguel were rather gloomy. They had managed to sell one *ternero* for 75,000 pesetas, but not the other two they had brought. 'It's the rain,' said Julio, 'they're not selling well. There are too many to choose from.' They visibly cheered up however as María started laying out her sumptuous repast. They discussed whether to lower their prices or just take the *terneros* back to the village and try again at the next fair. They were good animals and deserved a reasonable price and Miguel, having eaten, soon departed for the market again. His empty place on the bench was quickly taken up by María's brother from the village of Abedul, one of the most isolated in the region above Alcedo, where former *vaqueiro* pastoralists had settled and started farming the land. Room then had to be made for Severa's elder brother Gregorio and his son, who came from a village some 40 km to the west near Tineo.

The conversation turned to politics and the forthcoming elections. Gregorio had been a boy when the last elections took place in the 1930s. They all agreed that the prospect of being able to vote freely was strange but exciting.

By about five in the afternoon, just before dusk started settling in, the trucks had been loaded and had gone. The market, except for a few villagers and remaining animals about to depart, was virtually empty. In the town across the river the bars were full and before long the dancing would start. The older people who had not already departed on horse or muleback to their villages, obtained lifts from the few car owners. On the way home they would stop at roadside bars to reminisce on the fortunes and misfortunes of the day It might have been daybreak before they got back had it not been for wives, sisters and daughters chivvying them on: for there was work to be done in the morning.

Felipe, who had brought his donkey for sale, was very sceptical and compared the fair with those held in earlier days. Then there were fewer animals and none of the 'new-fangled machinery' so much in evidence now, and negotiations were conducted in a less hectic manner. 'We have a saying here,' he added, 'abundance makes waste'. But then, while others were talking about the sums of money they had got for their animals, no one had shown the slightest interest in Felipe's ageing donkey.

Animals and economic viability

Most domestic animals are destined for the pot in one form or another, within the village or elsewhere. Animals suffered to die naturally are cats and dogs, and occasionally donkeys and mules may be included in this category. Young *chatos* or *terneros* are not eaten if stillborn or born with a malfunction, for fear of catching some disease. They are dumped some distance from the village and become carrion for dogs and wolves. The semi-wild horses frequently escape the abattoir by falling foul of marauding dogs, wolves or even the occasional bear.

In the past these mountain villages were almost entirely subsistence-based and the local markets were used for trading sheep, goats, fowls and other produce including fruit, berries, snails, a variety of nuts and sometimes knitwear. Since the civil war, however, with better communications and access by road, village economies have become market-orientated, concentrating increasingly on cattle rearing. Although the older generation retains a sentiment of close association with animals, there is perhaps a lessening attachment among the younger villagers. Once beholden to an external market system life and work have to be geared to the exigencies of that market, which is controlled by many factors beyond the behest of these small communities. Inevitably over the decades since the civil war adjustments and compromises have been made in the villagers' philosophy towards animal husbandry and the farming of their lands. There is for instance the constant reminder of the monetary value of animals in current market terms and a consequent need to know the best time to sell for maximum profit. This of course is dependant on various factors which may include weather conditions and the availability of feedstuffs through the winter to bring animals up to their most advantageous physical shape for selling. It also means cattle are being bred more on the basis of profitability than for reasons of tradition and perhaps better adaptation to the environment.

With the recently completed macadamised road to the village from Boinas it is possible for buyers to drive up to the village and buy calves direct from individual farmers. Although local fairs are popular and all the villagers continue to go to them, they are not so dependant on selling their animals there. In effect the new road gives them more options. In the past buyers would know that a farmer brought his animals to market because he needed to sell them, and that he did not wish to take them back to his village. This was not just a question of pride but rather a practical problem involving the economics of husbandry, as any delay in selling meant extra costs in feeding the animals. Equally, after the relatively inactive winter months, buyers knew that with the coming of spring farmers could not lavish so much time on the well-being of their calves, particularly during the time of the hay harvest. Knowing this, buyers would bargain down sellers who might lose as much as a quarter of their expected price. Nowadays, if a buyer comes to a village, although a farmer may not expect the same price as he might get in the market, his animals are snug and dry in their byres and may appear sleeker than they would after a long journey. Furthermore the buyer is hardly going to carry the cost of bringing his large transporter all the way up to an isolated village if he does not have every intention of buying. Thus to some extent the roles are reversed and the farmer is in a better position to set his price.

Most farmers in the village own mules which are used for a number of tasks. They may be employed to bring in freshly cut clover for animal feed in the spring, or for carrying manure on to the *tierras* prior to the spring sowing, or for light ploughing, harrowing and seed drilling. People ride them when visiting other villages and use them as pack animals when taking *meriendas* to the local fairs or to the haymakers working in the fields in summer. Donkeys are also used for many of these purposes.

Many villagers own horses or *jeguas* and may express pride in their numbers: occasionally they have as many as twenty or thirty. These are never put to any domestic use in Alcedo, although they are occasionally broken in and ridden in some other nearby villages. These horses are semi-wild and roam freely on the open moorland, the foals being born in the early spring. Providing they are not eaten by predators or struck by lightning, they may be rounded up during the winter. As a result some eight- to nine-month-old foals and elderly mares past parturition are taken to the San Blas fair in Tuña in February as well as the summer fair.

Although wolves command a deep respect, villagers frequently complain about their depredations on their horses. During the particularly severe winter of 1978, one man told me with apparent resignation that he had lost three fine horses in a week. Usually wolves hunt small game singly or in pairs. During severe winter weather however, when they may enter the village to scavenge, they tend to hunt in packs and can easily pull down fully grown horses. Their methods of doing this and their other modes of hunting are indicative of their remarkable cunning and intelligence.

Most wild horses, including Exmoor ponies, when approached or threatened in any way instinctively group in a circular formation: heads to the centre, rear ends and hooves outermost to fend off attack. These Asturian horses, descendants of the famous Asturcón, seem to have lost the instinct for self-defence. Conversely, the indigenous Asturian cattle automatically converge when threatened, predictably with their rear ends inwards and their heads and horns facing out. When resting on the ground, they tend to group themselves in this manner. Despite this wolves have been known to attack them with some success. Sheep and goats, despite the agility of the latter, tend to be easy prey and need constant attention, even in fields close to the village. The increasingly heavy losses of sheep sustained by villagers through the earlier part of this century were a direct result of depopulation and the consequent lack of young shepherds to guard the flocks. This and the market emphasis towards cattle sales saw the virtual demise of traditional herding practices.

In spite of a greater government emphasis in recent years on wildlife protection, especially of endangered species such as the Cantabrian wolf, there is little evidence of a recovery, which of course would conflict with upland farmers' interests. Indeed shooting wolves with a licence, and poisoning them without one, continued through the 1970s and may still be happening.

The breeding cycle of pigs is controlled not by market demand but by the *matanza*, around the time of the new year. This is the winter killing of pigs for the curing and preservation of the following year's meat supply. Most of the product of each house's *matanza* is consumed within that household, the rest being exchanged within the village and used as payment to those who assist with the summer hay harvest. Presents of meat are also given to kin and affines and godparents who may live beyond the confines of the village in nearby towns or more distant cities, and these gifts are a much esteemed luxury.

'When is it preferable for calves to be born, you ask me?' said a villager in answer to my query in 1978. 'In summer, of course, when the grass is green and has *fuerza* (strength) and the cows give more milk. But it seldom works that way now. The calves need looking after and there is much work to be done at that time of year: other work that is. There is the question of the best time to take your calves to market to sell them. There are the flies and insects in summer which molest the cows. No, there are many factors.'

Clearly the old villager was contrasting traditional with contemporary market requirements and the economic realities of timing for the maximum economic advantage. He had just failed to sell two of his calves at a fair and was understandably depressed. He was one of the poorer villagers. He had few cows which produced equally few calves; he was short on winter feed and tended to stick to his price owing to stringent finances. He was a very hard worker who preferred or was obliged to keep to the traditional methods of agriculture. Not for him the recently introduced silage system, nor the new tractor-carts from Italy.

He treasured his oxen and ten years later when we returned he was still relying solely on them. He had no heirs to inherit his farm or influence him towards modernisation. He still went to as many fairs as he could, even if he had nothing to sell. For him it was the occasion that was important, meeting old friends and relations from other villages, particularly his own, for he had married in and acquired his land through his Alcedan wife.

Another villager of a similar age had a sizeable herd of nine cows in 1978 and ten years later had expanded this to 30 including calves destined for market. He was not the largest stockholder in the village, but it was a substantial holding compared to most. He was more relaxed about fairs and, although always attempting to obtain the best price, he was prepared to bargain. Having four sons, three of whom were working part-time on his possessions, he had a lot of assistance. Unlike other villagers however, who had formed a bull-sharing cooperative, each contributing equally to the expenses of maintaining the animal, this man shared a bull with his brother-in-law who lived in Tabla. He also spaced his calves, unlike some who tended towards simultaneous insemination of their stock so that parturition and maturation of the calves would coincide with the winter fairs. In 1978 all his nine cows were with calf, having been placed with the bull at intervals over a six month period, so that the calves would be born between January and June and would be saleable at intervals from the following autumn to the spring of the next year. For various reasons he might decide to sell some early or hold them over till later. Such decisions might depend on how much help he could expect from his sons, and on the availability and costs of feedstuffs, both home-grown and from outside sources, for increasingly as their herds grew villagers were becoming dependant on imported feed. Decisions might equally depend on other commitments and contingencies, not least on estimated gluts or scarcities of saleable *terneros* at the various winter fairs, or indeed external influences causing fluctuations in market prices.

Not all calves are necessarily destined for market. If there was a need to replace or supplement a household's oxen, then two strong male calves would be matched, castrated and trained for the yoke. If a cooperative or shared bull was required within or outside the village to replace an old one, then a fine bull calf might be selected to sire future calves. If replacement milking cows were needed by the household or by neighbours, good calves would likewise be retained.

Writing of these animals in the abstract, the situation may seem very commercial and businesslike, almost like a factory system, but this is not the case. Indeed, villagers become extremely attached to their animals. *Chatos* or calves are not named but all grown animals are, some of which may have been with households for up to fifteen years. They are known by their different physical characteristics and personalities. Villagers will frequently refer to elderly cows with affection. They will tell you how old they are to the year, day and even hour they were born, how many calves they have bred, and about their habits, endearing or otherwise.

Oxen may be particularly favoured. Those from years gone by are spoken of with pride, for their great strength, prowess and intelligence. Sometimes this is demonstrated by a faded photograph from thirty or more years ago, framed with the owner standing proudly between his old favourites. Ultimately, though with sadness on the part of the owner, they too will be destined for the marketplace or for the winter *matanza* along with the pigs. Even when this happens, some find it virtually impossible to slaughter their own animals, particularly those they have known and appreciated for years. They will ask others to carry out the deed while they absent themselves to mourn. Relations with animals among these villagers are complex and frequently discussed among themselves: the rights and wrongs and the dilemma of wishing to preserve while needing to subsist.

Chapter 4

The *matanza*

A cada puerco le llega su San Martín

In a colloquial sense this well known Asturian saying would translate as 'every pig meets his Waterloo', San Martín being another name for the winter killing. It is a common epithet in Alcedo, where most domestic animals end up in the pot. The pig, however, does deserve special mention, for it is that unfortunate animal which is most favoured for slaughter during the *matanza*, which takes place in the village by custom between the last week or so of November and the last day of December. This killing, which provides villagers with all their following year's meat requirements, was until recently a tradition in which every single household participated. The custom was not peculiar to the village, nor indeed to Asturias, but occurred in rural communities throughout Europe for centuries until the introduction of abattoirs and state controls.

Attitudes of villagers towards this yearly event were variable. Not infrequently I would be asked if I had ever killed an animal or whether I would wish to. It seemed that wild animals such as rabbits or pigeons did not quite fall into the category of larger domestic animals and my response was in the negative. To which my interlocutors, who were invariably male, would respond by saying that I was *timido*. It was in a sense a test of character. If I had no inclination or wish to kill I was considered to have a somewhat shy or timid nature with the implication that I would not make a very reliable Alcedan villager.

Some villagers would then admit that they themselves felt the same way, perhaps from commiseration with my inadequacy but occasionally, I felt, genuinely. Others would maintain that it required *valor* which implied not so much bravery as strength of character, a sort of test of manhood. Undoubtedly, there was an implicit regard for those who did not shrink from slaying their own animals, which could include cattle as well as pigs. Usually, however, a householder would request an expert *matador* to dispatch the former. One villager, a *matador* himself, one of two in the village in 1978, justified his killing of a cow that belonged to him by maintaining that the animal was 'mean and ungrateful and gave no milk'. The traditional way to kill cattle was to split their skulls with a single blow of an axe, although some *matadores* from outside the village were beginning to use humane killers. Every male villager was able to skin and butcher a pig, but cattle demanded different skills.

At least cattle were allowed the dignity to stand while being pole-axed. Pigs were held down by force while a long knife was driven to the heart causing near instantaneous death. Unlike one of Pieter Brueghel the Elder's famous depictions of Flemish rural life in which a man can be seen sitting on a pig while singlehandedly dispatching it, time-honoured practice in these mountain villages is for several strong men to restrain an average sized animal. Faced with imminent death these beasts display a desperate strength, though whether their remonstrances stem from the indignity of being manhandled or from some premonition of their impending fate is uncertain.

As with other village cooperative activities such as the harvesting of potatoes, *escanda*, chestnuts and hay, various households work together to accomplish the *matanza*. Although some villagers maintain that they always have cooperation from a similar set of houses in the complex tasks associated with this yearly ritual, this is not strictly true. There is a perceived but not strictly maintained division between the upper and lower village in Alcedo, which is subordinated to the mutual desire for all to cooperate: an ideal towards consistency in social relations rather than an actuality. The village itself is known to outsiders for presenting a common front in local affairs and for its internal cooperative nature: its inherent mutuality. The very geography of the village, however, and the social proximity resulting from it, while creating alliances between houses also tends to break them. In the process new alliances are established, which for various reasons in their turn dissolve and re-group.

Reciprocity with the *matanza*, as with other exchanges of labour, is absolutely essential. No single household nowadays has sufficient able-bodied menfolk to undertake the winter killing on its own and it invariably requires assistance. This is reciprocated by the immediate distribution of fresh meat after the butchering, and usually two *banquetes*—a breakfast and a lunch—given to helpers on the day of the kill. The meat distribution is not limited to the helpers' households, but also includes other houses with which there are what one village lady described as 'priorities'. These she explained were 'family, friends and close neighbours and those with whom you have *compromiso* [commitments, pledges]', the last of course encompassing the former categories, while the term 'close neighbour' is flexible and indeterminate, as I have indicated.

In a sense the meat provided by the *matanza* is not just sustenance: it is a form of currency. Bread and other village food products are used in this way for everyday reciprocities, but meat, once salted or processed in other ways, is the major exchange item *par excellence*. It enables villagers to draw in outsiders to help with the haymaking, giving them gargantuan picnic feasts in the meadows, or in bad weather in the household dining area, in exchange for their work in the fields. The centrepiece of these picnic feasts is the rich diversity of cured and smoked or salted meats, so appreciated by outsiders, who might themselves be part of the extended family, guardians of the children, or just friends. Equally they might be close neighbours, with whom *compromiso* or commitments are held. Thus networks of relationships are established outside as well as inside the village, the *matanza* representing only a part of this subsequent interdependence.

A member of the village community is expected to reciprocate, regardless of personal inclination or aversion to particular people, even if openly expressed. The fab-

ric of the community life would cease in its customary form if people did not reciprocate, the *matanza* being one way of providing the means for this.

As each of the nineteen houses in the village had a *matanza* in the winter of 1978,
and the general procedure for each is essentially similar, the following will be a
summary account of the half dozen or so which, either partially or in their entirety,
I was able to witness, and which I describe here as one single continuous event. It
was a sheer necessity until very recently for such isolated communities, without
easy access to outside markets, to provide for their own sustenance. Meat is conceived to be an essential part of subsistence and the *matanza* represents its function
and integration into the social fabric of exchange.

Beyond its economic role, the *matanza* plays an important part in village conceptions: on philosophical views of existence. It has many of the elements of a form of
religious ritual. In western society there is a social ambivalence bordering on
hypocrisy which villagers cannot assimilate. Villagers do not have the metaphorical
confessional of the abattoir, that assuager of conscience. They have to contend with
the *matanza* in their daily lives, as is evident in their constant allusions to it in their
thoughts and conversation. Just as we give our children books about animals which
enact human roles as surrogate human beings—powerfully conducive in chan-
nelling children's minds towards a romantically poetic vision of animal life—so do
villagers consciously endeavour to protect their young children from witnessing the
killings. Perversely fascinated by the historical and sociological implications, but
equally appalled, I dreaded the impact of these events on the susceptibilities of my
own two very young children, who participated fully in the common experience of
all the other children of the village.[8]

The setting

The *matanza* may take place in any of the outbuildings of a particular house but the
customary place, and the one most frequently used, is in the lower part of the
granero. Although to some extent dependant on prevailing weather conditions, it
usually commences in about the third week of November, each household taking
about four days for the bulk of the work to be completed. With nineteen households in the village and each one following consecutively it would take two months
or more to complete the cycle. It is customary to terminate the last *matanza* before
New Year's Day, and hence there is pressure on houses to complete within the allotted time span. There is therefore considerable overlapping and as many as three
households may be working at any one time. Although households may slaughter
further animals in January, this is relatively rare, usually reflecting mismanagement
or some untoward cause such as a death in the family. If an animal has to be killed
outside the winter months as a result of an accident, its meat cannot be preserved. If
possible the carcass will be sold to a town butcher at a very reduced price, or given
away to neighbouring villagers. If an animal should be slaughtered outside of the

San Martín period, it is never done in March. This prohibition, though not explained by villagers, could be related to their concepts concerning death and rising tree sap and its association with blood: matters to which I shall refer in Chapter 12.

The most auspicious time during the six weeks of the *matanza* is in the period of the last quarter of the waning moon, which occurs in mid-December just prior to the winter solstice. At this time the meat is considered to taste sweeter, and the skin can be removed more easily from cattle. However, this apparently important but brief period of time is for most villagers more aspiration than fact, for each house calls on the assistance of at least three other houses when its *matanza* takes place and thus these other houses cannot simultaneously carry out their own slaughtering. A great deal of water is also required which the fountain reservoir cannot sustain, and over the six week period most of the cleaning of intestines for sausages has to be done in the river valley below the village. There is also the fact that cattle are only infrequently slaughtered at the *matanza*, so their skin removal is less of a problem. Nevertheless, the sweetness of the meat applies to pigs as well, and slaughter at the time of the waning moon is clearly still a preference exercised by some houses each year.

It is as previously mentioned very rare for the owner of a cow or heifer to kill his own animal. This is not just for practical reasons, but rather for sentimental ones. Villagers form strong attachments to their cattle during their life, particularly their milking cows and oxen. Beef is a required ingredient in one type of preserved sausage, but rather then kill an animal, it is normal for villagers to buy this meat from the butchers in Belmonte.

Prior to the *matanza*, pigs are fattened by being fed on chestnuts, ash leaves and maize. Ash leaves cut from the hedgerows in the late autumn are said, like the period of the waning moon, to sweeten the meat. Chestnuts are said to put more meat on the animal, and maize is said to increase its weight, although some villagers maintain it only adds fat. Should a cow, and it would be an old cow which is no longer milked, be assigned for the slaughter, then it too will be fed on ash leaves.

Normally, pigs are fed from household leftovers, mixed with greens such as *berza* or winter cabbage. On occasion they may also be fed on pig's blood mixed with gruel, rather as villagers eat pig's blood sausages, one of the three types of sausage made. As one villager commented, 'Pigs eat like us!' and in this, as in many other ways, pigs assume certain human affiliations in villagers' minds.

With regard to the killing of pigs a variety of views is expressed. These range from the concepts of *valor* to which I have referred, to completely opposite views when villagers quite openly deprecate the *matanza*. 'We are criminals,' they will say, almost shaming themselves. And although all participate these ambivalent feelings, openly expressed and sincerely felt, are not infrequently the butt of humour.

Often villagers come to watch the proceedings: they are almost invariably men, and small crowds can gather. On the occasion of one killing near the centre of the village a neighbour passed by and, pausing for a moment before he went on, he shouted to the participants good humouredly: 'You are all like wolves!' 'We are not,' was the quick rejoinder from within the *cuadro* beneath the *granero* where the pig had just been dispatched, 'we have to pay for it!' 'That makes you worse than wolves!' was the passer-by's rejoinder, amidst laughter from all the onlookers.

The killing

On the first day, the women are up at dawn preparing food in the kitchen, while men search out various items of equipment from the *hoyo* or *granero*, which is usually used as a tool shed as well as a larder. Until recently the *granero*, because of its multiple purpose, was always considered the most important of all the farmstead's buildings. That is why it takes the most prominent place and is so carefully built, being made entirely of fine durable woods rather than stone as with other outbuildings. Villagers are very proud of their *graneros*, many being centuries old. They were traditionally central to the *matanza* and are still usually the site of the butchering and subsequent preservation processes.[9]

The equipment required includes heavy ropes, leather thongs and wooden cross braces for hanging the carcass immediately after the kill. There are also heavy chains for rolling the carcass in boiling water, a very large wooden or concrete trough for containing the water and large urns which are hung over wood and broom fires to bring the water to the boil.

As on all occasions when households combine to carry out joint work, food is provided by the host house, either in the fields or in the household's dining-room or kitchen. For a *matanza* it is customary to provide both breakfast and lunch, both being gargantuan and a demonstration of household prosperity and largesse. By about nine in the morning, men from other participating households have arrived and with the head of the house and perhaps one of his sons they may number six to eight in all. They will partake of a breakfast consisting of a variety of cooked meats in batter, slices of smoked ham, large quantities of freshly baked bread and wine, followed by a chocolate drink and cakes. For this meal it is usually only the men who sit at the table, as they are most involved in the morning's work.

At about ten the first of three pigs is brought from an outbuilding to the space below the *granero*. It is a large old sow, squealing as it is brought in by the eldest son of the house, who is dragging it along by means of a rope. This squealing is probably the most upsetting part for the younger members of the community, all of whom should by this time be safely ensconced in the school house in the upper village.

In earlier days a pig's squealing would give away a *matanza* and would bring the village *vigilante* hot-foot to record the weight for tax purposes. Villagers still, even if only for the sake of the younger children, usually bind the pig's snout to stifle the sound. If it should prove recalcitrant, as this one does by refusing to move, there is a cruel but effective means of coercing it.

It is noticeable in this case, as with so many others in their daily lives, that men, and particularly younger men who wish to demonstrate their vigour and not be shamed in any way, will undertake comparative feats of strength. It is perhaps a question of pride for a man to show that he is as strong as anyone, and particularly important if he should stand to inherit his family's farm, for it is one way of showing himself capable: this may mean competing with a father who has lost some of his youthful vigour. To coerce a full-sized pig of nearly 130 kg single-handed over a distance of 100 m is no mean feat. The pig will stick in its trotters and just refuse to move. Should this happen a sharp iron hook is inserted beneath its jaw, attached to the rope by a ring and then pulled. The pain increases with its obduracy and the animal is immediately more compliant.

On reaching the *cuadro* six men take hold of the pig, making sure that it does not kick out with its extremely sharp trotters, its front and rear legs being bound with rope to incapacitate the animal. It is lifted bodily on to a low table-bench and held firmly by all the men, for a pig has immense strength. Then a member of the household takes hold of a long-bladed knife or skewer and with one rapid movement thrusts it straight to the heart of the animal, killing it instantly. As the knife is withdrawn, a woman—it is always a woman—of the household holds a bucket or a very large bowl under the rush of blood. After a minute or so, during which she stirs the blood with one hand so that it does not congeal or coagulate, the flow ceases and the bowl is removed. Immediately a long chain is placed with three turns around the inert body which the men lift and place in a 2 m long wooden trough. Scalding water is brought from the nearby fire in cauldrons and poured over the cadaver and into the trough. The men then set to with their knives and start scraping the hair off the skin: the older men dealing with the head and front parts, the younger with the lower parts and hindquarters. Occasionally adding more scalding water and rolling the cadaver with the chain in the trough they complete this process, which is carefully executed from behind the ears to the base of the trotters, in about twenty minutes. Then with an incision made in the rear legs, the tendons are extracted sufficiently to insert a stout 1 m pole, to either end of which a rope is attached, passed over a floor beam of the *granero* above, and hauled upon by all the men so that the cadaver is strung up feet first with its rear legs apart and its snout just clear of the ground.

It is at this point that various guesses are made at the pig's weight by those who are working on the cadaver and by numerous villager bystanders who have gathered to watch. Some of the onlookers may lend assistance if required, though their help might imply the need for a gift of meat, and they are therefore reluctant to offer it, even if only to save any embarrassment.

The pig is then weighed by means of a scale attached to a beam. Immediately after the weighing the owner or his son butchers the animal by slitting it from the base of its tail down the belly to the base of the jaw, causing its innards to hang out from the carcass. The stomach lining, lungs, liver and all the intestines are then taken away. The rest will be discarded.

The carcass is then lowered from the floor beam and carried up into the *granero*. The remaining two pigs, both smaller animals, are brought down simultaneously and are dispatched and dealt with in a similar manner. It is noticeable that the second of the two pigs is busily rummaging around the *cuadro*, seemingly quite content with its new-found freedom and quite oblivious to its sibling's fate close by. As with the first, both cadavers are also then carried to the *granero* above the *cuadro*, though in the process one young man, attempting to carry one of these single-handed in a show of strength, loses his grip and to the consternation of all and his own embarrassment, it falls to the ground.

Each of these processes takes approximately one hour to complete. By twelve noon the first carcass is hanging in the *granero* ready for butchering. That will involve only the menfolk of the owner's house during the following day. By about two in the afternoon, all three carcasses are hanging in a row, one weighing 130 kg and two 100 kg each. Taking into account that several kilos of meat will be given away immediately and that part of the weight is bone, this is still considered to be sufficient meat for a small family with two or three adults for the year to come.[10]

At this juncture the day's proceedings terminate for the men except for a huge six-course *banquete* in the house of the family holding the *matanza*. The menu for this is as follows: soup, rabbit with rice, four kilos of meat fillets and hams, followed by rice pudding—an esteemed recipe used by Alcedans—caramel pudding, various cakes, then cognac, cigars and coffee. The order of seating around the large rectangular table is much the same as the order of scraping pigs, with the head of the house at one end and the principal and oldest of the helpers sitting beside him. At the other end sit the women helpers. By four in the afternoon when the meal terminates the men have dispersed to take up their late afternoon activities in their respective holdings.

The preservation of meat

The Spanish by and large tend to characterise Asturias as a beautifully green and mountainous country whose people 'eat well', meaning that they eat a lot of meat. Alcedans themselves do not deny this. 'There [in the south] they eat more salads and vegetables and fruit, because it is hot country,' was the comment of one villager, implying that they are lazy by adding, 'Here we eat more meat because it is cold and we have to work very hard ... it is strong [meat] and it gives us strength.'

It is at this point that the women take over much of the work. On the first day they will already be starting to clean the intestines of waste matter. On the second day the butchering and salting take place, usually done by male household members without outside assistance. A carcass is first placed on a large wooden block in the *granero*. Using butchers' cleavers the haunches are severed and the back and foreparts cut into large sections. As soon as the men complete this task, parts of the meat sliced from the back are distributed by the women, one or two kilos a time, depending on the indebtedness or *compromiso* outstanding. This giving of prime fresh meat is normally reciprocated by others with their *matanzas*, so that in theory it does not represent any net loss in meat.

These exchanges, like all similar types of gift exchange in the village, are conducted surreptitiously. It is not good form to divulge or discuss with others outside the household, to whom meat has been given. As one villager put it: 'people should not know who is giving and receiving presents and you should not thank someone for a gift when others are present, but wait until you are on your own.' There is nevertheless considerable curiosity, especially among the village womenfolk, as to who has given to whom, and perhaps these attempts at confidentiality only generate more speculation. The givers and recipients of these particular meat gifts, although claimed to be the same from year to year, do in fact vary and because of the extreme secrecy involved, patterns of exchange are very difficult to ascertain. The type of meat given, whether cooked or raw or in the form of primary or secondary types of sausage also varies and constitutes a subtle and carefully graded system.

Appropriate reciprocities depend on numerous factors, such as other cooperative work or assistance given during illness throughout the year. They may also be instigated in anticipation of new obligations with different houses in the following year. In our own case we received meat in various forms from ultimately every house in the village. This may be because we gave gifts of various kinds to all houses on various occasions. So generous were these gifts of meat that it became something of an *embarras de richesse*, as from mid-November through to early January kilos of meat, both raw and preserved, began to accumulate, far in excess of our limited needs. This was complicated by the knowledge that we could not pass it on to others for fear of causing offence, and the advice we received from near neighbours that we should keep it out of sight.

The butchering continues through the second day. One or two large wooden containers are placed ready in the *granero*.[11] These are first lined along the bottom with a thick layer of salt. The hind parts of each animal are laid flat along the base of the container, each haunch or quarter being carefully salted first. Parts of these huge pieces of meat are pierced with a knife and filled in with salt wherever it is suspected that a residue of blood still remains. Villagers maintain that if not treated in this way the blood in time will turn the meat bad. Following the rear haunches the ribs and the various cuts from the mid-parts of the animals are placed on top, followed by the forequarters, thus replicating the natural order of the carcass. If there are any large gaps between the sides of meat and the salt, which is constantly being added (up to 50 kg may be used in any one container), then maize cobs are used to plug the gaps, so that no air remains trapped. The container is then carefully sealed with a heavy lid.

The salted meat is left in this manner within the container from fourteen to eighteen days. When re-opened, the various cuts of meat are hung on hooks attached to the roof beams of the *granero*. Villagers maintain that salted meat, properly cured, can last up to three or four years, but after that the meat tends to deteriorate.[12]

If the killing and butchering is considered to be men's work, then the making of the various sausages is women's work. Before most of the belly and ribs of the carcass is placed in the salt, much of the meat is removed. This, along with other edible parts of the animal such as the stomach lining, is used as a component for the three basic types of Alcedan sausage. The first of these is *morcillo*, a large type of sausage made from some parts of pig meat, some beef of poor quality and pig's blood. The second type, called *chorizo*, is made from inferior quality beef and pigmeat. The prime type of sausage, which may also be called *chorizo* 'first class' or *salchicha*, is made from prime pork and some beef. All three types have added ingredients and all are smoked over wood fires during a period of about fourteen days for about an hour each day, usually in the *granero* where, like the salted meat, they are hung from roof beams. The *salchicha* can be eaten smoked in its raw state. The other two have to be cooked before being eaten.

The manufacture of these sausages commences on the second day and continues through to the fourth or fifth day. It takes great patience and skill to wash, cut, fill and tie the intestines to make the sausages. Men say they cannot do the work as their hands are too clumsy and the intestines are easily punctured. If there is sufficient water available from the spring above the village, the primary work of washing can be done in the yard of the house (water having been recently piped to all houses in the village) or in the fountain in the upper village. But if, as is often the case, there is insufficient water, then it has to be done in the river in the valley to the east of the village. This can be very cold work and may take several hours, literally hundreds of metres of intestines from a number of *matanzas* having to be carefully washed inside and out. In 1978 it was snowing for much of the time and there was no water available and many people had to go to the river. With buckets and bowls containing all the intestines and other animal parts perched on their heads, one group of some eight women went down the steep incline early one morning, in single file to the valley bottom. There in the snow, as they cheerfully gossiped well out of earshot, they carefully washed the seemingly endless piles of intestines metre by metre, slapping them on the river stones, checking each centimetre for residual dirt or punctures. It was nearly midday before they returned to the village.

Depending on the size and number of the animals killed, a house can have about 150 kg of sausages to prepare, and this means very hard work for the women of the house and any other women who may from time to time assist with this process. Originally all the meat had to be cut up by hand, but fortunately mechanical mincers now obviate this labour. However, there is no machine to help with the mixing process, which takes time and strength. For this three huge wooden troughs are kept in the *granero*: one for each type of sausage. The basic ingredients that have to be added consist of three types of *pimiento* (capsicum or pepper). One of these is very sharp tasting, another sweet tasting, and a third one which is reddish is used to colour the sausage meat. In addition small quantities of garlic, salt and parsley are added and also white wine for the *salchicha*. These various ingredients are added in variable amounts to the different types of sausage.

Villagers frequently draw comparisons between their own product and manufactured types. One lady commented proudly when adding parsley: 'They don't put that in the meat sausages you buy!' Frequent allusions are made to the advantages of making your own product and eating your own meat, rather than meat from an animal you never knew. It is 'tastier' and 'healthier' and there is the unstated pride in being able to raise your own stock: something which urban dwellers can never do. They are dependant on others. Alcedans are dependant on no-one: they are their own masters.

'It is all done by machines with factory produced sausages,' was one villager's comment, including of course the slaughtering, as she added, 'but it tastes much better this way'. This to some extent may be a form of social justification for all the hard work that goes into the process, for without a very refined taste, which perhaps villagers have, it would be very difficult for the layman to note the difference between the village and the factory products.

The mixing and kneading of sausage meat in the troughs may go on for two days, the women taking it in turns, before the mixtures are ready for putting into the skins. To do this a small machine with an extended nozzle is used, rather like an old fashioned hand cigarette maker.

Having washed the intestine skins with great care, cut them in lengths, dried them and thrown away any damaged ones, the women begin the process of filling. As with a hand mincer the sausage meat is fed into the machine and the handle rotated, thus compressing the mixture as it fills each skin placed over the nozzle. These skins, all of which are made from pig intestines except for some larger cow intestines used for *morcillo*, having been previously tied with gut or string at one end are when filled then tied at the other end. Each is then examined carefully for air pockets which if found are pricked to allow the air to escape. Rotating the machine requires considerable physical endurance and men often take turns with the women to turn the handle.

The three types of sausage may total some 300 and in some houses more. They are usually equally divided into lots of about 100, varying in length from approximately 30-60 cms, hung up in the *granero* row upon row and smoked along with the salted hams. It is a fine sight to see a *granero* so full that it is difficult to walk inside without bumping into the products of the *matanza*, and the pride in this profusion is only too evident in the eyes of the householder: the culmination of years of pastoral care and four or five days of hard labour. In a sense it is the most graphic example of what it means to be an Asturian villager.

Plate 10 Scything the hay with Tabla in the background

Chapter 5

Order and cooperation

The corporate nature of village life

Outsiders always referred to Alcedo as *un pueblo muy unido*: a very united village. Townsmen in Belmonte would compare different villages mainly in terms of people they knew who lived there, or by some other feature, but Alcedo was always referred to as a corporate unit. When we first arrived the villagers described themselves in similar terms, as *gente muy noble*. This could be translated as people having various attributes, including 'of good blood', 'of good faith', 'generous', 'loyal', 'of distinguished ancestry', or a combination of these characteristics. Whether the inhabitants of Alcedo are indeed more united or more noble than those of the hundred or so other villages in the immediate vicinity of Belmonte is a matter for conjecture.

It may be that Alcedo is unusual in the region of Belmonte in that it has retained, or sustained, a sense of traditional corporateness in a way that comparable communities have ceased to do. The causes for the gradual demise of many of these mountain communities are various, but usually relate to the changing aspirations of the younger generation who, with the advantages of education and better communication with urban centres, have largely abandoned rural life and its attendant inconvenience and hardship for the economic benefits and comparative luxury of town life.

The civil war caused great disruption to many of these communities, not so much because they were directly involved in the conflict, as Alcedo was, but because many of the younger generation suffered enforced separation from their domicile as a result of it. This separation was part of a continuing tradition of younger villagers of both sexes who did not inherit land or livestock of seeking work elsewhere or emigrating. The war and its aftermath—the poverty and deprivation these communities suffered—only tended to increase their depopulation, particularly by the young. Since then the building of roads, the spread of consumer goods and the changing role of the church in community affairs, coupled with a declining population, have tended to undermine the old tradition of self-sufficiency. It may be that its peculiar geography and relative isolation, at least until the 1970s, allowed Alcedo to retain a certain autonomy and corporate identity longer than its neighbouring communities.

Village government and organisation

After the decline of the suzerainty of the Lapedo monastery in the early nineteenth century, the waning of the feudal impositions of the *palacios* in the early part of the twentieth, and the diminution of church influence resulting from the civil war, villagers gained a degree of autonomy perhaps unknown in the past. This autonomy however was regulated to a degree by an authority within the village. The first of these was the *vigilante*, a villager designated by local authorities to oversee village affairs and be responsible to those authorities. The second was the *regidor*, a villager nominated by his peers to represent their interests within and outside the village with those same authorities.

The introduction of a *vigilante* or invigilator came about during the nineteenth century. At that time he would have been responsible to church and manor for collection of the various dues or 'taxes' levied on animals. From the late 1940s onwards, however, the *vigilante* was probably granted wider powers within the village, and he was appointed by a local district officer from Belmonte or by the mayor of Belmonte himself. These appointments were made for life, and as he was not democratically appointed by the villagers themselves, the *vigilante* tended to be a rather unpopular member of the community; however, although resented he was nevertheless usually respected.

The role of the *vigilante* included the settling of village disputes. If these proved difficult to resolve they would be referred to a higher authority within the parish, or in Belmonte. He supervised any public works within the community and was responsible for the upkeep of paths and trackways both to and within village boundaries. He also oversaw the slaughter of animals, particularly at the winter *matanza*, and the then relatively infrequent sale of animals at market. Until the subsequent reorganisation of taxation based on land possessions, the market sale or slaughter tax was the only workable system by which to levy income from these mountain villages.

Villagers would not infrequently attempt to avoid this tax, either by not informing the *vigilante* of a slaughter or by concerted efforts to rig the scales. Usually such evasions were discovered, as after the war it was mainly pigs which were slaughtered for consumption and they had an unfortunate habit of making an awful noise when secured for this purpose; while villagers, including the *vigilante*, had a very good eye for the weight of an animal. Conversely, the *vigilante* himself was not unknown to favour certain neighbours for various reasons and to over-tax others. He might also be accused of filching some of the proceeds himself by fixing the books. Such accusations, whether just or unjust, caused distrust and recriminations.

With the change from an animal tax to one based on land, the role of the *vigilante* became redundant. A new system was inaugurated in the late 1960s for a representative called a *regidor* to be elected by the villagers themselves. This democratically elected official had to be the head of a house or his representative and could hold office for one year only.

In the late 1970s a special meeting for voting in a new *regidor* would be held in which every senior household member or his representative was expected to be present. Other male villagers could attend this meeting, but not the women. The latter would organise their own meetings separately, mainly to arrange rotas for preparing particular feasts or village festivals.[13] For their meetings the men would usually convene in the village shop. Slips of paper, each representing a household, would be placed in a hat. All were blank except one which had a cross on it. Whoever drew the marked slip would be the *regidor* for the following year. Each year those who had previously been *regidor* would not participate in the draw until only one remained, after which the process would commence again.

On our return a decade later the system had been altered. Starting from the fountain at the southern village boundary and progressing northwards, each house, including the two remaining *barrio* households in Tabla, would in turn take on the duties of being *regidor* each year. I am not sure why this new system was adopted. It is however possible that with a few of the houses no longer wishing or able to participate through lack of active male representatives, the lottery system proved unpopular. It was also thought preferable to know whose turn it would be next, to allow the *regidor*-elect time to prepare.

The *regidor* is regarded as the village spokesman. He is the person who receives communications concerning village and parish matters from the senior *regidor* in the district who lives in another village closer to Belmonte. The *regidor* may call a meeting in the village shop to discuss such matters. Written communications which do not require discussion, such as a list of those with outstanding tax payments, will be posted on the door of the barn just below the shop. In the event of a visit to the village by the more senior Boinas *regidor*, or from the mayor or other officials from Belmonte, the village *regidor* is expected to officiate and to entertain the guests in his own house with a feast or some other sustenance. Such official visits are however rare. He is obliged to convene meetings at which various matters may be discussed, including any current disputes. One such dispute in 1988 involved the owner of the shop and it was thought more appropriate to hold subsequent meetings in the old school house, which was considered to be neutral ground. A decade earlier the main issue that came up at meetings was the paying off of the outstanding debt for surfacing the road up to the village, which had only recently been completed. Part of the costs of this had been covered by government funding, but the rest had to be provided by the villagers themselves, each house in theory contributing a similar amount. Much of the sometimes heated debate at these meetings would centre on why some houses should pay less than others on the apparently escalating costs of work already completed.

Most payments concerning taxes, or other debts such as for the road, are settled through a villager's account with one of two banks in Belmonte. Some villagers are however still reluctant to use banks in the belief that they charge them for keeping their money. In fact, distrust of banks is endemic and may be related to the time of the civil war, although at the time few villagers would have had sufficient liquid funds to place in a bank. Some villagers still keep their money in wooden chests in some secluded place.

One of the wealthiest villagers decided to buy a Santana Land Rover and the purchase transaction took place in the bar of a Belmonte *pension*. The vendor, a car salesman from Oviedo, was astounded when the villager brought out an old cigar box with rolls of 100, 500 and 1,000 peseta notes, all carefully tied up with string, and then proceeded to count out the 200,000 pesetas required.

Perhaps the *regidor*'s most important function in villagers' eyes is overseeing communal work. Although each villager is responsible for the upkeep of his own property, there are paths, cart-tracks, walls, bridges and certain buildings which are common property. On an appointed day the *regidor* will ring the *capilla* bell and heads of houses or their representatives, who might be unmarried brothers, sons or sons-in-law, or even grandsons, will assemble in the centre of the village with their shovels, pickaxes, oxcarts and whatever other items may be required for the task in hand. The party will then move off to commence its work, which may be to rebuild a nearby wall, repair a collapsed culvert or fill in a badly potholed cart-track some kilometres from the village.

These gatherings are usually an occasion for a certain amount of jocularity as well as hard work. Anecdotes and stories are told and retold. Items of village gossip may be discussed within certain limitations, and there is a constant flow of repartee concerning the ineffective efforts and laziness of fellow workers: all apparently taken in good heart. It is an occasion when villagers who may find it hard to be sociable or even exchange greetings on other occasions, on account of some dispute or suspected insult, may find themselves working side by side and feel obliged to converse.

These working parties, in which the *regidor* himself has to work just as hard as everyone else, are therefore not just for keeping the village and its environs in a good state of repair; they are also social ameliorators, where disagreements can be temporarily put aside and when a man's actions and willingness to cooperate are under the full scrutiny of all his neighbours.

Cooperatives

Communal working groups are not the only form of village cooperation. These small and isolated communities are totally dependant on mutual help and reciprocities. Villagers say that one of the main reasons for the abandonment of many *vaqueiro* communities is the lack of able bodied neighbours to assist should a cow have a difficult parturition, something that happens all too frequently with the introduction of new breeds of cattle geared more for market demands than for the villagers' convenience. Should for instance the unborn calf turn and lie across the womb, instead of being born head first it may come hindwards. Although the cow may manage on its own the calf is likely to be stillborn, the umbilical cord having strangled it or been severed before it can breathe. In such situations quick action is required, and if rope and up to six pairs of strong arms are not available to draw the calf out promptly, it may be lost. Pastoralists cannot afford to lose even one calf, and if neighbours are not there to help in emergencies they can no longer raise cattle. There are numerous examples of villages being abandoned when they fall below a minimum level of population; this applies not only to *vaqueiro* villages but also to agro-pastoralists like the Alcedans, who are now equally susceptible with the greater emphasis on cattle raising for market.

There are other forms of required participation in the village and one of these is the *cooperativa*. These came into being early in the twentieth century and have since developed and expanded. By the late 1980s the cooperative had become the alternative mode of village economy, dependant on external commodities and markets rather than on neighbourly relations and reciprocal networks as in the older subsistence based economy. The cooperative may be seen as an attempt by villagers to regain some of their former autonomy in the face of their increasing reliance on traders and middlemen to supply external commodities such as animal feedstuffs, fertilisers and modern farm machinery. This expanding movement is however part of a wider network of self-help schemes which are now a dominant feature of village life.

In the late 1970s cooperatives internal to the village had developed around certain functions deemed by villagers as necessary to sustain their economic viability. Without these most villagers felt that the very continuance of their community might be threatened. Examples of this new cooperative spirit were the construction of the new road to the village and the open field expansion on common land for the growing of various crops. This required investment in hiring deep ploughing equipment and an operator, as well as large amounts of fertilisers, fencing posts and wiring. Not all the villagers participated, but those who did benefited from this development at the time.

The bull society was another example of a village cooperative, coinciding with the introduction of a breed known as the *colono* which, with its long and heavily fleshed back and rump, was sought after by the meat market. Villagers knew that their own traditional all-purpose Asturian cattle, which until then had served them well, were less marketable, and despite the problems of the *colono*'s unsuitability to the Asturian environment and its difficulties of parturition (owing partially to its long back) a society was formed to finance the acquisition of a suitable bull to provide, when crossed with the native breed, more acceptable calves. Not all villagers could afford to invest in the society, or indeed were convinced of the wisdom of bowing to market forces. They were therefore excluded from the society, although an earlier system of each household taking turns to provide a bull to serve the whole community still existed and continued alongside the new venture.

Another example concerns the customary manner in which villagers used to flail their *escanda*. This now rare type of spelt wheat, which has not been grown in the village since the late 1980s, was harvested by being broken off at the node below the head. The *espigas* or hair on these heads is particularly tough, and villagers lightly burned great piles of the heads to singe off the *espigas*, using special forks to move them around so they did not burn to cinders. Then using a traditional leather-thonged thorn stick they used to flail the heads to separate out the grains.

At the turn of the twentieth century a water mill was built next to the small river to the east of the village. It could not only mill the grain, a process which until then had been done with hand mills, but also incorporated a huge water-driven mechanical flail. Unfortunately, although the apparatus worked well and was in constant demand, it was inoperable throughout the summer months because of lack of river water to drive the machinery. Summer is the time when bread is in most demand because of the many visitors working in the hayfields, so most villagers had to revert to traditional methods at this time, until in the 1970s a group decided to form a cooperative to purchase a diesel powered machine to process the grain.

Like other cooperatives this one inevitably excluded some who for various reasons were unable to participate. Although villagers could still use the water mill for grinding wheat as that required less water, the flailing equipment ceased to be used even in winter as there was no longer any initiative to overcome the problems of lack of summer water and the need for constant running repairs. As a result a number of houses stopped planting *escanda* and bought flour for breadmaking from outside the village.

With the inevitable problems associated with operating the new equipment, not least frequent breakdowns and the prohibitive cost of fuel, it too was abandoned and by the early 1980s the highly nutritious *escanda* flour, the traditional basic ingredient in breadmaking, had been replaced by standard commercial brands.

These cooperative ventures were not new to Alcedans, who had after all set up their own generator for electricity earlier in the century. Admittedly this provided only very low light levels and only marginally alleviated the continuing need for oil lamps and candles, but it signified a joint endeavour. They had also devised their own system of piping water to village houses; again this was not entirely effective but in spring, when the water table was high, it lessened the need to obtain supplies from the fountain. The mill itself, and earlier mills it had replaced, had also been joint ventures with little or no assistance from any outside source.

These early cooperative developments however, which also included the establishment of a school in a disused house, had involved all the villagers. They were joint ventures which required far less capital investment, where those who had little or no available cash could contribute through manual labour. These ventures tended to unite rather than divide, substantiating reciprocities and a sense of community. Inevitably recent cooperative developments have involved greater capital investment and although economically attractive and beneficial to the members, they tended to exclude others who could not afford the outlay. Consequently they tended to cut across networks of reciprocities and values based on mutual help relating to a whole range of yearly activities. These developments, based on a regional cooperative movement, had become increasingly effectual and influential by our return in 1988.

Neighbours and reciprocity

> *Hagas bien y no mires a quién.*

> *Quién es su hermano—el vecino mas cercano.*

These sayings, often repeated by villagers, are subtle comments on good neighbourliness. According to the first you should do good to others and not count the cost. In many small actions of assistance, or in making gifts of food, villagers deny any ulterior motive and on occasion things are undoubtedly given spontaneously. Indeed, Asturian villagers have an enviable reputation for their generous nature. Nevertheless, no villager would be so naive as to think that he or she could accept from others without some form of return. No community could function without reciprocities. Mutual assistance is a *sine qua non* of existence and the second refrain, 'Who is your brother—your closest neighbour' is perhaps a more pragmatic comment on the realities of village life, though difficult to realise in such a closely compacted village as Alcedo.

All households are responsible for the general maintenance of their own properties and their economic viability, though assistance may on occasion be sought from neighbours in times of difficulty. The four main traditional yearly harvests are however occasions for mutual help. These four are the haymaking from June to August, the harvesting of *escanda* in September (which had ceased by the time we returned to the village in 1988), the potato digging in October and the *matanza* from late November through December. A fifth harvest was traditionally the gathering of chestnuts in November, but since about the end of the 1970s this has ceased and few now bother to gather the nuts. There is also the late summer cutting and gathering of bracken for winter bedding for the cattle. The September charcoal burning was another occasion for village participation. It was however peculiar in the sense that only men assisted and the blacksmith reciprocated in various ways including repairs on metal tools and the shoeing of mules, horses or cattle in part and indirect exchange. With improved access to the village by road and the consequent availability of commercially produced charcoal, this activity ceased during the 1980s; though the smith, who like other villagers is also a farmer, continues to work for the village and others in the parish when required.

Although the village can still be regarded as essentially a community of farmers, there are degrees of commitment to the actual farming of the land today which would not have been in question prior to the 1970s. The actual participation in the farming cycle by each of the nineteen households in the village in 1978 has implications for the traditional patterns of mutual assistance among houses. It should be remembered that a combination of factors including the development of regional cooperatives, the introduction of modern technology and a shift away from a mixed farming economy towards a more cattle based one are now changing the traditional exchange patterns from those of the 1970s described below.

In 1978 there were nineteen houses in the village in constant occupation, and three further houses only partially occupied for parts of the year. The latter are excluded as being virtually outside the mutual exchange pattern. Of these nineteen houses five were only partially involved in mutual exchanges and will also be excluded from the following discussion.[14] Two houses mentioned previously, those of the shopkeeper and the blacksmith, are peculiar cases. The former has been excluded as although in most aspects it was still engaged in farming its essential orientation had moved towards more commercial shopkeeping interests. The blacksmith's house is however included in the active category, as despite the smithy it retained all the accepted obligations with other traditional households.

Thus in the late 1970s there were still fourteen houses continuing traditional reciprocal arrangements through the cycle of the farming year. I have described above a serial pattern of obligatory reciprocity which involved and united the whole village under the aegis of the *regidor*. Mutual assistance in harvesting divided the village into a southern group of six and a lower northern group of eight households, the two remaining active households in Tabla aligning themselves with the latter group. This division tended to centre on inter-house ties of kinship and mutual regard and respect. Within these two groups there were frequent exchanges between two houses, and less frequently among several houses, based mainly on kinship ties which could however change from year to year. Thus although to outsiders Alcedo is regarded as *muy unido*, within the village there are recognised distinctions and separations.

Of course reciprocities crossed over the divide, but the majority of exchanges of labour, particularly those concerned with the harvest, seemed to operate within these two spheres which, for historical reasons of inheritance, were distinct in character. Those houses to the south, on the ridge rising up to the fountain, all had sibling ties, either *en casa* (that is as either male or female inheritors of a house) or married to *en casa* spouses. This group was characterised by very close marriage ties, even to the order of first cousin, for two or more generations. Thus almost every member of each house had a close biological affinity to members of every other house, which perhaps characterised the mutual reciprocities of this group. In contrast, the other group of households, extending northwards along either side of the ridge on which the *capilla* is situated, was much less closely tied by kinship. They seemed however to be no less supportive of one another.

Within these overall groupings it would be most unusual for all the able bodied members of one house to work simultaneously for another house. Normally one or two males from one house would reciprocate labour with another house, the women doing likewise with a different house. For instance, during the *matanza* men might assist with butchering, salting and packing the meat in bins, or smoking and hanging it up to dry, while women assisted with the process of sausage making. Likewise at haymaking men scythed the grass and conveyed it to the barns, while women spread the cut grass and stacked it to make hay. With some exceptions,

Plate 11 Scything overlooking chestnut woods in the western valley

men's work and exchanges of labour involved physical strength, while women's involved creating change: meat to sausage, grass to hay, *escanda* flour to bread.[15]

When a house has, for whatever reason, fallen behind in its harvest work, there is an implicit obligation on all other houses, despite the division mentioned above, to come to its assistance. Every active household should help another to complete its haymaking before the village begins the *escanda* harvest.

Although I have emphasised that close kin in different houses usually reciprocate with one another, they do not do so exclusively: it is rather a preference than an obligation. An example of non-exclusivity occurred at the time of the sudden death of an elderly but still very active villager. As a result of their attention being centred on the old man's brief illness, death and the ensuing wake and funeral the family, whose active members included a middle-aged niece, her husband and two children in their teens, were quite unable to harvest their *escanda*. This resulted in a working party of between twelve and twenty coming to pick the crop with the family. This group came from a number of households from both sides of the village, though the old man himself had lived in the lower northern section.

A house in the northern section of the village with three able bodied men (a father and two sons) usually exchanged labour with the mother's sister's household in Tabla, but not exclusively. When not engaged in their own harvesting or that of the Tabla household, they would assist another household of three elderly villagers with whom they were only distantly related but who had no children and therefore no heir. Normally in such an unusual circumstance the property passes by law to the owner's co-lateral kin or their descendants. When this happens the beneficiary is usually unable to farm a second property, particularly if it is in a different village, and consequently it will be broken up and rented, sold or just abandoned. Alternatively, the owner may decide to will the property to another household which may or may not be related but which will guarantee the continuation of the house and its land and therefore benefit the whole village. If two sons in a family wish to farm but only one can inherit, a solution would be for the other to inherit a neighbour's possessions, which might have happened in this example. The three elderly villagers, two of whom were women, needed all the help they could get, and this was in a sense freely given, as clearly they were not in a position to reciprocate to any degree. However, this altruism on the part of the family came to nothing, as some years later a prodigal adopted nephew returned to the village unexpectedly and indicated that he would like to take over the farm.

The three examples of reciprocal arrangements given in this chapter—communal work, cooperative societies and labour exchange between households—are all openly accepted and institutionalised modes of village organisation. A fourth system of reciprocity is the exchange of gifts between individuals who are usually emissaries of their respective houses. In a sense all these different exchanges overlap and it is an oversimplification to treat them separately—for instance, a gift may be exchanged for labour—and they are all part of village government and cohesiveness: if the rules of cooperation are abjured the community will be undermined.

The giving of gifts tends to be discreet, at times secretive and strictly personal, though it is usually beneficial to others in a house and forms an essential part of the overall reciprocal ethos of the village. These are material gifts, usually of food, which are frequently given to relations or neighbours within the village and infrequently to relations outside in return for, or in expectation of, some favour or offer of hospitality. These are all essentially women's gifts and between women: a man's gift is his labour. Although the gifts are almost without exception food such as honey, sweet cakes, cheese, vegetables or small livestock, gifting tends to centre on two essentials: bread and meat.

Each house has its own oven and baking customarily takes place every two weeks.[16] It happens not infrequently that a house runs short of bread prior to the next baking and a neighbour will give sufficient loaves to carry it over. In a sense this is a personal loan between two women, but it benefits the household and will be reciprocated in turn. Meat on the other hand is given to a number of neighbours during the *matanza*, sometimes to all the houses in the village. The type of meat given reflects the importance of the debt to be returned and the esteem in which the recipient is held. Such exchanges are always discreet and preferably made without the knowledge of other neighbours. At times it may involve subterfuge, although villagers maintain that no one can keep secrets from the eyes of others. On receipt the meat is placed out of sight to prevent others from not only seeing that the gift has been received, but also noting the quality and quantity of the cut. Such subterfuge can occasion awkward situations which women like to recollect with good humour. It is possible that this clandestine gift-giving is traditional practice; or it may derive from the time of the civil war, when lives might depend on such exchanges and starvation haunted the lives of many. These different forms of exchange were probably fairly typical of similar western Asturian villages. What may be unusual here however is their continuance into the late 1970s and their relative complexity, which may have given Alcedo the local reputation of being a very united village.

Villages situated at a higher altitude than Alcedo are not in a position to harvest crops such as chestnuts and *escanda* which involve reciprocities, though their pastoralist economy requires greater amounts of hay for winter feeding. Villages at lower altitudes are less dependant on winter feed, having milder winters and fewer animals to keep, their economies being based more on *tierra* and kitchen garden cultivations which by their nature are less dependant on reciprocal arrangements.[17] The conditions of the Alcedans' peculiar environment and their need to sustain a near subsistence economy may have a bearing on their patterns of exchange which, at least until recently, seem to have been a key factor in the apparently unified nature of their social life.

Plate 12 Oxen in the *cuadro*

Chapter 6

House and family

> 'He is my best friend: we grew up together. '
> 'What is his name?'
> 'Gordo—the fat one!'
> 'No, no—his real name.'
> 'Alerio.'
> 'Yes, but Alerio what?'
> 'Ah—Alerio de Mateseva.'
> 'Surely that is not a family name?'
> 'No, that is the name of his house.'
> 'But what are his parents' surnames?'
> 'I don't know!'
> 'Would anyone else know?'
> 'I doubt it. You had better ask him.'

Good advice perhaps for the recently arrived fieldworker, but sometimes people are shy about giving their names. It might seem rude to ask such a direct question. In fact this indirect enquiry revealed some interesting points. Firstly the use of nicknames: a rather derogatory one in this case. Secondly, the naming of a person according to his domicile, not after his parents: something which applied to both sexes. Thirdly, the fact that a close friend of this man did not know his surname and the comment that it was doubtful that anyone else in the village would know it either.

Some days later, pinned to the barn door notice board in the centre of the village, I came across an official-looking typed letter containing a list of names. It was a register of those members of the *parroquia* or parish who had not yet paid their annual land tax to the local authority in Belmonte. A glance at the names, which related to a number of villages in the locality, revealed that many surnames were similar from either the mother's or the father's side, as one might expect. What seemed more surprising was the repetition in different combinations of the listed Christian names as for example in the following:

Juan Antonio García Garrido
Antonio Juan García Garrido
Antonic Juan Garrido García
Juan Antonio Garrido García

and so on. A big enough problem for the tax man, let alone the itinerant anthropologist. No wonder the villagers stuck to their house names. The fact that a man might be called by his second Christian name as often as his first seemed to add to the problem. Villagers were well aware of the dilemma and the following anecdote of a conversation between a village boy in Alcedo and a visiting priest had already been related many times amidst great jocularity before it was told to me.

> A visitor to the village, a priest, asked young Gonzal (an abbreviation of Gonzalo) of Casa Gonzal, what his name was.
> 'My name is Gonzal, padre, but they call me Toni.'
> 'Good—that is my name too, but people call me Anthony. And what is your father's name?'
> 'My father's name is Antonin, but we call him Toni.'
> 'Oh—then what is your grandfather's name?'
> 'His name is Anthony, padre, but we also call him Toni.'
> 'Well that is nice my lad—all of you with the same name. But how do you know one from another?'
> 'Ah, that is no problem, padre. I am the youngest. My father is older and my grandfather is the oldest!'[18]

Nicknames would seem to be an obvious way around the problem, but in fact these are hardly used. If we exclude abbreviations like Poli for Hippolito and Toni for Anthony, which strictly speaking are not nicknames, the only obvious ones, again rarely used, are Celo or Pepe as alternatives to Juan. The only other nickname I came across, apart from the above-mentioned Gordo, was Luís *con coche*: the first car owner in the village. Another villager, a rather heavily built and authoritarian elderly man, was known only by his surname. I do not think its invariable use was intended affectionately: perhaps more from respect, as other elderly villagers were also referred to in a similar manner.

House appellations when used as name affixes would seem therefore to be an obvious solution to a person's identity. However even here confusions may arise, for although a few houses are known to have kept their names for at least a hundred years, the majority have not. Some change their names from one generation to the next and some at even shorter intervals. Thus two people might apparently belong to different houses when in fact they belong to the same one. On one occasion a lady was referred to as 'Valentina de Pacholo de Gaitano de Celo', all three surnames currently in use to describe the occupants of her particular house.

Just how a house comes by its name is difficult to ascertain, but it seems that in the past it was more likely to have been named by fellow villagers than by the current, antecedent or ancestral owners. The name might relate to some personal or family characteristic or occupation, or to some physical feature of the house itself. The house of the last *vigilante*, who died some years ago, is still known as Casa de Vigilante. The house of the former village clog-maker was passed to his eldest daughter who subsequently married a man from another village. As a result the house has changed its name three times since the nineteenth century from Zapatero after the old man, to Mela because his daughter kept bees, to its present name of Leonardo after the daughter's husband.[19]

Spanish surnames are required for birth certificates, baptisms and marriages and for drawing up dispositions for dowries, inheritances and wills. The school roll-call was read out using proper surnames, but out of school students would refer to their colleagues by their houses and surnames were soon forgotten. Some villagers point with pride to the name of their house as having been the same for generations. It shows continuity, unchangeability and steadiness, attributes which may reflect on its occupants. However, regardless of its antiquity or lack of it, the house name is the proper means of assignation. Nor is this mode of identification used solely within the village.[20] One young woman, on being addressed as belonging to a particular house by a very elderly man from another village, did not recognise the name and later was somewhat mortified to learn that it was the name of her house in the time of her grandparents. On a practical level the constant repetition of family names as a result of intermarriage leads to confusion. House names are more specific and convenient.

I do not wish to suggest that people did not know their proper surnames, just that they served no purpose within the context of village life. Very few knew the surnames of others, but there were exceptions. One was an elderly lady who said she had memorised the names of her colleagues when she was at the village school in her youth. Later, after leaving school, she learned those of most other villagers when she helped her elder sister who was the assistant postmistress for the *parroquia* in Boinas. Letters from relatives abroad and official letters concerning bank accounts or non-payment of taxes were all supposed to be addressed to recipients according to their proper names. The postmistress's sister was able to identify these people according to their house at a time when there were many more people living in the village and many more houses.

Just as men may acclaim the whole village of Alcedo as being *muy noble* meaning proud or good, so an individual may consider himself as bearing the 'nobility' of his house. Certainly for most villagers in the late 1970s house names of long standing were equated with the honour of the family. Young children would be referred to by their Christian names only until they became *mozos*. Then they would be recognised as responsible members of their house and be accredited with its name and reputation.

If a house retained its name over a long period this could suggest that there had perhaps been a continuity of sons *en casa*, whose progeny had reputuations untarnished over time. It might be a house in which generations of children had been good farmers or distinguished themselves as priests, doctors, teachers or officials beyond the confines of the village. Such a house would have a 'noble' name transcending contemporary differences between its present occupants and their neighbours. If a house changed its name for some reason, perhaps because one member had brought disrepute on it, or because it had been sold or changed hands in some way, its prestige might be reduced, but could equally be enhanced by its present occupants.

We are thus speaking of honour, not precisely in the individual or the family, but in the house. To this extent the house embodies far more than its name. It represents generations of a family and embodies ethical behaviour, morality, connections, continuity and pride. As one villager put it when someone from another house had behaved incorrectly: 'Their house is their concern; mine is my own.'

Associations of the family house

A house is alive when it is lived in.

It is sad—a house loses itself when no one is there.

A house is embodied with 'spirit', but this essence is shared with its inhabitants. If they should leave and the house is deserted, it loses its identity and becomes just another abandoned building which may or may not be put to other use. Decades later however it may still retain its name in the village's corporate memory, even if it has become a ruin.

'If you swept the house out at night,' said one old lady, 'you were sweeping out the good luck of the house: we would never do it.' But she added, 'We don't believe in such things now. I sweep whenever I can.' Despite the old lady's contention, sentiment is still a prevailing aspect of the house.

'It gave my mother great sadness,' said another elderly lady, 'when the house where we were brought up in Tabla was closed down, when we could no longer keep it up.'

Villagers maintain that this abandonment of houses only really started in the 1950s. Although it was towards the end of the nineteenth century that the village population began its decline, at that time it was a question of individuals leaving and the abandonment of a house was a slow process as its numbers dwindled. Now it is more traumatic for those who remain, as complete families have migrated from the village, leaving their house, *graneros*, barns and all their appurtenances. They leave behind an empty shell which villagers view with sadness as it becomes one more void in a village which older people feel will, like so many others in the region, soon be totally deserted.

Nearly all the older generation of villagers said they came from families of at least eight children. The average family around the turn of the century had about ten and one had fifteen. Some died at birth or in early childhood, but most survived. It was accepted that some of these young people would leave to marry into other villages or work in nearby towns. More often, however, they would emigrate abroad and although these separations were painful for parents who would probably never see their children again, they were an accepted part of life.

'The stomach is important,' said one old villager. 'If you want to live long, it must have plenty of good food; but the pot was just not big enough for all of us children when we were young and we all went off in different directions.'

Families are now much smaller, usually with no more than two or three children, and if they decide to leave there is no one of their generation to keep on the house. Should the young leave for the city they take the old with them if they cannot manage on their own and the house has to be abandoned.

'Now the young leave,' commented one young villager rather ruefully, 'not because there is no food, but because they do not like to work; and there is little joy here.'

The houses of the families who left in the decades following the civil war were occupied by those who had still been living in hay barns. This process of internal absorption gave the village the appearance of a stable community even in the late 1970s, despite the fact that there had been a fivefold depletion in the actual population since the previous century. New houses replacing the old hay barns were more spacious. There would invariably be a dining-room with its large central table, the symbol of hospitality and sumptuous feasting, a sign of a family's success, prestige and generosity. Separate bedrooms would lead off the dining-room and in the kitchen the Bilbao stove replaced the open fire, the former axis of family life.

'In the old days,' one villager recalled, 'the kitchen used to have a fire in the centre of the room: an open one surrounded by stones. Benches and small wooden stools were placed around it, so that your front was warm and your back cold. The smoke would go straight up through a hole in the rafters—the smoke went up, but the cold air came down! There were many hooks for the sausages and cooking pots hanging from beams. Many kitchens were just like that until a few years ago. It was the *cocina de leña*, the wood-burning stove, which changed things. They were much better. They warm you all over. Our kitchen was one of the first to get these big iron stoves.'

In 1978 however the Bilbao stove was gradually being replaced by propane gas. Lavatory facilities, even bathrooms, were being made in a few houses. There were no septic tanks however and this meant the new facilities remained unused. Chamber pots continued to be employed, the urine being thrown on to the cobbled tracks that passed through the village, while the cow barn was used for faeces. My children were initially puzzled that they were never allowed to use one of the new bathrooms, and were invariably directed to the barn. Villagers on the other hand expressed surprise that our children slept in separate camp-beds. Their own children always shared their beds, sometimes with their mothers: 'That way we keep warm in winter.'

It was the houses with daughters but no sons which tended to modernise first. One reason for this was that sons were more likely to go on to higher education after the village school. Agricultural college was the preferred choice as the knowledge gained could be applied if and when the son inherited the house and the family land. One proud mother said her son was the first person in the whole *parroquia* to obtain a grant to attend the university in Oviedo. But further education could be costly and no family could afford to modernise its house as well as sending children away to college.

Daughters seemed to be less interested in further education. They expected to marry and settle with their husbands either on the land or in whatever occupation they might follow. They were therefore seen as being less expensive, primary schooling being paid for by the state. Hence, if there was any surplus cash in households with only daughters, it would go towards increasing stock, replacing old farming equipment and modernising the house. Although the latter might be of little consequence to village neighbours, it did add prestige to the house in the eyes of outsiders, especially relatives. Equally, if there was a predominance of women living in a house,[21] the men could be placed under considerable pressure to modernise its facilities, as the womenfolk would be the main beneficiaries. In a house with a predominance of men on the other hand, a wife might find little support for such changes.

Inheritance is also a factor and there is a need to attract spouses for sons or daughters so that the property may continue as a viable unit. Where a daughter is likely to inherit the property and become a *mujer en casa*, and indeed for her to accept such a condition nowadays, she will hope that things will be made easier for her. Her expectations will be raised by relatives who work in the town or city and extol the virtues of modernity. Equally, it may well be to her family's advantage in seeking a husband for her if such modern conveniences have already been installed in the house where he will reside. Coming from a village background he may not esteem them, but he will want a wife who is content with her surroundings and does not pine for the luxuries of town life.

In the case of a son becoming *hijo en casa*, it is considered less necessary for him to have such conveniences in order to attract a good wife. Although they may prove an advantage they may equally attract the wrong sort of girl, even a lazy bride from the city with illusions about 'country life' and rural ways. A serious young man will seek a bride from a not too distant village, if not from his own. As part of her dowry she will be expected to bring either land if she is from the same village or livestock if she is not, plus household appurtenances including furniture, linen and embroideries. She will also be expected to bring a willing pair of hands and an ethic of hard work, constancy and resilience of character to cope with the exigencies of daily life and thereby uphold the honour of the house.

In the nineteenth century it would have been more likely for sons to be *en casa*. In the late 1970s active households were about equally divided between men and women who had inherited. Being head of the house does not give a person jurisdiction over that house. Nowadays the in-married man or woman is considered equal to a man or woman who has inherited a house. Inequalities between the sexes seem largely irrelevant among villagers. A man takes pride in stating that everything his

Plate 13 Bringing cows in from pasture and carrying kindling

wife does he can do should it be necessary in the event of her absence or illness. Women maintain that they can do likewise. However, any villager if pressed will admit that there are some roles more suited to one or the other sex. Women by and large look after household matters and although they work alongside men in the fields, they will usually be occupied in tasks which involve less physical strength. Conversely, although men can and do cook and wash clothes, they will usually rely on the female members of the household to perform these tasks, or female relations or neighbours should the need arise. Their work is more with the livestock and the upkeep of the *tierras*, meadows and other arable land.

'I am a slave to work,' was the comment of a mother of four grown unmarried sons and no daughters. Apart from her eighty-year-old mother-in-law, she was the only woman in the house. She had to cook, wash the clothes by hand, care for the smaller livestock, maintain her kitchen garden and on occasion work in the *tierras* and during harvest in the hayfields. Her nearest neighbour was a seventy-year-old lady whose family had all grown up and departed, living in nearby villages or in Oviedo. Her land had been mostly sold, though some she rented to other villagers. She came to the village on occasions from Oviedo to 'air the house', as she put it. The younger woman liked her neighbour and they got on well, but privately she would say of the older woman that she never liked to work. This was a rather severe indictment and implied that she had always been that way. Other old women in active households always continued to contribute in whatever way they could. When through infirmity or illness this was no longer possible they would tend to deprecate themselves, saying they were *no vale* or of no use. The oldest lady in the village was at least eighty-seven but she still felt that she had to contribute. Each day she would walk for kilometres searching for kindling and firewood and would return with a large roped bundle of sticks and branches on her back. A very small and slight lady, she still mustered the strength to carry half her own body weight. She persisted in this activity in both summer and winter, often causing anxiety to her family as to her whereabouts, particularly at dusk. Frequently they would search for her, fearing that she might be attacked by wolves.

'She has to work when she is not at school or doing her homework,' said one lady of her eight-year-old granddaughter, to explain why she could not visit our children after school one day. 'She has to sweep and clean the house, make the beds—and if she does not make them properly she has to remake them—and then she has to herd the cows each day: she has to learn!'

This lady was fortunate as she had a strong and capable daughter, the mother of the eight-year-old, while she herself was a very active woman in her mid-fifties. This meant that although there was a lot of work to be done, it could be shared. This was far less onerous than the mother of four's situation, which could only change for the better if the son chosen to be *en casa* found himself a wife.

This ethic of work was very much a part of every child's upbringing from a very early age, and it remained so throughout their lives. Hard work was equated with morals. If a woman was not considered a good worker, then her morality could be in question, something which might not only damage relations within her house and the village, but also her marriage prospects.

Family relationships

> *Para Roma caminan dos perigrinos,*
> *A pedir a dispensar porque son primos.*

'Two pilgrims are walking to Rome to ask for dispensation to marry because they are cousins,' is an old Spanish saying frequently quoted in the village. There was a time when the medieval church considered that anyone marrying closer than a seventh cousin was committing incest. As a consequence of the difficulties in enforcing such a decree, particularly in the middle ages when most of Europe had a rural population, the stipulation was reduced to fourth cousin and there in theory it remains to the present day.

When Alcedo had three hundred inhabitants and many more in the previous century, close marriages were comparatively unusual. Today with a population under a hundred it has become a problem. In theory these mountain village communities were exogamous and they would tend to marry beyond the confines of their own village. Asturian stories are full of allusions to young swains having to defend themselves against cudgel attacks by men of another village who might jealously try to dissuade them from wooing their own village maidens. With larger village communities, however, such as Alcedo in the previous century, there was less need to marry out. They could marry within the village without too blatantly transgressing church ruling. If they did, then a dispensation known as a *bula* from the local priest, for which they had to pay a fee, would obviate the problem.

In the nineteenth century there were few if any freeholders. The land belonged to the church or the local *palacio* to whom dues were paid. Once the land reverted to the villagers, their natural tendency was to increase the size of their properties so as to multiply stock holdings and provide better for their houses. Marriage alliances within the villages might seem to have been a way of doing this. However, while a man brought land as his inheritance, a woman normally brought stock and household appurtenances. Thus when men were *en casa* they might increase their stock through marriage, but not their land for the grazing of it. When however men began to emigrate and family sizes decreased, then women tended to inherit land, and it became an advantage for a male heir to marry an *hija en casa*, as in that way they could combine their holdings. Thus the incentive towards expansion of household properties through marriage as the population decreased was a factor in increasingly closely related households, there being less incentive to marry out as property could not be removed from the village. Thus multiple smallholdings of arable and meadowland have, over the past seventy to eighty years, increasingly been taken over through marriage alliances and are now owned by the relatively few remaining households.

A genealogical chart of the present village shows many marriages of close kin. There are even cases over recent decades where the children of two siblings within the village have married. Close marriage is more prevalent among the households of the upper southern section of the village, and although first cousin marriage is uncommon, second cousin marriage has occurred fairly frequently.

When we first arrived in Alcedo one of our neighbours said that 'we are just one big family in this village'. At the time I thought she was expressing her sentiment on the virtues of village cooperation, but it is literally true as all villagers are either kin or affines, or both. When greeting each other or in conversation, men who are on good terms with each other will call each other *cuñado* or brother-in-law. At first I took this seriously and was encouraged to do so by villagers who maintained the term was used in its strict sense. It was however used so often that I began to doubt this, particularly when I knew those conversing were not brothers-in-law. When after a few months I found I was myself being addressed with this close affinal appellation I realised that, even if there were many close relationships in the village and the term might frequently apply, in most cases it was just an expression of confidence and friendliness towards someone rather than an actual statement of affinity. Calling all acquaintances by such a term would obviate any embarrassment among the men of the village who, unlike women, were very vague about family relationships.

'We are all cross cousins in this village,' commented one villager and she was not exaggerating. Although she was not using 'cross cousin' in a terminological sense, simply meaning interbred, I found virtually no one who was not related to other villagers, frequently many times over. Very few of these relationships were of an order more distant than second cousin. The only affinal relationships were those of three spouses, two male and one female, who had married in from other villages.[22]

These close marriages are not just a recent phenomenon, although I only have evidence for this in certain families, and none of my information goes back more than three generations. There does not seem to have been such a high proportion of very close marriages in the past as appears to have been the case in more recent times. People are well aware of these repeated intermarriages within the village in the past. As one old lady put it: 'Everyone in the village was related in former times. The older generations were all family in one way or another. People didn't leave the village then very much. It was only later that people started going to Argentina and Cuba.'

Marriages outside the village occurred then as now, mostly within the immediate area to the west of the Pigueño valley. Such marriages into or out of the village tend to recur over several generations, and there are usually near or distant kin of the marrying-in spouse already living nearby. To some extent relatives are a protection, especially for a wife, and there are cases where affinal relatives have caused difficulties. One recent example of this, known to all the villagers, is of a young bride from outside the village being nearly starved to death by her mother-in-law. It is likely to be the bride's relations within the village who will help her to establish herself, assist her at the birth of her children and support her at times of illness or if she is temporarily incapacitated for whatever reason.

Relations between a wife and her mother-in-law are however normally equable. Over the years the dominant position of the latter in the household gives way to her daughter-in-law, who should gradually assume a role of domestic authority, though this position can be complicated should there be an unmarried sister-in-law also living in the house. With growing daughters a house may have several female members who can share the burden of daily work. It is more difficult for an in-married bride with an aging mother-in-law and only male children, as was the case in one household. Such a wife is indeed a 'slave to work', as the burden falls on her. Fortunately in this example the wife was born in the village and she had an elder married sister locally. During particularly onerous times, when feasts had to be prepared during the haymaking or the *matanza*, or when there were festivals or illness in the house, this sister would lend support well beyond normal neighbourly reciprocity. In such a house, however, the men are also more adaptable and willing to take on chores they would not normally have to do.

For the father in the house, one of the main areas of friction arises when his son has grown up sufficiently to feel he can assume greater responsibility and influence matters concerning the land and livestock, and make other onerous decisions. As a teenager he may vie with his father in matters of physical strength and in other ways become increasingly competitive and mildly aggressive. Arguments with the father may result. As he grows up he may try to influence his father in matters of family finances such as the selling of *terneros* and his own share in the proceeds. Conversely the father may maintain that his son is lazy and rebuke him if he does not get up in the morning to look after the cattle, clean out the byres, or get to the hayfields early on a hot summer's day because he has been out for most of the night at some fiesta.

Conflicts between male siblings resulting from expectations of inheriting the house and the land are usually resolved by one son, and not necessarily the eldest, becoming engaged. Once married with settlements made in his favour, he will tend to direct the household and the father's role will become that of an adviser. Old age will reduce the father to watching over the cattle grazing in the meadows or spending hours in the centre of the village, or in the shop, conversing and reminiscing with other village octogenarians.

When a daughter becomes *hija en casa* her in-married husband may direct the household or, if she is a strong personality, she may. Discussions among village neighbours as to 'who wears the trousers' are common whichever way inheritance is resolved, and mutual help within households tend to negate any sexual distinctions. There is no shame in a woman taking a dominating role in family affairs, even concerning the sale and purchase of livestock and in controlling the family purse. It may occasionally give rise to neighbourly gossip and amusement, however, which suggests that it is more the exception than the rule.

Although it is now considered fairly normal for a daughter to inherit, it is debatable whether this was always the case in the past when families were much larger. Houses which have not changed their names, implying that there has been a continuity of male inheritors, tend to command more respect. Nowadays the young do not necessarily wish to continue to live in the village, even if they are expected to inherit, as there are so many opportunities to find a living elsewhere. A father may have several sons, and none may wish to continue with the responsibilities of farming. This can cause bitterness and resentment. On my remarking somewhat injudiciously on the equanimity of one elderly village neighbour another one retorted, 'Oh him! he has no trouble with his sons—he doesn't have any!' Another villager, the father of several sons, who always seemed very even tempered, vented his annoyance on them by saying that he would never give up his house to any of them. A third elderly villager who resented the possibility that not one of his three sons wished to inherit, expressed himself in another way. Railing against their opportunities as a result of their education when he had had none, he expostulated, but not without humour: 'If I had had the chance my sons have now with their lives, I would have been a much better man than any of them!'

Undoubtedly some of the disagreements surfacing between fathers and sons in the late 1970s had to do with matters of education. Few of the older generation had been able to attend school. The school in the village was not properly established until some two decades after the civil war. There were sporadic efforts to give the young some education before then, usually instigated by villagers who had opportunities that others lacked. But such individual attempts tended to fall foul of the demands on the young from various houses to work the land and tend the animals. In one instance a parish priest took it on himself to rectify the situation. He was a most unusual man and is still remembered by villagers with respect and affection for his integrity, not so much because of his efforts towards education, but because he assisted the village in many ways, being always prepared to roll up his sleeves and work in the fields alongside his parishioners. For the most part, however, the older generation remained virtually illiterate. In the 1970s I found that only one house in the village contained some books and these belonged to the eldest son who was attending university.

The older generation have a great respect for education. Their doubts about it lie in the realisation that it tends to take the young away from the village to seek a living elsewhere, and with little ambition to continue the way of life of their forbears. The young are well aware of this and the relative shortcomings, as they see them, of their parents' generation. This manifests itself in various ways. For instance, parents are sometimes admonished by the young within the house for speaking in their traditional patois and not in 'proper' Spanish.

Differences however erupt with greater frequency regarding matters of traditional values and morality. The older generation feel that the young of both sexes spend too much time going to parties, dances and discos in nearby towns. When they were young, fiestas took place every few weeks either within the village or in those nearby and there were up to sixty young *mozos* and *mozas* in Alcedo alone. They could create their own entertainment and there was no need to seek it elsewhere.

In these remote villages, the postwar period limited the aspirations of the parents' generation, enabling the old order to prevail. Their comparative isolation through lack of transport and roads served to restrict their communication with the world outside. On our return to Alcedo in the late 1980s there was some excitement in the village because a public telephone had been installed some two kilometres away in Boinas. There was even talk of a telephone being installed in the village itself, something that would have been inconceivable ten years earlier.

There is another difference between the older and younger generation, between father and son. It concerns the change from traditional farming practice and the old subsistence order to the need to modernise farming in line with a market-oriented economy. This means greater concentration on livestock and less on arable farming. Although there is a reluctance to change among the older generation, they are well aware of the consequences of maintaining their more conservative style of farming, one in which the village has remained independent and self-reliant. The experience of civil war and its aftermath engendered a resistance to change and a suspicion of any overdependency on outside resources. Alcedo after all survived that long period of strife and shortages, whereas other communities did not. Yet the older people are all too aware of the consequences of not bowing to the inevitable and the wishes of the younger generation: their inheritors. They have no wish to see all the young depart, as has happened in so many other communities in the region, and for Alcedo to fossilise, gently decay and become just another abandoned village.

Among some of the older generation there is an almost exaggerated deference towards the young in their new-found knowledge and education. Inevitably however this creates tensions, particularly concerning household economy. What allotment of the household purse should be made to a son who markets and successfully sells cattle, or who negotiates a favourable rental on an absentee villager's meadow? What should be the extent of his pocket money? And what amount of the family purse should go towards further education? These are matters which have to be weighed against the need to invest in the expansion of livestock and the land and the continuation of the house as a viable unit. So house and family come under new pressures and areas of conflict to which before they had not been subjected.

When asked how he arranged the finances in his house an elderly villager was understandably reluctant to divulge much. At the time his eldest son of four was most likely to inherit the property, though his wife favoured another son. The eldest was working part time building a barn for a farmer near Belmonte. He went there two or three times a week during a period when his absence was not critical to his commitments to the household. His father regarded all the money that his son earned at work as 'his own and not for the house', adding, 'I always give him money if he needs it—I never hold it back.' As for the sale of *terneros*, the main source of income for the household, he maintained that his son would get a 'share' in any sale. This was despite the fact that most of the money gained in this way would go towards his youngest son's expenses at agricultural college, pocket money for a second son doing his military service, and financial help towards another son who was training to be a teacher. The rest of the sales money would help towards the upkeep of his land, the purchase of new stock and farming equipment, and entertaining relatives and guests during the time of the hay harvest. He was perhaps fortunate in having no daughters on whom he might have been obliged to make a settlement.

In contrast to his father's rather complex financial concerns for the whole family, the eldest son was more concerned with his own interests. 'I have *confianza* [accord, confidence] with my father on money matters. Yes, I get a percentage on *ternero* sales, but this is very small and amounts to about one tenth of the sale price. If I want money for something, I ask my father. If he should not be there in the house I may just take it. There is no problem.' He indicated that problems do arise when they have been unable to sell any cattle for some time. 'We call these lean times *vacas flacas* [thin cows]. When we feel better off, we call that *vacas gruesas* [fat cows]!'

Matters such as these concerning household finance should be discussed between the father and his wife within the confines of the house and not with neighbours. As the father commented: 'Two heads are better than one—we should have equal views.' If disagreement arises it should be resolved quickly. 'There are houses in the village', he added, 'where they won't talk to each other for eight or ten days after an argument. I think two hours is too long!'

While disagreements within families are usually of short duration, divisions between houses may last for years, even from one generation to the next. In former times such disagreements concerned failure to maintain field walls to keep animals in, the often unintentional ploughing into a neighbour's *tierra*, or the shifting of stone boundary markers. More enduring animosities between houses might stem from failed marriages, withdrawn inheritances, or recollections of political divisions, denunciations and betrayals during and after the civil war.

With many households abandoning their *tierras* to concentrate on calf breeding, and with less need for reciprocal labour in the fields, cooperation within the village is now less essential. Conversely, the increasing emphasis on the house and its continuing economic and financial survival creates tensions within the family, as the young, aware of market forces and cooperative needs beyond the confines of the village, put pressure on the older generation.

Plate 14 Large *graneros*, called *panera*, with eight stanchions

Plate 15 The photographer and first communion

Chapter 7

Childhood

It is customary when a child is born to say that it looks like its father: never its mother as this might be casting doubt on its paternity. 'If there is any doubt then we say it is the *padres*,' said one lady, half in jest, adding, 'don't tell anyone I said that!' Any doubt or suggestion of infidelity would cause endless gossip and recrimination, and the local priest is an unfortunate but obvious scapegoat for such an untoward happening in a close-knit community.

Whether illegitimacy is more frequent now than in the past, with the greater freedom given to *mozas* or young girls to go to dances and other events beyond the neighbouring villages, is a moot point. There were cases talked about from other villages. However, the older women were shocked on hearing that a girl in her early teens from another village had become pregnant while attending school in Belmonte. There was also a rather sad story of a young and very beautiful girl who lived in Tuna with her father, her mother having died some years earlier. A young man had made her pregnant and abandoned her by emigrating. The father found foster parents for the baby and the girl herself became a nun.

In the past young *mozas* would attend all the different village gatherings in the locality. Even in the days when Alcedo had several hundred inhabitants and fifty to sixty *mozos* and *mozas* at any one time, everyone knew what was going on and such a happening would be most unusual. Young *mozas* would invariably be chaperoned by a brother, elder sister or parent on these occasions. They still are today, but with difficulty, as with fewer local events due to the demise of local villages, and with access to motor transport, there is more movement between the villages and local towns to attend such festivities.

There have, of course, been numerous other opportunities for the young to meet: when tending livestock in the fields for instance, or shepherding sheep well beyond the confines of the village. If however any clandestine encounter resulted in a girl becoming pregnant, the father of the child would almost invariably be identified and would most likely be obliged to marry her. If the young man came from another village, then her parents might provide inducements for him to settle in Alcedo by offering him a part of the possession, and if his wife became *en casa*, he would become heir by proxy to the house and land. Normally in this situation, when a young man approached the parents of a girl with a view to marriage, formal arrangements would have already been negotiated as part of the marriage settlement. They would not be forced on the parents in order to retain the good name of a house.

Most young village men, however, would be very cautious about getting a girl within their own community pregnant. They pride themselves on being 'responsible' and are well aware of the repercussions if they are not:[23] disfavour within the village, a slight on the name of their house and the risk of being disinherited. There is however little emphasis, unlike in some other Mediterranean societies, on a girl's virginity when she is betrothed.[24]

Nowadays, when a village woman is approaching labour, she will normally be taken by car to Oviedo where she will give birth in a maternity hospital. This was a very recent development when we arrived in 1978, and women would give graphic descriptions of what hospitals were like, how relatives were allowed to visit at certain times only and how hygienic and spotless everything was: all unusual experiences. Until then births had taken place in the village in the customary manner. This was usually with a trained midwife or *comadrona* in attendance, though village women, mothers themselves, were still in charge. These women, known as *curiosas*, had learned from others and were very capable, though untrained in modern medical practices. Things could go wrong, as one very elderly lady commented. She had never wanted herself to become a *curiosa* as she might then feel responsible all her life for the death of a child or its mother. 'Anyway,' she added, 'I had no gift for it.'

If there were complications a villager would ride to Belmonte and bring back a doctor. Alternatively the woman in labour would be carried on a makeshift stretcher by a party of men in relays all the way over the high mountain pass to Belmonte: a journey of some five hours' duration in summer, more hazardous and prolonged in winter. But normally the birth would go without any problem. Womenfolk in the family and neighbours would take it in turns to keep the woman in labour company, talking to her, rubbing her back to ease the preliminary birth pains, and administering herbal infusions, particularly one based on rye which aided the dilation and contraction of the uterus. Delivery took place in the kitchen, the only room in the house with both water and winter warmth. It was customary, immediately after birth, for a *comadrona* or *curiosa* to pass the infant through the smoke of burning laurel leaves while reciting a prayer or incantation for its safe keeping and health. Most *curiosas* knew how to do this, but it required *voluntad*, the will or spirit to do it, to be effective. While some maintained it made no difference, others said there was always more excitement if the baby was male. 'We prefer penises to girls!' commented one woman.

'I could not then, nor can I now carry heavy weights,' said an old lady, 'because three days after giving birth to each of my children I had to get up and work. My mother was ill and her sister lived far away. My husband was a carpenter and had to work away from the house. There were no other women in the house. Neighbours used to help me with my work, though, and my father, while he was still alive, used to look after the animals.' She had had ten children in all, but three of them died before they were a year old. 'It is a matter of luck', said another woman with a similar experience, adding that others were more fortunate, 'Those with many womenfolk in the household—they don't even get their fingers wet.'

Depending therefore on the circumstance a woman might do light work two or three days after giving birth. Others might have to resume heavy work in the gardens or *tierras* after only a few days, leaving the infant in the house with the mother-in-law. In summer it was not unusual for a baby of only a few weeks to be taken to the fields during haymaking and remain there for most of the day in a basket in the shade of a tree. The mother kept a constant eye on the basket, occasionally throwing small stones in its vicinity to frighten away any *bichos* or small animals, a cause of concern especially in the sultry and humid air before rain breaks. Such *bichos*, especially snakes including the highly venomous asp, seemed according to villagers to have a curious inclination to enter these baskets. To forestall this they placed dried laurel leaves inside the basket, and inside the baby's swaddling clothes, to act as a deterrent.

Baptism

Apart from what villagers regard as the 'old beliefs', such as the association of laurel with birth, contemporary customs are intrinsically part of the more formal and orthodox rites associated with church baptism. According to villagers this should be done between two days and two weeks after the birth of the child. Orthodox belief apart, there are practical reasons for this. 'You always have to carry your baptismal papers with you when you travel anywhere in Spain,' commented one villager, 'and you can't marry without them either.'[25] She did, however, concede that in the cities there are many people, among them non-Catholics and 'foreigners', to whom it did not matter.

When a child is born older relations of the family may offer to be *padrino de pila* or *madrina de pila*, that is father or mother of the baptismal font. If no one offers then the parents will have to ask other relatives to act for the child. If, as usual, the baptism is to take place within a few days of birth, the mother is unlikely to be present, nor is it expected. Thus in a sense the *madrina de pila* is the mother's replacement at the brief ceremony, but she may also have longer term obligations. These may include attending the child's confirmation and marriage, although in the latter case it is usually the bride's font father and the groom's font mother who are asked to attend by the bridal pair. They are then known respectively as *padrino de boda* and *madrina de boda* or the father and mother of the marriage.

A priest officiates at the baptism, either in the village *capilla* or in the parish church at Quintana. If no priest is available, as would have been the case during the civil war, or in winter when deep snow in the pass above Belmonte prevents him coming, or even should the parents not like the priest, then villagers maintain that any man or woman who is a communicant can officiate. At the service the officiant will tell the font parents that they may have an obligation to bring up the child, in the absence of any other relative, in the unlikely event of the demise of both parents.

Formerly font parents would be sought among close relations living within the village. A mother's or father's sister or brother would be the likely choice. Now however with greater emphasis on emigration and education, it is more likely that relatives living outside the village will be sought as this will enable the child to have outside connections when it grows up and both parties may benefit from the reciprocal arrangements which will result. Should the child go on to further education, or take up employment in the locality of the font parents, who may be husband and wife, then he may live with them, his parents reciprocating by sending them gifts of bread and meat. These relationships can take on the appearance of *compadrasgo* (in the sense of co-parenthood and mutual support) for the younger villagers, as they work part-time in shops or bars belonging to their font parents, or butcher pig meat for former villagers living in nearby towns (cf. Pitt-Rivers 1976). Some people still however tend to favour village font parents, for traditional reasons concerning good neighbour relations and local reciprocities.

Baptism soon after birth is preferred as in the case of an early death, a child would be regarded as impure in the eyes of the church. This would have implications for the parents, not least that the child could not receive a proper burial. If a child is frail at birth then it will be baptised immediately, and in city maternity hospitals there is usually a priest on hand who will do this. Some villagers are however quite casual about this and an example was given from a nearby village of a fourteen-month-old child who suddenly died without having been baptised. 'There was actually a priest in the village where it happened, so this was the parents' fault,' one villager explained. 'They could not have a service at the child's funeral. The only thing that could be done was to bless the sepulchre or niche, when the body was put in it in the cemetery.'

From the time of the civil war baptism with a priest officiating would have been very difficult to arrange. This may be a factor in the negative attitude expressed by the majority of men in the village concerning the religious aspect of these rites. For them the necessity of baptism for the purposes of registration is most important, followed perhaps by the possibility of establishing gainful and prestigious relations as font parents outside the village.

Prior to the war there was a resident priest in charge of the *parroquia* centred on the church in Quintana, a village in the valley below Alcedo. Subsequently the various priests administering the whole region were brought together in a seminary in Belmonte. Sharing a common residence was both more economic and more convivial, as for some the isolation of living in their parishes was depressing. This move did however tend to distance the priests from their villages and parishes, though the road building programme made access easier.

Some resident priests left as a result of financial stringencies on church funding and disillusion over their apparently intransigent village communities. A younger order of priests who might have replaced them felt there was more important pastoral work to be done in the cities and large urban areas, particularly in the south. Numbers therefore slowly declined. In the late 1970s there were only three priests left for this vast mountain region, and when we returned in 1988, there remained only one priest in residence in Belmonte and one elderly priest based in the upper

Pigueño valley. This meant that the priest in residence had not only to officiate in the regional capital of Belmonte, but also to travel to thirty or forty villages and other small communities to tend to their pastoral needs. It was an impossible task and inevitably he began to lose touch with individual parishioners and whole communities. His initial pastoral enthusiasm and friendliness, particularly towards Alcedo, had sadly abated with the greater burden of responsibility and work.

Even in the late 1970s however the partial withdrawal of pastoral care meant that special services, such as for baptisms, first communions and even weddings, tended to be amalgamated with important religious occasions so as to minimise the number of visits the priest made to each village. Thus it happened that a particular baptism in Alcedo took place at the same time as the most important festival for the village, that of their patron saint, San Vicente, in late September 1978. The following is an approximate account of the the combined service which took place that day.

The service should have taken place in the small *capilla* in the village earlier in the day but the priest was late, having already given two services that morning in other nearby villages. Parking his car near the village centre, he walked up the path to the *capilla* and rang the bell three times. As it was an important day for the village, with many visiting relatives and friends who had come to attend the afternoon's festival as well as the extended family of the child to be baptised, there was a congregation well in excess of sixty women and children and a few men. The *capilla* could only contain some fifty people sitting and standing, the menfolk for the most part remaining outside the open doorway.

After putting on his vestments the priest commenced the mass and baptised the infant, wetting her head with water from the font. The child, being several months old, was accompanied by both her mother and father, and by her *padrino* and *madrina*, in this case her mother's father and mother. Clearly the large congregation was a pleasant change for the priest, a small, rotund and prematurely balding man from the south of Spain, who was about to depart from Belmonte for reasons which were the subject of much village gossip. He remarked on the fact that only four people had attended the parish church in Quintana whence he had come, and said he found it disturbing that so few had attended, 'when I had come so far.'

His address then centred on the baptism, referring to the time during which the font parents would have duties to the child, until she came of age at eighteen. He said that did not mean their obligations would then cease. 'Nor does it mean,' he added, 'that a child on reaching that age can just renounce God, as some seem to think.'

'Christianity is not something you can renounce easily,' the priest continued, 'especially when it is instilled into the young at an early age. It is the fault of the parents if this happens to a child in later life. There is more to being a Christian than baptism and taking communion. Parents ought to insist on their children going to church. In the old days there were *madrinas* and *padrinos* because the former would substitute for the mother who would still be recovering from the birth [a reference in this case to the delayed baptismal service]. The font parents have a role, but it is the parents'—the mother's and father's—obligation to give their child Christian education. Parents should not leave that to the font parents.'

After this admonitory note, the priest went on to comment on the symbolism of the ceremony of baptism: the significance of water, candles and whiteness (the wrappings of the baby). After commenting on the association of water with purity he continued: 'The lighted candle represents the resurrection of Christ. That is why we use candles during burials. The child's baptismal dress represents innocence, as innocence has no colour. When children die and are buried, it is in white. When an adult is buried, it is in black, because you can't be sure of their innocence. All children—even the King's children [Juan Carlos had recently assumed this role following the death of Franco]—come to this earth in a sinful state and they are baptised into a state of purity. They are reborn again into the Christian life. You change from being a pagan [a probable reference to the 'old beliefs' still retained in some of these mountain villages] into a Christian.'

This form of address, of approbrium and explanation, was a theme common to most of the sermons given by visiting priests during our time in the village. Though patronising, it has an uncompromising directness that orthodox sophisticates in urban churches might find disconcertingly simplistic and forthright.

No sooner had he commenced his sermon than a collection basket was passed around rather noisily among the congregation. 'No one is obliged to give anything,' the priest interjected, 'only if you feel like it.' He was evidently rather cross over this ineptitude and the interruption it caused, saying that this would be more properly done after he had completed his sermon. But he was also expressing some concern for village sensitivities, as many felt that the priests were always asking for money when they were already paid for what they did, and indeed, a fee for the baptism had already been paid by the parents.

To add to his discomfiture and to the distraction of the congregation, a bat started circling around just above their heads, obviously disturbed by this unusually well attended intrusion into its normally silent domain. As everyone seemed to be watching its gyrations the priest again interrupted his address, saying rather petulantly, 'A bat would have to come now to distract you!' evidently irritated by their lack of attention to what he was saying. This third service of the day and all his journeying in the course of the morning had obviously taxed his patience.

Clearly this baptismal service was not going as it should, for at the end of his sermon the priest announced that no one had invited him to lunch. It is customary in the village for the family of the baptised child to invite the visiting priest to a meal, as indeed it is customary to do so after a wedding or a first communion. As this was also the day of the village's patron saint and as a group of women in the village had prepared a feast for the occasion, the parents of the child had felt that such a meal was unnecessary as the priest could have stayed on for the feast. Unfortunately, this priest was not liked by the villagers and there were some who would say that as the family had paid the fee for the service, why should he also get a meal? Priests, with one or two notable exceptions, were seldom very popular. Nevertheless, he had come a long way and it might have been a courtesy to have shown him more hospitality. As it was his implied request remained unanswered and he left on an empty stomach, preferring not to stay for the feast.

Childhood

> You should teach children by good example when they are young. They won't learn when they are older. Just as a tree bends when it is a young sapling, but cannot when it is has grown to maturity.

This quotation concerning motherhood and a child's formative years is fairly typical of the use of analogy and metaphor in everyday speech among villagers. Poetic simile is intrinsic to their sayings and verses, but also frequently comes into daily conversation. Like all country people they make frequent allusions to the natural world about them.

A father usually has a playful, joking relationship with his young children, although they do not see very much of him during the day. He is normally up at dawn and away in the fields and *tierras* or on the uplands tending his animals, or at the market, returning after the child has gone to bed. With a son this relationship becomes more formal when the child reaches an age when he can start working or helping his father in tasks about the farm and receiving instruction from him.

Although a son is closely bound to his mother during his formative years, a daughter's relationship with her mother is particularly close and in normal circumstances persists through to her womanhood and marriage. One old lady, unmarried but a good observer of village life and mores, observed, 'Parents love their children: boys and girls equally. But boys can go off to dances and *fiestas*, and travel about more freely. They are less of a responsibility. Girls are more of a liability. You have to look after them so they don't go astray.'

Another old lady with many children and grandchildren, who had experienced the problems of bringing them up in a mountain village, put it slightly differently. 'Children are like their parents because they are very quick at copying things. If the parents behave well and if they spend time teaching the children what is right and what is wrong—as most parents do—' She did not finish her sentence but after a pause added wryly, with a laugh, 'They pick up the bad things more easily than the good!' Another mother put it more succinctly: 'Never lie to your children and they will never lie to you!'

Parental authority is thus still very much a part of village life, a benevolent one in the case of the father, but less so for the mother who has greater responsibility. Men tend to tease, not just their own children but their neighbours' children also, especially the girls. Women are more severe. One day when a mother realised my wife was not sure where our two daughters had gone in the village, she seemed quite shocked and chastised her, saying, 'You should always know where your children are!' This is a mother's obligation, particularly when her children are very young. At times it seemed to us that there was a note of rebellion in this responsibility and perhaps some resentment that men did not help more with their children's upbringing.

From a very early age children participate in activities around the house and in various seasonal occupations on the land. They are 'taught' village ways. Their grandparents will tell them stories about the past, about village life and particular personalities. They tell them about the *monte* (the countryside beyond the confines of the village) and wild animals—bear and wolf stories abound—about beliefs and curing, and local folk-poetry and refrains encapsulating much local wit and wisdom. Children learn by emulating their elders in the care of animals and cultivating the land. They also learn the basic tenets of village life: not to lie or be deceitful, to be tolerant of others and to reciprocate. Children however are human beings subject to whims, dislikes and selfish behaviour and many instances are cited of bad behaviour amongst the young. Small village communities tend to have long memories and some unfortunate event may be recalled decades later, reminding the young that their misdemeanours may not be forgotten. This kind of potential sanction may inhibit bad behaviour.

Veo, oyo, pero me callo (I see, I hear, but I say nothing) is a common saying in the village.[26] In its literal sense, it implies a certain deceit, a lack of openness, a sort of conspiracy to silence. On the contrary, however, it is a dictum of village wisdom and most will abide by it. If misdemeanours are committed by the young, or if there are troubles in a house, advice may be given but no one interferes. 'It is their house' is an oft-used phrase which applies equally to young or old, and ultimately wrongdoing in the young is the responsibility of their house and a reflection on it.

Up to the age of three or four children are seldom out of their mothers' sight. Whether a woman is in the house, milking cows in the *cuadro* or barn, washing clothes at the fountain, or in the fields or in her garden, her children will accompany her. Older boys tend to be left to their own devices and are allowed considerable freedom to move around the village. From an early age a boy will spend time with his father in his various activities in the *cuadro* and accompany him to the *tierras* and the meadows. A girl will spend more time with her mother and is encouraged to assist in small tasks. By the time she is six or seven she will be expected to work part-time around the house and the *cuadro*, even if she is also attending school.

There is, as already indicated, a very strong work ethic within the village. To be lazy or work-shy is equated with moral laxity. In the same way too much studying and reading—not considered as work—may send one mad, something I was frequently cautioned about. Hard work is virtuous and girls in particular are severely reprimanded if they show any sign of recalcitrance. Corporal punishment is unusual for girls, but for boys a slipper applied to the backside seems sufficient to deter most potential offenders.

Raiding orchards for apples and pears after dark is not an unusual seasonal activity for young boys, but most anti-social behaviour is confined to simple misdemeanours such as snowball and manure throwing (particularly at girls), window breaking (usually accidental) and stick fights. The last, an old Asturian pastime, can become quite dangerous, particularly with regard to the heads and eyes of combatants. However, among children these are usually mock fights and girls if attacked will run off and hide until the excitement recedes.

From a fairly early age boys and girls tend to separate. A boy of more than five or six who plays with girls is mocked by his peers and the same applies to girls, with the exception of siblings within a house. Younger girls mix easily with older ones, likewise younger with older boys, and there is little sense of competition between age groups, or of age stratification. 'Nor is there any jealousy among the children,' commented one village mother. 'In villages around Tineo there is, a lot of it, but not here!' This apparent lack of aggression and competitiveness may be because all the village children come from similar homes. None are more privileged or noticeably wealthier than others and this basic equality of life is reflected in their behaviour. Good manners are also important as one mother explained, 'If you learn to behave when you are young, you can always be educated later'.

With their predominantly outdoor activities in an inclement climate, children tend to be very hardy and seldom succumb to any illness following the first critical year after birth, when most deaths occurred in the past. However children, like adults, are believed to be more vital and stronger in the 'blood' in Spring, blood being equated with rising sap in plants and trees at this time of year. Perhaps the most common complaint among children is worms. 'If a child just wants bread and water, that is a sure sign,' said one mother. 'We all get worms here—like the animals.' To cure this, they boil a plant called *asento*, similar to camomile, in water. They give this tea to the children first thing in the morning before eating and it is considered to be very effective.

In early spring all the children go off in groups to collect snails, which they sell to a merchant who comes to the village every year and pays them by the sackful. Parents always express some anxiety when the children go off for their annual search, as most of the snails are found in the interstices of stone walls alongside paths and cart tracks and surrounding fields beyond the village. These walls, catching the early sun, are also a favoured abode of snakes at this time of year, particularly that of the small extremely poisonous asp which has caused the death of villagers in the past.

If snakes cause most anxiety for parents, it is dogs which seem to cause most for children. Frequently they will run away if a dog, even a near neighbour's dog, approaches them. This is odd behaviour as by and large village dogs are not vicious, and children never show any fear of other animals. Such apparent fear may be associated with dire warnings about rabies, though dogs showing signs of rabies may in fact have eaten poisoned meat left out for the wolves.

As girls grow older and reach pubescence, their hair is usually cut very short and will remain bobbed for the rest of their lives within the village. Even our own children, though still very young, were considered by the women to have over-long hair. Discussions would arise about this, the men disagreeing and saying they should be allowed to keep their hair the way it was! At the same time girls take on and share the more onerous household responsibilities: formerly they learned to embroider and to make bread. They become part of the *moza* group of girls until they are married. A boy will start working alongside his father at this age and become a *mozo*. He will also adopt more formal relations with girls of his equivalent age group in the village.

Boys are less protected in their upbringing than girls. While not encouraged to do so they may witness the *matanza*. Girls will avoid this if possible and frequently express concern for the animals to be slaughtered, although most villagers discourage any false sentiment about the killing of animals. Boys, even the very young ones, will also watch with interest whenever a bull is brought in to serve a cow, if opportunity arises. Their introduction to the facts of life tends to be a natural transition through observation of rural activities around them. Girls however may not be allowed such freedom and indeed are protected to some extent from sexual concerns. Once a girl's period commences there may be further restrictions: 'You have to look after yourself,' was the comment of one elderly village woman. 'You must stay away from greenness—that is from meadow grass and newly scythed hay— during your period. You must not wash clothes, or wash your hair, nor take a bath. You have to look after your body when you are in this condition.' It is however doubtful whether these prohibitions, which may have been enforced in the old lady's youth, would be taken seriously by the young of the present generation.

Once the young have become *mozos* and *mozas*, relations between the sexes become more ambivalent. In earlier times, *fiestas* would take place frequently. On such occasions the young would form groups and a type of ritualised insulting would take place in the form of proverbs and refrains being capped by each group in turn. This might involve singing and shouting as sometimes these groups were at some distance from each other. Prior to marriage, older *mozos* and *mozas* might form relationships, known as *amigos de bailar* or dancing friends, but these would not necessarily lead to marriage.

Schooling

'In our time education didn't matter—it was not important,' was the comment of a lady in her eighties. When another old villager remarked: 'We never used to look after children nearly so well as we do now,' he was not just referring to their material needs, but more specifically to education. Many of the elderly villagers remarked on how fortunate the young were now with their education and undoubtedly the older generation feel themselves at a disadvantage. Perhaps this is less so for men, because at least some of them were given the chance of a very basic literacy, but women simply never had that chance. To some extant this imbalance still prevails.

One old man said his father never learned to read or write. 'I only learned to add up and do sums because of my work in Madrid—I was a public transport driver and needed to count up money. But we learned very little or nothing in the way of schooling, and the women learned nothing at all. But then there was less need for them to!'

A village lady in her sixties brought up the subject herself in the following way: 'When I was young there was no school here like there is now. We had a sort of school, but it was just a wooden table in a village house. I learned to write my name, but no more. It was not serious then as it is now—papers and books are just lines to me.' And as she said this she crossed the page of a newspaper that lay in front of her with her finger. 'Just lines and lines,' she repeated. Then, with a shrug of the shoulders, she laughed a little. 'Now it is different!' she added.

A younger man, a small boy at the time of the civil war, spoke of village education in in the 1940s, before any formal school was established. There used to be travelling teachers, usually students themselves in need of money and sustenance. Villagers would pay them and feed them but it was a very sporadic affair as they came and went. At the time there were some thirty boys, but few girls attended as they were not thought to need an education.

'We were taught,' he continued, 'to add, subtract, multiply and divide. We would get quite good at this at a very basic level. But there was little emphasis on reading or writing. A few of us could do that, that is, if we emigrated and learned elsewhere. The priests could teach us the Catechism and we would hold the 'book' in church, but in fact we knew it by heart—we couldn't read it—this was our religious education.[27] But the priests did not want us to read and write. They were against [a general] education. But we did learn poetry by heart—there was a book we used to share between us, which had a thousand poems in it. But this was Spanish poetry, not like our own refrains. I remember some of them even now. One went *Adiós Rosina! Adiós Clavel!* and then there was one that went *Asturias patria querida! Asturias de mis amores!'*

The narrator went on to recite long extracts from these and other poems which he did with fluency and evident emotion. I found this poetic inclination, common to many villagers, a disarming and rather humbling experience, coming from a generation who claimed to be virtually illiterate. But I was to find these mountain villagers extremely adept at creating their own forms of spontaneous verse, and they constantly made allusions to traditional refrains and sayings in their daily conversation. Then, as if to assure me that their schooling was not all recitation or done by rote, the narrator said that they used to be set puzzles and riddles to solve as a test of mental agility.

'I remember one we were set. It went like this: there was a man who had with him a wolf, a *berza* [cabbage] and a goat. He had to cross a river and could only take one at a time, and he knew that the goat would eat the cabbage, and the wolf would eat the goat, if left on their own. So how did he do it?' At this point the narrator paused to see if I could solve it and as I hesitated he grinned broadly. 'Well! he first took the goat across the river, leaving the wolf with the cabbage. He then took the cabbage across, bringing back the goat with him. He next took the wolf leaving the goat, so the wolf would be with the cabbage. Then he returned again to collect the goat. So they were all once again reunited on the far bank.'

On reflection this anecdote seemed to me to have particular relevance to the village. At the Somiedo fair villagers admired the goats which were herded in large flocks on the open plateau. Unlike sheep, goats had never been a part of village economy. This initially puzzled me until villagers suggested that goats, being more individualistic than sheep, tend to wander, which makes them particularly vulnerable to wolves. They are also voracious eaters and very agile. This would make gardens and particularly the only green-leafed winter staple, the *berza* cabbage, equally vulnerable. Thus if goats were not consuming a village staple, they themselves would be consumed by wolves, which makes them a poor asset. Perhaps the narrator's riddle is well known beyond Asturias, but the choice of representations seemed peculiarly apt for the village school in Alcedo: as an explanation in husbandry.

In villagers' recollection there had been no serious teaching in Alcedo prior to the civil war. One lady in her sixties recalled that her father, who had been educated elsewhere and had become a *partidor* (someone who apportions wills and divides property), had taught in his house in the village. 'He taught doctrine,' she added, 'that is reading and writing, but only in the winter time.'

After the war villagers were too preoccupied in the restoration of their livelihoods and the community to be overly concerned with education. By the 1950s, however, itinerant teachers were coming to the village for brief periods and giving lessons in the houses where they stayed. This was not very satisfactory and in the late 1960s villagers decided to jointly purchase a disused barn in the centre of the village from its owner who had emigrated. They converted the upper storey into a classroom with desks and chairs. The problem then was to find a full-time teacher who would be willing to stay in a remote mountain village without a proper wage. Although they could not afford to give the teacher a full salary they could give her all the sustenance she required. Thus each house in the village with children attending the school would take turns to supply milk, wood and her various food requirements. This system operated on the same pattern as village cooperative work, starting with houses near the fountain and working down through each house including Tabla and then back to the fountain again. When a new teacher arrived they would tell her to let the children know what she needed and the things would be brought to her. One teacher who stayed for four years received so much that she was able to partially provide for her parents who lived in Oviedo.

Teachers liked the village despite its remoteness, partly because people were so generous and partly because they were well removed from any educational supervision. Most, both itinerant and permanent, were still in training and had not completed their diplomas. When teachers became government funded and received a proper salary some villages no longer gave them food, but Alcedo always continued to provide for them gratis. On the other hand the village was frequently cut off by snow in winter and, perhaps more disconcerting for some, the dialect was almost incomprehensible. One lady teacher from Madrid actually broke down in tears for this reason and had to leave.

The education authorities first stepped in to help fund teachers in the 1960s, then on a more permanent basis in the early 1970s. They also supplied and installed the first television in the village in the schoolroom in the mid-1970s. It never functioned properly however as the recently installed mains electricity was both erratic and very low voltage. This official backing for the school was in part due to the efforts of a priest who contributed greatly to the village in many ways. For two years towards the end of the 1960s when the village had no teacher, he came up daily to teach himself until the post was filled. Subsequently he arranged evening classes for a small group of young villagers he had taught, so that they could take their Baccalaureate.[28] Two of these young people went on to further education, one to university in Oviedo, the other to train as a teacher himself.

The first permanent teacher came in the early 1970s and stayed for four years. Initially appalled at the prospect of Alcedo, she later became very attached to it. As one villager put it, 'She wept when she came and she wept when she had to leave!' 'We were very obliged to her,' was another comment, 'she taught the girls to make beautiful *labores* (embroideries) which were each worth more than a thousand pesetas!' It was quite an undertaking for any teacher to educate children of both sexes, ranging from four to fourteen and all in the same classroom. The subjects she taught included Spanish grammar, French, social studies (which included history and natural history) and mathematics. She also taught drawing, singing, embroidery and needlework.[29]

By the late 1970s there were only sixteen children attending the school including our own two daughters. They were divided into nine separate grades according to their age and although fourteen was the upper limit two of the children were older as they had fallen behind in their studies. The new priest from Belmonte came up every two weeks to visit the school and give the children religious instruction, using picture books and slides to illustrate his talks.

The school year was divided into three terms, the last terminating by the third week of June because the children had to help with the hay harvest. The teacher herself, coming from a *vaqueiro* village above Belmonte, also left at that time for the same reason. As her husband was in the *guardia civil* and could not absent himself for such work, she had to help in his village as well as her own.

The children would always stand up when anyone entered the classroom and wait until requested to sit down. They would address the teacher directly as *señora* and when referring to her would call her *la maestra*, as would all the villagers, who held the teacher in great respect. The teacher herself said that the children were always well mannered in class. This was not in her experience the case in Belmonte nor in other urban schools. She seldom raised her voice to admonish a child and there was never any need to resort to corporal punishment in any form.

Within the classroom the children were situated according to age, the youngest at the front, and there was no division between boys and girls.[30] Once outside the school, however, the children would tend to separate according to sex. Girls were expected to tidy up the classroom at the end of each day, while every so often it fell to the boys to clean out the old sheep steadings beneath the classroom, used as the school's toilet.

Though respectful to the teacher, children were less so towards the priest on his fortnightly visits. Some took the opportunity to ridicule him by making faces when his back was turned. This might be regarded as merely mischievous, but could also reflect parental attitudes of eclecticism and indeed resentment towards the church and its representatives' intrusion into secular schooling.

Village schools like the one in Alcedo were relatively rare in the region of Belmonte in the late 1970s. Once the number of children attending a school fell below a certain figure the local authorities were compelled to close it down as they could no longer sustain the expenses of maintenance and a teacher's salary. Early in the 1980s only nine children were attending the school and it had to be closed. Smaller families were a factor in this decline in numbers, but when whole families left the village the decline was rapid and inevitable. The *parroquia* school in Boinas also had to close down, which meant all the children had to go to the state boarding school in Belmonte. This had a profound effect and was an outcome that could hardly have been foreseen when villagers first advocated the benefits of educating their children.

'It all started some twenty-five years ago now,' commented on elderly lady with some resignation, 'when whole families, not just individuals, started departing from the village ... It gives much sadness to those of us who are left. In a few years' time there will be no school here as there will not even be nine children of school age left in the village—they will all have to go to Belmonte.' She was of course quite correct in her prediction, only it happened sooner than she expected.

On our return in the late 1980s there was no village school, just an empty room. The few children of school age stayed all week in Belmonte and, provided they had the means to get back, they returned to the village at weekends and during the holidays. Villagers did not like this. They considered that it was bad for their children, not because of the teaching, but because of the separation from their families.

'Children hardly know their parents,' complained one villager. 'They are just like any other person, as they see so little of them. They lose their love for the land and for the village. It changes them. They are like orphans.'

The outcome of the villagers' initiatives to modernise educational standards, and the repercussions of these on traditional values, were summarised by an articulate young woman who had married in from a village near Cangas de Narcea. 'All the children from my village have to go to Cangas from six years old onwards. They stay there during the week and return at the weekends. My husband thinks this is very bad. Firstly because the children become accustomed to town ways. They see many things they would not normally see and hear, here in the village. They get used to town ways, not country ways. This is why the young are all leaving now from the villages. The second factor is that they catch many illnesses, such as colds and influenza. When one gets it they all get it. But more importantly, when they are ill they don't have their parents to look after them. That is not natural. Before there were more schools in the villages, but you had to pay. Now there are state run schools. You don't have to pay, but your children are taken away from you—and from the village.'

It seems a sad indictment of what was intended, a rationalisation of education for the good of all, but with little thought for the peculiar circumstances of these mountain village communities. In fairness however, it should be said that over the past decade there has been no appreciable decline in the population of Alcedo. The young seem to be adapting and applying new technologies and although the traditional ways are fast disappearing, the land is still being farmed.

Confirmation

On one of his visits to the school the new curate asked one of the younger pupils, aged ten, if he had learned his Catechism. He replied in the affirmative: that he had indeed familiarised himself with the instructions prior to his pending confirmation. Two weeks later, on the Sunday of Corpus Christi, he came with his close family to the *capilla*. The curate had rung the bell at 2.15 p.m. Several children with their parents had already come to the chapel, which they had decorated for the occasion: ferns and foxgloves were placed in the aisle and close to the altar table, on which were red roses. A single red rose had been placed beside the wooden carving of the Virgin of Covadonga on the left of the altar, while on the right in a niche the figure of San Vicente, the patron saint of the village, remained unadorned. The young boy was wearing a new suit for the occasion while the other children, all of whom had recently been confirmed, were also wearing their best clothes.

Although the *capilla* was reasonably full with some attendance from other nearby villages, it was noticeable that a number of houses were not represented, not even by their children. This may have been due to a recent rift between the young boy's family and some of their neighbours; however, a number of houses in the village took very little part in church affairs as a matter of principle.

The curate started by explaining the significance of his various vestments as he donned them, there being no separate vestry. After preliminary prayers he gave his address, speaking of Corpus Christi as a day on which the church can honour the meaning of God and Christ. He then turned to the subject of the confirmation.

'It is not just the clothes which are important—the dressing up for this occasion—but rather your actual taking of your first communion, and not just your first one, but all the communions you will take in the future. This is just a beginning, and your parents should set a good example in this.' He then spoke of the sacrificial lamb of Moses and of the continuity between the Old and the New Testament. As he mixed water with the wine he referred to the former as 'humble water: the symbol of ourselves,' and the wine as 'the blood of Christ'. He then referred to Christ as being the head and ourselves as the body, quoting St. Paul.

As the young boy received his first communion from the hands of the curate a photographer, who had been standing near the altar and had handed the curate the water, took a flash photograph. Then other children, followed by their parents and others, also took communion. Later the congregation gathered outside the *capilla* door, overlooking the village, where the photographer took more colour pictures. Meanwhile the curate gathered his vestments together and joined those outside where the children were giving the boy his presents: small sums of money placed in sealed envelopes. Then the family moved off together with the curate to partake of the customary *banquete* in their house.

Photographs are important possessions in most houses in the village. Sometimes these are very old and faded monochromes of parents or grandparents, which may be framed and hung on the wall of a dining room. These rather poignant reminders of the past are in very formal poses: the men in dark suits, the women in black and always facing the camera. Now some houses keep their photographs in albums which they treasure and prominent among the pictures they contain are colour prints of confirmations and weddings. When no villager owned a camera it was accepted practice to hire a photographer from a nearby town for such an occasion.

Some women in the village considered confirmation to be the most important occasion in a young person's life. One mother had her daughter's first communion cards specially printed, saying that it was not only the most important event, but 'it is also a happier event than marriage, because children still retain their *ilusiones* at that age.' She thought that every house in the village should be invited, that recently confirmed children should attend, and that everyone should give presents. In practice, she admitted, this never happens.

Presents are usually in the form of money and most houses, even if not attending the service, will give them. In 1968 one young man received about 13,000 pesetas on confirmation, worth about £65 at the time: a considerable sum, most of which would have been donated by close relatives. While we were living in the village in 1978, a girl received 28,000 pesetas, a reflection perhaps of the growing prosperity of the village. Not only money is given, however, and watches, earrings, embroideries and tablecloths may be given to a girl, while others may give food, particularly sweet breads and eggs.

Some villagers were less than enthusiastic about this occasion, viewing it pragmatically more as a necessity than a rite of special religious significance. One old lady remarked, 'You have to be confirmed in order to marry later on, that is within the church, for you have to take communion then.' An elderly man, now an atheist but admitting that he had been confirmed when he was ten years old, was rather more dismissive of this trend: 'There was no fuss about it then. Now however it is all luxury and costs lots of money.' He was perhaps overly cynical, but there were many villagers with similar views at the time.

Plate 16 The 'wolf-men' visit the village

Chapter 8

Village youth

A vital force

> No hay carretera sin barro,
> Ni prado que no tenga hierba,
> Ni mozacina de quince
> Que no tenga la cara fea.

> There is no highway without mud,
> Nor meadow without grass,
> Nor a girl of fifteen
> Without an unsightly face.

This is a typical village proverb about a young girl's preoccupations with acne. Conversely, *El mozo cresciente, tiene el diablo en el vientre* refers to an older boy having 'a devil in his vitals', which could have either digestive or sexual connotations. Although the words *mozo* for young man and *moza* for young woman are still used in the village, they do not seem to have quite the implications they engendered in the past. Older people, particularly women, seldom speak of the former numbers of houses in the village, nor of a total village population; it is almost invariably 'the time when there were [forty, fifty or sixty] *mozos* in the village'.

There is always a sense of pride in this, for in many ways the *mozos* (meaning both males and females as a group) are the image of the village. If a village has few *mozos* this could imply that it is simply a small community, or that it is in decline or of little significance. Conversely, the presence of many *mozos* implies a healthy, vibrant and perhaps expanding community. It expresses a sort of vitality and exuberance or *joie de vivre*, especially in the minds of the older women. (A man might more commonly refer to the time when he had a particular pair of oxen.) Comparisons are apt to be made between the state of affairs in the village now and in the past.

'The young now think we older villagers are stupid, but I think that we used to enjoy ourselves more than they do now.' This elderly lady in fact had a very difficult childhood. Her father was disabled during the civil war and her mother relied on her, the eldest of the family but still a young *moza* of only fourteen, to help with the other children. These included a newborn daughter to whom she became a surrogate parent until her mother could manage herself: 'I was made her *madrina* [godmother]', she added rather proudly.

Another villager maintained that she learned to use a scythe like a man when she was thirteen and how to make bread when she was sixteen. 'Nowadays none of the young are being taught to make bread', she added. However, in spite of the more onerous obligations of the young in those days, it seems they still managed to enjoy themselves.

Young people are considered *mozos* between the ages of about fourteen and thirty unless, as in the case of most women, they marry. When a boy becomes a *mozo* he ceases to be a child and takes on adult responsibilities. A young man will help his father care for the animals in the *cuadro*, in the steadings beneath the house, in the meadows and in the common grazing grounds. He will go to fairs and help his father sell and purchase animals and attend, if not at first actively participate in, the winter *matanza*. He will in fact take up all the daily tasks of an adult villager, and as such he will be aware that one day he may inherit his parents' land and house. He may participate in discussions about inheritance with his parents and siblings, and if he is the eldest son he may assume that the role of being *en casa* will in time fall to him. He may have to decide if this is really the life he wishes to follow and if so he will have to prove he is capable of such responsibility. He must be a hard worker and civil towards neighbours with whom in time he will have to cooperate. But first of all he must find himself a wife: a girl brought up in the village tradition, who will bring land or stock to add to his household possession. Formerly this would have been part of her dowry, but nowadays villagers prefer to view it as her inheritance at the time of her betrothal. However, it may happen that an individual may do all these things and not inherit; for various reasons the house and land may go to a younger brother, or a sister.

A young *moza* should perform all the tasks expected of any woman in the village. As a younger girl she will have assisted her mother in the house, but as a *moza* she will be expected to take on more arduous duties. She will learn to cook and make bread, to care for the animals and prepare the various meat products from the *matanza*. She will learn to harness oxen, clean byres, stook and dry hay, cultivate the kitchen garden and harvest maize, potatoes and *escanda*.

Many of the preoccupations of an adolescent girl are not so different from those of a boy. Even if she has brothers she may find that circumstance dictates she is to become *hija en casa*: an occurrence perhaps more frequent nowadays than in the past. This means it becomes her responsibility to find a husband. Preferably he should be from the same village or an adjacent one, bringing not only cattle but also land to be farmed along with her own. If she makes a bad choice in her marriage she may forfeit her inheritance.

In the past when there may have been a dozen siblings in one household, the parents had considerable choice about which of their children should inherit. Younger members of the sibling group had little chance of becoming *en casa* and would either marry other villagers who were inheriting family property or marry into another village. The majority of the siblings would eventually move away, unless they remained unmarried, in which case they could if they wished stay all their life in the family house. This could be to the advantage of a household as it meant an extra pair of hands to share the work, and allowed for the expansion of stock.

For villagers the *mozo* group is seen as being 'new blood' and the future vitality or life force of the village. *Mozos* are the guardians of tradition as they sing the old songs and learn the *refranes* or proverbs and create new ones. Each year they re-enact the festivals: walking in the dew of San Juan, engaging in the *romerías* and forming the *corros* or circles for the traditional dances and quick witted repartee of debate. They express hope and aspiration and retain their *ilusiones*, unlike some of the elderly villagers who may have become saddened, cynical and even slightly corrupted by circumstance.

Sheep

As previously indicated, the villagers of Alcedo were semi-pastoralists of sheep until the late 1950s. They had sufficient cattle for milk and the plough, but sheep were central to their economy along with agriculture. Estimates vary, but on average each household maintained between twenty and thirty sheep. With forty or more households in the village, this meant a combined flock of well in excess of a thousand. 'The slopes of Manteca were white with sheep,' was one man's comment, and as nearby villages also grazed their sheep on this mountain's common land, his description was no exaggeration. The flocks might mingle during the day to be separated before dusk, which meant that young herders of both sexes could fraternise while watching their sheep. As one old villager commented with a hint of nostalgia, it was an ideal time for wooing and courtship beyond the confines of the village.

The herders came almost entirely from the *mozo* groups, who would take on this not unpleasant duty in turns. The village herd was divided into two flocks of five to six hundred animals. During the summer the flocks might only require one shepherd each, but in winter and during the lambing in spring they would each require two. Each house in turn provided two *mozos*, and an individual could expect to herd at least once a week. Later, when the village population began to decline, pre-adolescent children, even ten-year-olds, were required to watch the sheep. When this happened things began to go badly wrong with the traditional form of herding.

The sheep were always brought into the *cuadro* at night and kept in byres beneath the houses which are now used for cattle. The very low ceilings of these byres may bear testimony to their former use as the cattle have to lower their horns to enter them. 'I remember the noise the sheep would make beneath the house,' one old lady recalled, 'especially when there were lambs—it was a din! Each house would take it in turn to do the shepherding. We used to go down through the village in the morning calling out the sheep, and the flock would accumulate as each house sent out their own and then we would go off together.'

They would spend the whole day with the flock on the slopes of Manteca, accompanied by mastiffs and other large dogs with nail-studded collars to protect them against wolves should they get involved in any fighting while guarding the sheep. According to another villager the young shepherds did not always take their surveillance too seriously: 'We used to meet up with other flocks from other villages—from Quintana, Abongo and Puente Castro. We would gather on the *verdes*,[31] and talk. But later,' he added rather ruefully, changing to the third person as if in his day they had been more responsible, 'they would allow the sheep to wander on their own—the wolves could get them for all they cared.'

Wolves usually hunt in pairs. If they come across sheep guarded only by a mastiff one of the wolves will make itself obvious, attracting the dog's attention to it. No sooner has the dog left the flock to see off the intruder than the second wolf will move in on the temporarily unguarded sheep. According to villagers wolves will use the same technique with young shepherds. When approaching sheep they will stalk them, moving very low to the ground and sometimes on their stomachs, through the low cover of undergrowth and open grassland. Although familiar with this technique shepherds and dogs were often caught out and if a mist came down, as one villager recounted, it was easy for the wolves.

'Miguel's father was quite recently up the valley above the village watching his five sheep grazing in a meadow from a nearby hedgerow. A mist suddenly came down the valley and obscured the sheep from his view for a moment. In less than two minutes the mist cleared and there were his five sheep: they were all dead!' This may seem like indiscriminate killing, but wolves will always return later, usually under cover of darkness, to eat the carcass.

Every household had a lead sheep with a bell around its neck. The other sheep in the flock would always stay close to the particular sound of this bell and on returning to the village in the evenings, each household flock would follow its bell-leader. This was not an infallible system however and in the confines of the village, with a thousand sheep milling around, I thought that there must have been problems. However, as one experienced shepherd pointed out, 'They could be quickly distinguished by the small marks or cuts in their ears—but,' he added, as if to assure me that sheep were perfectly intelligent animals, 'each sheep knew its own *cuadro*—returning them to their houses at the end of the day was not a problem.' Recalling what the old lady had said about the noise of the sheep, he said, 'The noise she referred to earlier was probably when they were brought in off the mountain in the evening rather than the morning. If they had lambs which had been kept in all day and you had thirty or forty ewes and about as many lambs all looking for their dams—you had a lot of noise!'

Whether shepherding was always entrusted to the *mozo* group is unclear, but in a community where agriculture was regarded as of equal importance it would be logical for the young to care for the sheep and the more mature to cope with cultivating the land which required more physical strength. Problems seem to have arisen not with a sudden increase in the predatory population of wolves, but with the precipitate decline in village population in the late 1940s and 1950s. An immediate result of this was a reduction in the number of *mozos* available to care for the sheep, aggravated by the perceived need for the young to be better educated in the village, resulting in less time being available for shepherding.

Households found that they were no longer able to provide two *mozos* when their turn came and substituted younger children, older members being too occupied with their daily agricultural pursuits to pass a day on the mountain. This meant that the sheep were not so well guarded and began to sustain heavy losses through the depredations of wolves. At the same time there was a gradual shift to cattle herding as households reduced their flock holdings. Cattle produced a better return at markets, were able to defend themselves against wolves and therefore needed less continuous attention. However, they did require good grazing land and large amounts of winter feed. Many households accustomed to sheep herding on open common land and with relatively small holdings of meadow and hayfields, were less able to make this change.

Sheep were also providers of wool, and until the demise of cooperative sheep herding, villagers made most of their own clothing. They also grew and wove flax for linen, but sheep's wool provided for most of their needs and it was normal to see the women, particularly *mozas*, carding wool, spinning it on spindles and knitting. The dialect (and *bable*, the Asturian dialect) term *filar* (Spanish *hilar*) means 'to spin' and is very similar to the word *fila*, used by villagers to describe visiting neighbours, to sit around talking and telling stories while the women spin and knit. This was one of the many occupations of *mozas* and these gatherings in different houses were a nightly event in winter. With the resort to manufactured clothing after the civil war, although these visits continued in a desultory way they lacked their essential motivation, which was for women to demonstrate their skill and take pride in providing clothing for their families. A few houses still retained a minimal flock of up to six or eight sheep in the late 1970s and they were still making some clothing, particularly stockings, from their own wool. However these sheep had become something of a liability for they required constant protection and most households were too busy to have time for this.

The fundamental changes over the past several decades do not however just relate to husbandry and the economics of village life, but also to social customs and village morale. The decline from upwards of a hundred *mozos* before the civil war, to approximately sixty after the war, to a group of twenty in the late 1970s, signifies to the older generation a downturn in village fortune. As I have previously indicated it is a circumstance Alcedo shares with numerous other mountain communities in western Asturias, but is a matter of relatively little importance to the younger generation of the farming community. With modernisation of farming techniques, better communications and a fundamental change from a near subsistence economy to one based on trade goods and cooperatives, and an open market system with an emphasis on subsidies, banking and profit margins, they now see things very differently. Although they may not regard the older generation's wariness and entrenched nostalgia as mere *tontería* (stupidity), they feel themselves to be more realistic and sanguine about the future and view current changes as necessary and inevitable, as factory farming replaces animal husbandry.

Wolves

Whenever young children wander far from the village, or an elderly person does not return from collecting firewood by dusk, people will always say that the wolves may get them. This at times is not just a joke but a genuine fear, particularly among women. When I walked far from the village during the daytime my wife would be told, half humorously, that I should take care or the wolves would eat me! Despite their depredations wolves are greatly admired for their hardiness and intelligence. Perhaps more than the bear, which villagers consider to be like humans, the wolf retains a supernatural element in village consciousness. This does not make it any less of an enemy, responsible for human deaths in the women's view, though this is a charge which men tend to refute. Although attitudes are changing, wolves still hold a peculiar fascination for villagers. Their presence, particularly in severe weather in winter, when they may be heard howling in the vicinity and on occasion enter the village in search of food, is all prevailing. As one villager remarked after hearing them nearby: 'They do not like to eat snow—they will soon be here!'

To some extent young men associate themselves with wolves. 'Men are more wolves than wolves' is a typical jest expressed by the young *mozos*. I would not suggest the *mozos* think of themselves as wolves, but there is an implicit analogy here, borne out by frequently reiterated remarks by women who make such comments as: 'Men are like wolves—they are much stronger than us! Men just laugh at our fears, but we women are more imaginative. Men are not afraid [of wolves].' Mothers discipline their very young children not to wander far from the village by the implicit threat that if they do they will be eaten by the wolves; and they relate numerous stories of encounters they or others have had, and their narrow escapes.

All the villagers knew the story of a destitute old man who had wandered into the village one day to beg for food, like so many others in the decade following the civil war. He was very frail and in rags. The villagers helped him with food and sent him on his way to the next village some four kilometres further on. He set out and was never seen alive again. They found his body half eaten down one side. The women maintained that the wolves had killed him, although there was no evidence that he had not just collapsed and died and become carrion for the wolves.

They cited a more recent occasion concerning a child who had wandered and apparently disappeared. Perhaps this was too close to village susceptibilities and involved neighbours and relations, but no-one seemed to want to elaborate on the tragedy, the men appearing defensive and embarrassed, saying, 'Oh that—that was just a story,' implying that a mastiff on the loose could be a formidable animal.

What was interesting here and in the telling of other such tales was that men invariably came to the wolf's defence. It was as if the wolf had a basic morality and would never offend his fellow denizen. Accuse the wolf (all wolves were regarded as male) and you would be accusing the menfolk of the village. Yet, when wolf hunts were organised by syndicates from the city, village men would often join in as beaters. No women ever joined in this sort of escapade, which was strictly a male preserve.

The Spanish wolf (*Canis lupus*) is a formidable animal weighing up to forty kilos. Nowhere else in western Europe does this animal survive in the wild and unless protected it is unlikely to survive for long. It is illegal to kill it unless an official permit is obtained, though in the past when their sheep and horses were attacked villagers did not always seek permission. Urban sportsmen obtain permits and villagers tend to ridicule these slightly pretentious outsiders with their feathered hats, hunting garb and glistening weaponry, implying that the wolf is much too smart for them. On the rare occasions when they despatch a wolf they will have a photograph taken with the animal stretched out in front of them, reminiscent of a tiger shoot in the days of the British Raj. The beaters stand around looking uneasy. 'It is only a very young wolf,' confided one villager, 'it is not much bigger than a cub.' In contrast to the hunters who are jubilant after a long hot day in the mountains, the Alcedans seem subdued and slightly embarrassed at this display.

Yet villagers kill wolves themselves, not with the gun but with poison. This is put on the carcasses of animals recently killed by wolves, so that when the predators return to eat their prey they will also die. In Alcedo this practice is frowned upon and no villager would admit to the use of strychnine. 'Elsewhere that might happen, but not here,' was the usual response. Without guns themselves, however, although fully aware of the rarity of the wolf and the need for its protection, they use poison to atone for the carnage these animals are capable of causing to their stock. Sheep are not the only victims; wolves also hunt down horses, and particularly foals. Even cattle are not exempt. There is a palpable sense of grievance when this happens, as such losses can be critical to a household's well being.

Chemists and others from whom poison can be obtained are expected to be on the lookout for purchases of this nature, but there are always ways around this. There is, however, an implicit rule that poison should not be left on the carcass of a recently killed animal for more than two days. After that the remains must be disposed of and are usually buried. That is considered time enough for wolves to return to their kill, but insufficient for other animals, particularly dogs, to get to the carcass. After taking the poisoned meat wolves immediately seek water with fatal results. Dogs however tend to return to the village if poisoned inadvertently, and in their agony bite, causing concern over rabies. Poisoning is therefore a calculated risk and villagers admit that most wolves are just too smart to succumb to this device. They can immediately sense that humans have tampered with a carcass, and leave it strictly alone. For a hapless few however it is a cruel death.

It is customary in these mountain villages that when a wolf is killed its body is taken around all the neighbouring villages. The animal is first gutted and then stuffed with hay, sewn up and strapped to the back of a donkey, its hair ruffled up to maximise the impression of size. One that was brought to Alcedo during its tour through the villages appeared to be almost as large as the donkey which was carrying it (Plate 16).

The object of this custom is partly to demonstrate goodwill between villages and a sense of shared participation in their common fight against a perceived enemy which destroys their livelihoods. To reciprocate in this gesture of goodwill the men who bring the wolf (to whom I shall refer as the wolf-men) receive rewards from households as they perambulate along their route, or await the arrival of spectators to view the victim near the centre of each village. These rewards may consist of loaves of bread, eggs, *empanadas*, *chorizo* or *morcilla*, apples, cider or whatever may be at hand, which may also nowadays be money.

These perambulations generate great excitement and there are numerous exchanges of news and gossip, especially if the wolf-men have relatives in the village. In this instance the two wolf-men came from a small village near Mieldes, above Soto. They had killed the wolf some three days earlier in the third week of March, at a time when wolves are apt to move to lower ground after the long winter to seek sustenance when their cubs are born. This coincided with a lull in the agricultural season, just prior to the seeding of the crops, so the men had time on their hands. They stayed for about an hour or so in the centre of Alcedo before moving off again to the next village. During this time the village turned out almost to a man to view the wolf, passing comments on its immensity and apparent ferocity, the mouth braced open to display its huge canines. The young passed admiring glances at the wolf-men who were evidently enjoying, in a deprecating way, their temporary elevation in status.

They had completed the round of the various houses and received either food or money, sometimes as much as two hundred pesetas. When they saw me with a camera, they joked goodnaturedly: 'That will be five hundred pesetas!' I gave them what other householders had given them and they were obviously pleased. A man nearby remarked rather caustically: '*Broma o no broma, vd. toma!*' implying that, joking or not, nowadays it was all business! A woman standing next to him appeared unimpressed by the sight of the wolf. 'It is venom stuffed with straw!' was her brief comment, leaving some doubt as to whether she was referring to a poisonous or a poisoned animal.

It might have been possible for the wolf-men to perambulate almost indefinitely in this manner around local villages, for this could prove to be quite a lucrative pastime. However, they needed to return to their village to care for their holdings and plough their *tierras* before the spring seeding. As for the wolf, it would soon begin to spoil and smell in the early spring sun and required burning or burial before the wolf-men's visitations became distasteful. The wolf-men were representatives of their village and like all villagers they were bound by certain conventions, by the rules of reciprocity and neighbourliness. If they accepted gifts in the name of their village then it was their moral obligation to share them with their fellow villagers, particularly if, as is usually the case, others were also involved in the wolf's demise. The moral of the following story is concerned with this aspect of neighbourliness and customary reciprocities and it is the *mozos*, the young adults of the village, who see that customary traditions are observed. They are in the best position to act if, for some reason, the norms are not observed.

A corporate sanction

'Some poison was put on the carcass of a young calf wolves had killed.' The narrator did not specify who had put down the poison, but she implied that it was someone from a nearby village. 'The father of old Fernandez and his uncle came across the carcass and decided to keep watch on it.'

The implication was either that the men wanted to find out who was responsible for this illegal act, possibly with a view to reporting the matter, or that they themselves wished to abscond with the wolf, should one be poisoned. Either way, their intentions did not seem honourable in village terms, as neither the carcass nor the land on which it was found belonged to them.

'They kept a watch on it for a day or so,' continued the narrator, 'then one morning they arrived to find not just one but two dead wolves in the vicinity of the carcass. They opened the wolves up, cutting out the entrails and gut and stuffed them with grass. Then, with the stuffed wolves strapped to the back of a donkey, they made a tour through the nearby villages. After two or three days of visiting many villages they had collected a huge amount of meat, *chorizo*, bread, potatoes and much other food and even some money. But they made no division of these gifts among us here in the village. They didn't share with anyone, but kept it all to themselves.' The narrator was emphatic on this point, repeating it so it would be clearly understood.

'After they had returned one evening from visiting the villages, Lisario, who was then a young *mozo* himself, got together with some others of the *mozo* group in the village, and stole up on the Fernandez house during the night. They untied the wolves which were hanging beside the harness in the *cuadro*. They took them down to the centre of the village and placed them on a great pile of ashwood they had prepared beside Casa Genero.' This was a very public place right in the centre of the village. 'It was a big bonfire and the wolves were burned—the fire was seen by many nearby.' The narrator emphasised the public nature of the burning, despite the fact that it happened during the night, and the implied sanction against the brothers.

'When the father and his brother woke up the next morning and were ready to go off again, they went into the *cuadro* and found the wolves had gone. "Where are the wolves?" they asked of each other.' The narrator made quite a play on this episode in her story, re-enacting in mime their surprise and amazement. 'They asked all their neighbours about the disappearance. Then someone suggested that the wolves might have been burned on a bonfire in the centre of the village. They went down there and found some charred remains of the carcasses and they were furious. They went around asking everyone who was responsible: who made the bonfire? But all, to a man, said they didn't know. "Who knows? Who knows?" they said, or they were silent and just shrugged their shoulders.' With some satisfaction in her voice the narrator concluded, 'And they never did find out who was responsible. Never.'

This story, despite being fifty years old, was still told with great relish as if it had happened the previous day. It reflects well on the *mozos* of that generation, particularly on Lisario and his house; equally it reflects badly on the house of those responsible for this blatant breach of village etiquette. The narrator was not unbiassed, having some personal antipathy towards the descendants of that particular house; but the fact that the malefactors were never to know who had been responsible for the burning meant that no retribution could be made, and over the years the conspiracy of the *mozos* had been a continuing sanction and reminder to those who might otherwise think of transgressing village codes.

On first examination the story seems to be about a relatively minor offence, the stealing of another man's property. As this apparently did not involve a fellow villager, it could be partially excused. The inexcusable act was not sharing the spoils: meanness and selfishness are qualities that villagers will not tolerate. The community depends on the spirit of exchange and this accepted reciprocity, this chain of giving and receiving, should not be gainsaid. It was not that the villagers needed the food: the story relates to the late 1920s, well before the civil war and its aftermath of near famine. It was the lack of generosity, not just to an individual but to the whole village as a corporate group, of which the men were culpable.

The bonfire is described as being very large and made at night in the centre of the village, where many people are said to have seen it. The culprits' house however lay on the southernmost fringe of the village and they would have been unaware of the bonfire: matters which emphasise the central importance of the *mozos'* action and its corporate nature. The villagers ensured that the culprits knew what had happened to their wolves, so that they could not assume for a moment that this was just the whim of an ill-intentioned neighbour, but knew it was the action of the *mozo* group acting on behalf of the whole community. This corporate disapproval was to endure, for no one would say who was responsible and the sanction was reiterated each time the story was told. A punishment to fit the crime indeed: a narration as a metaphorical executioner.

This also points to the relevance of the *mozo* group. No individual house or group of houses could have made this sanction on another house, for that would have been regarded as mere envy. It fell to the *mozos*, who in a sense represented both no one and everyone, to act as a corporate group on behalf of the village: as influential scions of tradition and guardians of morality. In any other context this episode might have been regarded as just another village prank.

Football, charcoal-making and insults

Every year there is a football match between the *mozos* of Alcedo and those of Boinas. It is a contest between mountain and valley people, Boinas and its attendant villages lying in the valley some three hundred metres lower than Alcedo. The event alternates between the valley and the highland location and in 1978 it was the turn of the Alcedans to host the match.

The only flattish ground near the village was some three kilometres distant, in a large hayfield close to the near-deserted village of Abongo. On one side of the chosen pitch was a low stone wall running its entire length. On the other side the ground rose steeply towards the *monte*. Both goal lines were relatively unimpeded by walls or rising ground, while the pitch itself was reasonably flat except for numerous molehills. The goal posts were fashioned out of tree branches and pieces of brushwood.

The two teams, each numbering ten *mozos*, were dressed in motley array. One young man—a visitor from Oviedo whom the Boinas *mozos* had commandeered to make up their numbers—was dressed like footballer, but no one else was. There was no linesman or referee. As one player later explained, 'If anyone fouls, or any fighting starts, we all step in to separate them.'

The game commenced at 7 pm and was completed three hours later at nightfall, when the ball could scarcely be seen and when even the oxcarts laden with hay had ceased to rumble past down the lane at the end of the pitch. During these three hours, even after a day's work in the hayfields, there was no half-time, nor any break at all. The players just kept going with furious energy. If one player became temporarily exhausted he would go to the edge of the pitch, or sit on the wall until he had recovered his breath. If two players by chance retired from the same side, either through tiredness or injury, then a player from the opposing side crossed over and substituted. The energy displayed by the young and not so young *mozos* was remarkable.

The only slight pause occurred when the ball was kicked up the hill, when there would be a throw in; but on the other side of the pitch the wall effectively preempted this, as the ball bounced off it back into play. If the ball went over the dead ball line at either end, play usually went on, rather in the manner of lacrosse. Goals provided a momentary breathing space for jubilation and a kick-off in the centre of the field, but in all that time only twelve were scored, four to Boinas and eight to Alcedo.

Each goal of course brought great excitement to the respective supporter groups. Alcedo supporters outnumbered those of Boinas by about four to one; but as Boinas could only muster three, two *mozas* and an elderly man, Alcedo supporters were not numerous either. What they lacked in numbers however they made up for in volubility. Like over-zealous bobbysoxers the Alcedans, apart from two elderly women, were all *mozas* who leapt up and down with excitement every time their team approached the opposition's goal. The almost continuous string of insults which they yelled at the unfortunate opposition caused the other group of supporters to retreat to the far end of the pitch shortly after the game began.

Insults, couched in free verse or humourous asides, were customary form on such occasions. In Boinas the previous year dozens of their fans, far outnumbering the Alcedans', had behaved in the same way but apparently to less effect:

> You think you have such brilliance,
> But you only use a pot cleaner,
> You think you are so clever,
> But you play with your knee!

This refrain, one of several chanted by three young *mozas* throughout the game, had been composed by them the previous evening. In imperfect rhyming couplets it seemed superficially innocuous and prosaic. The last word in the first line, *brillo* (brilliance), which is also the name of a well-known brand of cleaner, assonates with that of the third line, *listo* (clever), while that of the second, *limpiador de olla* (pot cleaner) corresponds with *rodilla* (knee): apparently a straightforward if slightly banal stanza.

Like all refrains, it is couched in innuendo. The word 'pot' is an allegorical reference to a person's physique as being fat or unfit, while *rodilla*, although an allusion to playing football with the knee, with a slight vowel shift becomes *rodillo* (which rhymes with *brillo*), meaning a rolling pin or hard cylindrical object: an apparent allusion to 'the fat man who plays with his penis.' The *mozas* seemed to be directing their chanting at a specific individual in the home team.

Following on from this stanza the *mozas* alternated the last two lines with other variations such as:

> All you eat to make you so weak
> Are sausages filled with mule meat!

These lines terminate in the words *flaco* (weak), and *morcillo de mulo* (mule meat sausage): a further ribaldry with apparent reference to a mule's, and by analogy one of the players', inability to reproduce his own kind.

Of course at a football match with many players, no one knows precisely to whom such insults are being made. However, one rather corpulent Alcedan *mozo*, whose nickname was Gordo (Fatty) at one point left the game and approached the three *mozas*. Having taken their comments personally, he asked, with evident good humour, why they were insulting him. 'I am after all playing for your side,' he pointed out. The eldest of the *mozas*, evidently rather embarrassed, pointed to his large corporation. To which he, glancing at her ample bust, responded, 'But I *like* your big bosom!'

This sort of ribaldry, part of the normal yearly ritual at this event, had this time been a little too shrill and insistent. As both teams took this personally the three *mozas* responsible were cold-shouldered by all the *mozos* that evening at the customary post-match dance in the Boinas bar.

A few older village women came over from their haymaking for a brief spell to watch the game and seemed to be taken aback by the *mozas'* chanting: at any rate they feigned shock by covering their faces with apparent embarrassment. My wife later asked the *mozas* if it was customary to use such language on these occasions, to which the eldest girl replied, 'Here in the mountains, yes, we talk like this!' Although this was not entirely true, some weeks later, in mid-October, I witnessed another example of chanting and shouting insults during charcoal making. This time it was the *mozos* who were responsible.

The area chosen to carry out the work lay some twelve kilometres from the village in the mountainous country to the southwest, an area overlooking a neighbouring village occupied mainly by (former) *vaqueiro* cattle herders. I had set off on the long walk very early with the village farrier and several other men, most of whom were *mozos*. During the arduous work of digging deep pits, filling them with brushwood and firing the wood to make the charcoal, the men bantered continuously among themselves. In intervals of relaxation they told one another risqué anecdotes, mainly concerning fellow villagers. Some of these were told in the presence of the farrier's wife, who had arrived around midday with a large *merienda* in saddle bags slung from her mule.

Throughout the day the young *mozos* would chant and shout with the full force of their lungs whenever they spotted anyone moving about the village across the valley. The older men did not join in and later the farrier turned to me half apologetically: 'I am afraid,' he said, 'you will think of us as being very bad people.' Using the local dialect, the insults were couched in the form of rhyming couplets, but they were spontaneous and included references to women's anatomy. One *mozo's* couplet referred unashamedly to a woman's private parts as being 'hot with desire' for him. Normally recipients of such jocular abuse would respond in a like manner, but these villagers remained strangely silent.

The refrains

This apparent licence for untoward behaviour, together with their former prominent role in village affairs, seems to grant *mozos* a freedom of expression and action denied to older members of the community. When, however, I discussed these matters with an elderly villager, particularly extolling the couplets chanted at the football game with their innuendo, she considered them contrived and was rather dismissive. 'It is not the same thing,' she maintained. 'In our day, when I was a young *moza*, we made them up on the spot: they were spontaneous.' In fact many spontaneous refrains were variations on known ones. They were not just spoken, called or chanted, but also sung, often while *mozos* stood or sat around in a circle or *corro*. When the *mozas* said very bad things, as they often did, the *mozos* would chase them with their sticks. 'They would never hit us,' the lady added, 'they would just threaten us!'

'When there were sixty or seventy *mozos* from this village alone,' she continued, 'we would make up several *corros* and *hacer lanzas* (think up witty responses). One person in the group would start by singing a refrain—perhaps a traditional one or one he or she had just made up. Then another person in the circle would respond to it and then someone else would cap that and so on. It could go on for an hour or more: it was wonderful entertainment!'

There was an element of rivalry in the *corros*, which were in effect competitions between the young *mozos* and *mozas* to ascertain which group had the quickest wit. They could 'win' and gain favour from the opposite sex and build up an admired reputation as village savants. Nor was this activity confined to Alcedo. On festive occasions the *mozos* would travel by well-worn paths over the mountains to other villages where they would dance and form *corros* to compete with other groups.

There were also impromptu occasions. A *mozo* from Abedul, in the manner of the charcoal gatherers, used to stand on a hill above the village and challenge the *mozos* of Alcedo. He was considered to have had an extraordinary natural ability. 'He was so good,' said one elderly lady, 'that he could always cap anything our *mozos* called out in response—he was greatly admired.' Then, with a laugh, she added, 'and some of those exchanges were *muy picante* [very spicy].'

The *mozo* group may also use these verbal exchanges as a commentary on many aspects of village custom and behaviour, both collectively and individually. In this sense refrains can be used as a form of social sanction through their implicit moral censure. If for example, as in the case of the wolf story, a person offends village susceptibilities, he will find himself the butt of such impromptu or set exchanges by the *mozos* at festivals, dances and Carnival.

The refrains can take many forms and although they can be improvisations many are well known, not only locally but elsewhere in the province. To know these may add a certain degree of sophistication to a *mozo*'s repartee. An example might be as follows:

> *Ay! Asturiana, cuanto te quiero!*
> *Porque tienes unas ojas azules,*
> *Como la luna de enero.*

> Oh! Asturian girl, how I love you!
> Because you have blue eyes
> Like the January moon.

This is said by a man at about the time of the full moon to the woman he is courting, to which the woman may reply:

A la luna de enero
Le falta un día,
Y a tí te falta todos,
Para ser mío.

The January moon
Will be full in a day,
But it will take forever
For you to be mine.

There are several possible renderings of this response to the suitor's overture, but the assumption is that a full moon is being referred to. As it is also a 'blue moon' and therefore, like her eyes, very rare, the answer must imply that the suitor has no chance whatsoever. Such a well-known refrain may however also be used in various contexts by the *mozos* when issuing a challenge. The following more local verse was recited by a *mozo* of one village to the *mozas* of another:

Al origen del río
Ya no hay varas que cortan.
Las mozacitas de este pueblo
No quieren contestar.

At the source of the river
There are no sticks that cut.
The young *mozas* of this village
Do not wish to respond.

This refrain refers to a high mountain village with little vegetation, where there are no branches (*varas*) for staffs (*bastones*) and the *mozas* are unresponsive. The innuendo lies in the use of the word *varas* and the *mozas'* apparent indifference. *Bastones* are carried by all men, and young children learn to fight with sticks at an early age. In old prints Asturians out courting or at festivals are always depicted holding sticks or cudgels in their hands. They are a symbol of manhood and used in settling disputes, particularly over *mozas*. I frequently heard stories of a young man wooing a girl from another village and being chased away by the local *mozos* who used their cudgels to beat him off. In this context, and in the knowledge that *mozos* threaten *mozas* with these staffs when insulted by them, the refrain clearly implies that where there is no wood to make cudgels, there are no real men to react against the insults of women. They do not engage in *corros* and contests of wit, the implication being that they are rather stupid.

Among other forms of refrains are those specifically related to place and time, for example the saying that when the first snow lies on Manteca in late autumn, the chestnuts are ready for gathering. Such sayings represent a sort of working calendar for yearly activities. Most of them are specific to the village and its immediate surroundings and represent a form of folk knowledge passed down over the generations.

After living in the village for some time I found that when I greeted neighbours, both young and old, they would frequently make some obscure comment and watch for my reaction. I soon learned that these comments were playing on the words of particular refrains. If I recognised the origin of the quip or indeed attempted to cap it, then I would receive an approving nod. While the formal style of the *corro* at the *romerías* of the past is now lacking, the tradition remains and surfaces in unexpected ways.

In the late 1980s, when we were attending a large family gathering for a *banquete,* a chance remark set the lady of the house off in the manner of her youth. She flushed visibly from a compliment paid to her by a *mozo* at the table and quickly quipped an epigram couched in the words of a well-known refrain. For the next few minutes those around the table reverted quite naturally to the old style *corro.* There was a constant repartee of refrains, witty allusions and rapid asides bandied back and forth around the table, everyone joining in the competition to the delight of all. Indeed for a moment it was as if the more elderly in that circle around the table had themselves re-assumed the role of *mozos.*

Fiestas *and Carnival*

> Every fifteen days or so we used to have *fiestas;* and then there was Carnival: that was the the most important of them all!

Fiesta here is taken in its broadest sense as a social gathering or party. This old villager's comment is a modest one, for included in this category are the entertainments, referred to above, called *fila.* This was a time when neighbours, and especially women, would get together in different houses during winter evenings to gossip, eat sweet cakes and drink wine or cider and spin the large rolls of sheep's wool into thread, and sometimes with the *mozos* present they would sing, dance and *contestar* (hold refrain competitions).

Besides these spontaneous household get-togethers were the frequent and much larger gatherings held outdoors in summer and in barns in winter. Villagers danced to the *gaita* (bagpipe) and tambourine in *corros,* men and women alternating, maintaining the circle by locking little fingers with their neighbours. As the numbers swelled more *corros* formed, each one containing thirty or more dancers. Sometimes, on more 'official' occasions, a large banquet was laid out on flat ground to the north of the village. An occasion for this was the official opening of the road in

August 1978, when dignitaries arrived from Belmonte. In the evening there was dancing to pipes and a small band and the *mozos* formed *corros* to *contestar*.

After each major harvest throughout the year there would be a *romería* or *fiesta*. Often *mozos* from other villages would walk over to join in these gatherings, the *mozos* of Alcedo reciprocating so that large numbers of young people would be constantly moving back and forth between neighbouring villages.

As important as Carnival in the recollection of villagers was a festival known as the Dew of San Juan, which fell within a day or so of the summer solstice. This was both an orthodox celebration and a traditional rite. It centred around two customs, one of which was still continuing in the late 1970s.

The first concerned *centeno* or rye which, although no longer grown in the village, was formerly widely used. 'We used to make bread with it, though it didn't rise like maize or *escanda*,' commented one villager. 'About now [21 June] the rye would be very high in the fields.' She indicated a height well above her head. Then she added, 'All the *mozas* used to walk through it when it was soaked with dew— we used to get very wet!' When I later mentioned this comment to another elderly village lady she appeared a little embarrassed, but then laughed. 'Oh! the dew of San Juan,' she exclaimed, 'Yes—when I was a *moza* we used to celebrate that. At about midnight on the night of the *fiesta*, we would slip away from the dancing [to a nearby rye field]—sometimes we were joined by the young married women too, and we would get completely undressed, then we washed ourselves in the dew of the rye. Young *mozos* used to do the same', she added, 'but in a separate place.' This she said, made them more beautiful (and gave them, virility, health and luck) and afterwards they gathered clover to place about the house.[32]

The second custom, still prevalent in 1978, was the habit of placing sprigs of walnut leaves over the doorways of barns and houses in the village. These were collected at the same time, when the dew of San Juan was still on them. An old lady explained that it was the custom for young *mozos* to collect these and place them on the houses of their sweethearts, who might 'guess who had put them there!' These sprigs and unspecified flowers would also be placed around the fountain at dawn on that day. *Vaqueiro* villagers did likewise but used ash sprigs, as walnut did not grow at the higher altitudes of their villages. It was also customary at this time to take out all the animals, except pigs, from the *cuadros* in the early dawn: 'We all went out before sunrise, while the dew was still wet in the meadows,' said a villager, 'and we took with us all our cows, sheep and goats too, so they could walk in the dew.'

> *Luna nueva de febrero,*
> *El primero martes el carnival.*

> After the new moon of February,
> The first Tuesday is Carnival.

'We always know when Carnival is,' said one villager, 'by the phase of the moon and by this saying—we call it here *entroydo*, which means the beginning of the year.'[33] In 1979 the only celebration of Carnival was that undertaken by the children in the village school. The date had been changed from that described in the refrain to coincide with Shrove Tuesday (27 February in that year). For this occasion the children got dressed up in various costumes representing tramps, nurses and witches among other guises. All wore face masks and one boy carried a drum, another a tambourine. There was great excitement as the little band of fifteen, including our own two children, set off from the village in the late afternoon towards Abongo several kilometres away. 'If they try to go there,' remarked one villager,' the wolves will get them!' Fortunately at dusk they turned back and having visited Tabla they commenced singing, dancing and reciting, stopping at each house from the northern end of the village. Acting out their various characters, they received presents of money, food and even wine, so that towards the end of their perambulation some of the them became quite tipsy. By 10 pm they had accrued nearly two thousand pesetas, a lot of cakes and an assortment of sweets and on the following day they had a *banquete* in the schoolroom, presided over by the teacher.

'It is just an imitation of what Carnival used to be,' remarked one villager. In his day thirty or forty *mozos*, up to seventy if joined by young people from other villages, would make their way around Alcedo at night in their masks and disguises, frightening the women and young children. Unlike the schoolchildren, the *mozos* were dominating in their manner and sometimes threatening to the point of intimidation. The event would go on all day and all night and sometimes for longer. During the daytime everyone joined in various pastimes, games and pranks. The ritual game most villagers recalled, perhaps because of its gruesome nature, took place on the small green in front of the *capilla*, where a cockerel was buried in the ground up to its neck. All the participating children would be blindfolded. Then, each armed with a short stick, they would attempt to locate the head. The one who located it first won the bird: almost certainly dead after such an escapade.

Another event that would take place at nightfall was the 'burning cart', a ritual described by several villagers, when the *mozos* would load an old cart with mouldy hay, set it on fire and send it careering down a steep slope towards another village in the valley below.[34] Like meat for humans, hay is essential winter feed for animals; therefore bad meat and burnt hay represent inversions of the normal patterns of exchange and are characteristic of the role reversals common to Carnival.

'It is our custom to give meat at Carnival,' said one old villager. As the festival falls a few weeks after the *matanza*, there is an abundance of it. It was frequently said that a lot of fat should be eaten at this time of year. 'This is most important,' the old man continued, 'this is what matters for your good health. *Chorizo; morcilla;* it makes you strong. It fortifies you!' Fruit of any sort, however, was considered by the older generation to be 'cold' and to be avoided at this time of year.

Although meat was plentiful at this time, it was 'bad' meat which the *mozos* took as presents to nearby villages at Carnival. This could be meat from the discarded remains after the *matanza*, or meat which had simply gone off. On their fellow villagers the *mozos* would play other meat tricks. If a man had big ears they would wrap up cow's or pig's ears in a parcel and give it to his family; or they would give animal teeth to someone with unusual teeth, or who talked too much. Animal testicles might be given to a man and woman known to be carrying on an extra-marital affair. Such gifts would be accompanied with songs and apt refrains or mimes by the donors, to add piquancy to their 'benevolence'.

'Carnival has nothing to do with girls,' commented one villager after witnessing the schoolchildren's outing. He then recalled that when he was a boy, before the civil war, it had nothing to do with any saint's day, nor indeed any association with the church, but that it did concern the *mozos* of Alcedo and all the neighbouring villages. 'The *mozos* of this village would go to other villages and *mozos* from other villages would come here. The handsome men,' he continued, using the term *bonito* or pretty, 'would get dressed up as women, and we would have two huge *banquetes*: one during the day and one at night, with lots of meat and *berza* (winter cabbage). My wife's father when a *mozo* used to dress up as a blind man, led by another *mozo* on a length of string. Playing an old barrel organ, he would accompany himself with songs. He knew many songs. Other *mozos* would get dressed up as old ladies with bent backs carrying a stick or spinning wool, as mothers carrying their babies, as elegant ladies or flower girls. One man surrounded his belly with cow bells, tying them to his belt, so that when he jumped about they clanged so loudly that he could be heard as far away as the slopes of Manteca. Many things were given to the *mozos* as they came around and banged on the gates and the doors of the houses.' The man's face lit up with enjoyment as he recounted these exploits. 'They banged a pan or a pottery jar on the house walls to announce their arrival and would be given food, drink and money and in turn they would sing. One *mozo* from Puente Castro used to sing so well that he made a lot of money this way.'

A *vaqueiro* lady married to a villager maintained that when she was young the *mozos* did not dress up, although they also regarded Carnival as the most important event of the year. The young men of her village would go around from house to house but they did not receive money. 'They didn't wear disguises and they didn't make fools of people, but they went around each house and sang songs and recited refrains and in return they would receive meat, but mainly *chorizo*, bread and chestnuts.' They would also dance, the lady continued, but as they had no *gaiteros* (bagpipe players) they would use pots and other implements to beat out the rhythm. 'We would dance a lot and make many jokes and later the *mozos* would go off to other villages to continue the celebrations throughout the night.' Her recollections came from a time after the civil war when the church for a while exercised far more influence over village life. It was opposed to the Saturnalian aspects of Carnival and her description may reflect this change which has continued into the present, although in 1979 some vestiges remained of the former behavioural patterns associated with this pre-Lenten time of riotous revelry.

I noticed that on the day of Carnival, apart from the fact that male villagers were not working in their customary way, there was a perceptible change in their behaviour. One elderly man asked me into his house and offered me a glass of brandy, which was most unusual on a normal working day. 'Is your wife alone in the house?' he asked in a rather confidential manner. Then after making a risqué joke about girls who are still virgins, he commented on the fact that today was Carnival, adding, 'We are bad people you know!'

Later in the morning a close neighbour whom we knew very well invited himself into the house and asked for a drink of brandy, behaviour which under normal circumstances would be considered extremely rude. When my wife remarked on the day being a rather cold one our visitor, normally a rather polite and shy man, emphatically contradicted her: 'No! It is very hot!' Clearly he was using her innocent remark on the weather as a metaphor for a state of being of a more personal nature, and as he took a lengthy look at my wife he added, 'and all the women have been running about in the nude!' Obviously this was a joke and its evident Rabelaisian connotations were not lost on my rather embarrassed wife. As if this were not enough he then launched himself into several stories of a rather risqué nature, to her further discomfort. Then as if momentarily appreciating that his behaviour was untoward, he more characteristically started condemning the church for the present state of Lent and Carnival. 'We all eat lots of meat on the day of Carnival,' he said, 'but it is a mortal sin to do so afterwards!'[35] He emphasised the word 'sin' ironically and continued: 'It makes no difference now, but it did once—but the priests aren't interested in Carnival or anything else that concerns us poor people.' Later at a *banquete* the same villager asked my four-year-old daughter if she would like to share his bed! Clearly intended as a joke to tease my daughter, such a remark nevertheless seemed entirely out of character for an otherwise reticent man. Then a *mozo* sitting next to him, a young man of normally unimpeachable decorum, suddenly announced that he and several other *mozos* were off to a nearby village in the valley because, as he put it amidst general laughter, 'the *mozas* there need us!'

These are just a few examples of the attitudes and general banter characteristic of that day of Carnival. Some of this unusual behaviour was directed at my family simply because we were being treated in exactly the same way as all other villagers on that day. This calculated and generally accepted mode of behaviour, very different from the norm, is presumably a residual manifestation of the former tradition.

The following kinds of behaviour are therefore characteristic of Carnival: gifts of bad food in the form of inedible meat and burnt hay (and its destruction); gifts of extraneous animal remains symbolising the habits or physical appearance of the recipients; the use of masks as disguises; the separation of the sexes; occupational role reversals and transvestitism; the cockerel game for normally protected young children; general bad manners; and a sexually explicit, insulting form of discourse.

The following table illustrates the complementary oppositions represented by this behaviour:

Normal daily life	*The time of Carnival*
exchange (meat)	exchange (bad meat)
preservation (hay)	destruction (burnt hay)
openness	disguise
normal dress	abnormal dress (transvestism)
mozos (men and women)	*mozos* (men only)
courtesy	bad manners
children protected	children unprotected
discretion	licentiousness

Although the whole village participated at one stage or another in Carnival, the dominant role was played by the *mozo* group of men. The dramatic decline in numbers of *mozos* after the civil war may have been a contributory factor in the discontinuation of Carnival. However there were also other causes: 'They stopped Carnival because the men used to drink a lot,' commented one villager, 'and there would be fighting and other behaviour which created bad relations within the village.' It is likely that these 'bad relations' stemmed from the aftermath of the years of civil strife and the inevitable divisions created between houses and families; divisions only exacerbated by a rejuvenated post-war church which did not favour secular rural traditions such as Carnival.

Plate 17 Scything the hay

Chapter 9

The age of responsibility

Inheritance

Although villagers say that it does not matter whether a son or a daughter inherits the house, traditionally a son was preferred. With families of up to ten or more children being not uncommon, there was always a likelihood that one of several sons would inherit. The intention to marry was however a prerequisite, and if a younger son married first, and showed himself capable and willing to work and administer the possession, he might well gain preference over an elder brother. Nowadays this may equally apply to daughters.

It is customary that only one offspring can inherit the possession. Villagers maintain that this prevents the fracturing of the various individual holdings within the community. With the large families of the past, if all siblings had inherited land the viability of any house's holdings would quickly have broken down. The one who is ultimately chosen to inherit does not, however, ever acquire all the land and animals, nor does he even receive the majority of the individual holdings initially.

Normally, he (or she) will receive one-third of the total holding of *tierras*, meadows, hayfields and other arable land in his own right once he has obtained an acceptance of marriage and prior to the wedding (Lisón Tolosana (1976) describes a similar form of inheritance in the Galician mountains). Most houses had inventories of their holdings in the past; this is now a legal obligation on the basis of which taxes are paid. Thus after lengthy discussions within the family regarding this preliminary allocation, with the view of the *paterfamilias* usually prevailing, a formal paper or *manda* will be drawn up by a notary in the regional capital of Belmonte, assigning to the chosen inheritor certain allotments of land which will henceforth be considered his property. He will however continue to work the whole farm with his father as before.

On the death of his father (or mother if she is *en casa*), the inheritor will receive a further third of the possession and will take control of the house and the steadings; however his implicit ownership of these may be assumed earlier as his parents become unable to carry the full burden of the working day. When both parents have died the remaining third of the possession is distributed evenly according to the number of children in the family. If for instance there are ten siblings, it will be distributed ten ways. Thus the main inheritor gains a further one-tenth of the remaining third.

This arrangement is, on the face of it, rather hard on those siblings who only inherit a fraction of the last third of the total possession. The primary concern, however, for all houses in the village, is to hold the possession together and to keep it as a workable unit for the next generation. The remaining siblings will in time depart from the house unless they remain unmarried; otherwise, as one villager expressed it, 'The wives (or husbands) would quarrel!'

Normally, the main inheritor will receive only land. He may also however obtain animals through his own acquisition or via his bride. His wife, especially if she comes from another village, will have received animals in her dowry. These 'animals' would have been sheep in the past, but nowadays tend to be cattle. Pigs, mules, donkeys and *jeguas* do not count for these purposes, although they may in time come his way.

Like the first and second distribution to the inheritor, the third will also be mainly land, though it may include animals and possibly household belongings. At this third and final division the inheritor's siblings will normally sell him what little land they inherit, as it will be of no use to them unless they marry within the village. However, even siblings who emigrate abroad may sometimes wish to hold on to their land, while others may keep it in order to rent it out to other villagers, even to the main beneficiary. Thus it is not always certain that the complete possession will be passed on to the inheritor, but the system does ensure that the bulk of the parents' holdings will remain intact and workable. Animals may also be sold back to the inheritor so that, at least in theory, the main beneficiary will be in the same position as his father before him: a position that may be enhanced by an advantageous marriage.

Villagers maintain that since the civil war the dowry or *hual* is no longer a part of the marriage settlement. This may have been largely due to impoverishment at the time which resulted in villagers having little to give. However, despite this refutation, young *mozas* were obtaining or being given items towards the time of their marriage. But whereas in the past possessions belonging to the house—either animals or land—would be part of the marriage arrangement and might be viewed as an advance on inheritance (i.e. the final third), this is less likely to be the case today and a young bride, apart from household items, may have to wait until the final distribution.

Any definitive explanation of these distinctions is very difficult to arrive at, as apart from the general rules set down regarding inheritance, every situation is different and each house within certain limits makes its own arrangements. To this extent it is likely that the alleged discontinuation of the *hual* is more a reflection of present fiscal and social attitudes. All such arrangements should be ratified by a notary and an official *manda* should be drawn up. This can be an extremely costly to less wealthy villagers in terms of both time and money.

As indicated previously, endogamous marriages seem to have been regarded as preferable in the past. Reasons for this may include the need for redistribution of land or stock in relation to marriage settlements; and the fact that a bride leaving a village might be regarded as a depletion of its resources, whereas a man marrying out took nothing away from the village apart from himself. However, a more basic need in a small community's survival lies in cooperation among houses and it is an obvious advantage for marriages to take place within the village. Then, at least in theory, there is no loss of land or stock, and reciprocity in the major farming activi-

Plate 18 The *cuadro* and gate lintel

ties of the year is guaranteed. Hence one possible reason for the traditional inter-village rivalry among *mozos*: the cudgel fights were not just misplaced anger, *machismo* or thwarted love, but matters which concerned village and inter-house solidarity and perhaps survival. Nowadays individual aspirations, socially advantageous marriages and the lure of modernity mitigate against such communal solidarity. In the face of such pressures the mere survival and viability of these communities towards the end of the twentieth century seems remarkable enough.

Another form of inheriting or acquiring a house and its possessions is more common today than in the past when there were large families and many siblings with aspirations to work on the land. This is inheritance by a neighbour when a married couple is childless, or where all offspring prefer to seek their livelihood elsewhere, leaving no obvious successor. With the increasing need to acquire more land, particularly good meadows and hayfields for raising growing numbers of cattle, this can become a very sensitive issue as houses discreetly vie with one another to acquire the inheritance. This can adversely influence the communal ties and cooperative work so essential to a good ambience in a small community of farmers.

If a couple have no direct descendants to inherit, they may consider leaving their property to another relative such as a niece or nephew. Such potential heirs can however be problematical for they are not beholden as are direct descendants. When a farmer has spent his life caring for his possessions like his ancestors before him, the thought of his house and barns lying empty and falling into disrepair, his meadows covered in brambles and his chestnut trees, orchards, stone walls and hedgerows uncared for, grieves him greatly. There are many old dwellings in the village now disused and gradually disintegrating: a constant reminder to those whose houses and possessions may go the same way. Sentiments on such matters are often vehemently expressed.

'Isn't it sad that we have no children?' commented one elderly spinster, who lived with her childless sister and brother-in-law. 'When we die we have no one we can give all this to—it will go to the devil!' Then, with an expansive gesture of her hands, implying that they might as well enjoy the benefits of their labours while they could, she added: 'We should eat well!'

The evident bitterness in her voice was not however because her sister and brother-in-law had no children of their own, but because years before, with succession in mind, they had adopted a nephew of the husband's and things had not gone as planned. The boy's parents had both died at an early age and he had been brought up as a son by his uncle, his Alcedan *en casa* wife and her unmarried sister. He attended the village school, worked on the farm and all went well until he completed his military service. On his return, against the wishes of his foster parents, he married an Alcedan girl and left the village to set up a bar in a nearby town. Either because he married the *moza* without their consent, or because earlier he had expressed no wish to inherit, no settlement had been arranged for him to receive one-third of the property according to normal practice. His foster father was so upset that, according to his sister-in-law, he nearly hanged himself. 'After all,' she said, 'he had raised him as a son. When he left we did not eat for eight days.' After that the foster father never visited his adopted son even though on one occasion he passed by the door of his bar, and the young man never visited his foster parents despite occasional visits to the village.

This also caused a division between the adopted son's house and the house of the *moza* he had married. At first, they would not speak to each other, not even in greeting. On one occasion several years later, while taking her cows to the meadow, the elderly foster mother greeted the *moza*'s father in an attempt to be conciliatory. He remained silent. 'So you are not going to talk to me?' she asked. 'Haven't you talked enough?' he replied, alluding to that lady's propensity to gossip about the dispute. After that they have never spoken again.

Ten years later, perhaps fifteen after the initial breakdown, things seemed no better and the foster parents had developed a close relationship with a neighbouring house. Without any apparent heirs to the property, it was natural that other houses would become interested in a possession which would one day become vacant. An extremely hard worker but getting on in years, the foster father still meticulously observed his communal and neighbour obligations with only his wife and sister-in-law to help. He was nevertheless still in need of more assistance than he could possibly reciprocate, particularly at harvest time. This help was forthcoming from a son of the house of one neighbour in the late 1970s and from another neighbour's house some years later. Understandably no villager would ever admit to any ulterior motive in such apparent altruism, primarily regarded as an act of friendship or good neighbourliness towards someone badly in need of help.

The circumstances and possible resolution to this particular problem of inheritance were further complicated by the adopted son attempting to improve his relations with his family by sending them small gifts, apparently to heal the breach between them and with a possible eye to his inheritance despite the fact that no formal agreement had been drawn up. However, it was not the foster father who was *en casa* but his wife. Her consent would be needed to give away the possessions, and she had ceased to anticipate the return of the 'prodigal' son. 'When we grow old,' she had said, 'we will lend fields to those who help us by getting wood and washing clothes for us—things that will be difficult to manage then—in exchange for the use of the fields. We might equally give the fields away before we die, or when we die, to those who help us.' It seemed clear that at that time she had no intention of allowing the adopted son to re-establish his previously disregarded inheritance.

If the owner of a property dies intestate, then state law becomes operative. According to villagers this means that 'half the valuation' of the house and its property is absorbed by taxes or estate duty. The remaining half is divided between near relatives and dependents. This happened in the case of a villager in a neighbouring village to Alcedo, who suffered a fatal heart attack. He had a very good holding and was a conscientious farmer, but as a result of his mischance and the fact that he had no *manda* drawn up, his possessions had to be dealt with according to the law. Although he had no children himself there were dependents, but in the ultimate distribution the bulk of the second half of the property, fell to a nephew and a sister, both of whom lived elsewhere. As one villager, who was a close friend of the dead man and knew of his pride in his holdings, ruefully commented: 'It is no good to either his nephew or his sister. It is a waste. Now his inheritance is scattered. The land is unusable. It is of value to no one!'

It is in the villagers' interests that this sort of thing does not happen. The widespread evidence of abandoned field systems seems to bear testimony, not just to population decline or unwillingness to work the land, but to a lack of provision for the future and the breakdown of family relationships. The abandonment of property progressively weakens the social and economic cohesion of a whole community, leading to its ultimate demise. Thus when neighbours lend assistance beyond the normal call of reciprocity, it is not just self interest with a view to inheriting from those without obvious heirs. It is rather for the sake of the continuation of the community as a whole, and in this way may be regarded as altruistic.

In 1978 there was an obviously prosperous house in the village with fine traditional outbuildings and two young and able sons, either of whom could potentially inherit, but whose possessions were badly placed. They had sufficient land for the gradual change from sheep pastoralism to intensive cattle raising, but their meadows and hayfields were scattered and distant from the village. This meant they faced harder work for less return than others whose holdings were better placed.

A close neighbour of this house, an elderly widower whose children had left the village, still owned a considerable amount of land. For years he used to visit the house every day to obtain milk and occasionally for meals, and had his laundry done by the womenfolk. He was very grateful for their solicitude and they in turn were very attentive to him. All went well until the early 1970s when rumours reached him that the two boys, though invariably polite to his face, were mocking him behind his back. This affected the old man's relations with the house and he began to look elsewhere for help from other neighbours. By the late 1970s the elder of the boys, now a responsible young farmer *en casa* with a wife and two children, found that he could no longer sustain the upkeep of the possessions, despite being ably assisted by his still unmarried younger brother and their ageing father. Their old neighbour had died, his house and possessions for the most part fractured. Some had been given away to other neighbours who had latterly helped him, but most of it, though still held by relatives no longer in the village, lay abandoned. None went to his nearest neighbours who had helped him years before.

The young family, who had earlier entertained hopes to inherit at least a part of the old man's land, had to leave the village for Oviedo, together with their parents and a grandmother who had never been further afield than Boinas in the valley below. The father became a taxi driver and his mother, a very proud lady, took up domestic service to help make ends meet. The magnificent old farmstead now stands empty, gradually decaying, a mute testimony to the damage that loose talk can do, while the village has lost not just one but two households.

Although in theory families who leave Alcedo retain their houses and land by renting them out to other villagers as an assurance for the future, in practice it frequently happens that properties become available through sale to young people who are not *en casa*. One daughter of a house in the village, for example, who was not herself *en casa*, inherited a *tierra*, a meadow and part of a field. When she married, her husband, who came from a distant village, sold the house he had inherited there and with it bought a house vacated by a family in Alcedo. With this modest beginning and by means of renting and where possible purchasing other vacated plots of land, the couple increased their holding, ultimately making it a viable farming possession.

In the past, in the case of large families with relatively small holdings, the division of property could be quite complicated, especially if, for instance, it had to be divided among many siblings. For such a division a *perito*, someone skilled in the division of properties, would be consulted. A sibling might find himself inheriting a portion of a field, part of a *tierra*, or even half or a third of a cow. These anomalies were usually resolved by selling these various parts to the *en casa* sibling. Some however retained their ownership and if they died with no obvious heirs, their surviving siblings sometimes tried to claim back their allotted settlement. This could be a very complicated business, especially when it involved household possessions such as clothing, blankets, sheets, cutlery and pots and pans. Sometimes such claims led to acrimony and unhappiness between close relatives, particularly when they no longer lived in the village and arbitration was difficult, or when neighbours or other relatives had taken possession of these items in the belief that the deceased had had no heirs.

Dowry

'Nowadays the young marry for love,' commented one old villager, who obviously disapproved of this. However, even now, no man who wishes to inherit his father's house and possessions and spend his life as a farmer will consider marriage on those grounds, at the risk of being considered a fool or merely irresponsible. While men are reticent about their reasons for marrying, women are less so and one village wife somewhat bluntly commented: 'You know in Asturias we have a saying about men and marriage. We say, "If a donkey was made of silver, a man would marry it."'

In fact most villagers would agree that marriage is, and always was, something of a compromise between genuine affection and economic consideration; and beneath the humour and self-deprecation regarding their motives, they know that marriage and its corollary inheritance are inextricably interwoven. From the village's point of view a bad marriage can undermine the viability of the community, particularly now that the population is declining, and some go so far as to contend that bad marriages have brought about the near demise of the village. Women cite examples of good wives *en casa* married to spendthrifts who sold or abandoned their land, disinheriting their children; or good husbands *en casa* whose wives drifted away, unable to cope with the tribulations of village life, leading to the abandonment of the house and its possessions. The villagers of this region of Asturias recite the following refrain on the theme of dowries:

> El Norte is the daughter of El Gallego,
> And when she asks him for her dowry,
> He gives her rain.

When it is appreciated that El Norte (the north) is also the name of the north wind, and that El Gallego (a man from the province of Galicia which lies to the west of Asturias) is also the name for the west wind, this little saying may be interpreted on three different levels. Firstly, it describes what almost invariably happens when a wind from the north shifts to the west. It brings rain, frequently very heavy, which can be disastrous at the time of haymaking. Secondly, as the rain is unwelcome in this already wet mountain region, the wind could be called ungenerous. It could therefore be construed that El Gallego is rather parsimonious with the dowry he gives to his daughter. A man must be judged by his actions and generosity towards his neighbours, and especially his own children, can do much for a father's reputation and that of his house. Thirdly, we come to politics. During the civil war and its aftermath, relations between these two north-westerly provinces of Spain were put to a severe test. As will be discussed in Chapter 11, the main thrust of the Nationalists which ultimately subjugated western Asturias in 1937 came from Galicia and was spearheaded by Galician battalions. This is something that Asturians, and particularly Alcedans, have not forgotten, causing some ambivalence towards their nearest provincial neighbours. Nor are villagers slow to point out that Franco himself was a Galician. Thus the fact that the girl's father was El Gallego, a Galician, places him in the role of a man (a wind) who would by nature lack the generous spirit of an Alcedan villager, giving her only rain as her dowry. This refrain demonstrates layers of context and meaning which I think all Alcedans would implicitly recognise and which emphasise the fact that literacy is not a requirement in creating a subtle and deeply felt oral literature.

When a young *mozo* is about to marry, villagers will know who his bride-to-be is and opinions are formed very quickly. Among the women these often relate to physical characteristics. 'She is not pretty, but she will bring lots of money!' was the comment on a pending bride from another village who was known to have been well endowed by her family. 'When I came to the village as a bride thirty-five years ago,' said one elderly lady, 'neighbours said I was too thin at the waist, and that I would be no good for work!' When her son married, he brought into the village a bride who was neither pretty nor possessed of a generous dowry, but she had great physical strength and did much to restore the ailing fortunes of her adopted house.

A *mozo* may not, depending on the circumstances, have to make the decision to marry until he is approaching middle age. For a *moza*, however, it is different. She begins to prepare herself for marriage from as early as the age of twelve, when she will start to make a collection of items called her *hual*. This is partially a dowry or trousseau, as it contains many items given to her by her parents and other close relatives. It may include such things as bed linen, tablecloths, towels, clothes, underwear, cutlery, glassware, pots, pans and other items that may prove useful to setting up a home at the time of her marriage. The *hual* may include items embroidered by the *moza* herself.

The marriage always takes place in her own village and in addition to her *hual* she may expect presents from friends and relations. In the past, food for the marriage feast would have been given rather than presents, though money is preferred. Older villagers still tend to give customary gifts such piglets, hens, eggs and various sweetmeats at the time of the wedding.

'Nowadays we don't have dowries,' observed an old villager, and went on to describe the pre-war tradition of loading oxcarts with a bride's dowry when she left home to reside in her husband's village. The whole village would turn out and the attendant crowd could number hundreds. The occasion would be one of solidarity and festivity, especially if the bride was popular, beautiful and went with a generous dowry. She went as a representative, not just of her house and family but of the whole community; and in her departure with her laden oxcarts, she was viewed as a symbol of the village's prosperity and generosity. A girl marrying within the village would not have such a celebratory send-off, while a young woman emigrating might depart almost unnoticed except by her family and neighbours. Thus although a girl's family would prefer an endogamous marriage to enhance their possessions, for the village at large an exogamous marriage was an occasion for celebration.

The laden ox-carts, on one of which the bride would be perched, would contain furniture including a bed, kitchen and dining ware, linen, sheets, embroideries and her own personal possessions. Alongside the oxcarts, as they processed through the village led by her family, would be several sheep and goats and a cow or two as part of her dowry. Perched above the heads of the throng, she would lead the procession through the village to the accompaniment of singing, shouting, fire-crackers and the piping and drumming of *gaiteros* and *tambor* players.

Slowly the procession would move out of the village and down the long winding cart track to the valley below; gradually the concourse would disperse except for a few of the younger *mozos*, a number of children and the bride's immediate family, all of whom might still be in attendance many hours later on arrival at the village of her future domicile. If this lay far away from Alcedo, it could be years before she set eyes on her home again. Thus a village *fiesta* could be a very poignant occasion for the bride.

Courting and wedding

> You have to be careful who you marry.
> Some women have very hard heads—even horns.

'When I was a *mozo* we all used to come over from my village for *fiestas* to this village. That was when I was courting. My sister was *en casa* in my village, so I had to look elsewhere. When I married my wife, who was *en casa* here, I brought with me a cow, a few goats and some money in my pocket.' The old man, then in his mid-eighties, could still easily recall that time in 1918 and how his parents and those of his bride-to-be had come together to arrange a marriage settlement, which was finally completed and written down by a lawyer in Belmonte. All did not go well for the couple, for having only recently returned from South America and with the Spanish Moroccan war still continuing, the young man dreaded conscription by the military. So his wife, with one baby and pregnant with a second child, had to remain behind in the village while her husband took ship to Havana.

Although there was parental pressure to marry within the village, and outside spouses were not always accorded the same respect as those from within, exogamous marriages were fairly frequent even in the early twentieth century and the old man's story was not untypical of the time. However, as an elderly lady commented, 'We all knew about the young *mozos* in our own village, but when one came from another village you didn't know anything about him. You must know someone in order to have confidence in him.' The parents of any prospective bride would send a member of their family to check up on a *mozo* from another village.

'If he came from a bad family,' she continued, 'then you would have had to advise your daughter not to have anything to do with him. A *mozo* cannot enter a *moza*'s house until he has proposed to the girl. He can take a walk with her and talk to her in the pathway, but not in the house, unless he has some official business to discuss with the family. Around here of course we know everyone.' This lady, a spinster herself, perhaps had a rather idealised view of courting. This view is enshrined in old prints and pictures of country life in Asturias, in which a potential swain, dressed in traditional attire and with a heavy stick in his hand, stands on one side of a partly open door talking to his girlfriend who stays discreetly within the house, or leans over the closed lower half of a stable door.

Young *mozas* were always chaperoned by an elder sister or female relative at village *fiestas* and other venues, and mothers always tried to ensure that a family in another village kept an eye on their daughters. Some would not let them go without an invitation from a host family. A young *mozo* would be very cautious in his behaviour towards a *moza* from another village if she were under the protection of a family in his own.

Despite these precautions a young *moza* could get into trouble and become pregnant, causing considerable embarrassment to her family. The associated shame and dishonour common to some Mediterranean societies was not however prevalent. My wife related the dire consequences of inchastity before marriage and even worse, cases of adultery, in former times in Greek villages. The women present were truly shocked, particularly at the idea of stoning. It brought tears to the eyes of one old lady. 'Oh, no!' she protested, 'it is not like that here. We could never do such things.'

As I have indicated endogamous marriage was considered preferable for economic reasons, but as one old lady ventured to say: 'A good man from another village is better than a bad one in your own'. Bad in this sense meant someone who was not a hard worker: this was always a test of character. So long as a young *mozo* was conscientious and showed willingness to work on the land, it was generally assumed that he would not be irresponsible, or be cruel to his wife, or desert her.

The formalities of betrothal were described in the following manner: 'The young man goes to the house of his *novia* to ask her father if he may marry her. This we call the *compromiso* (pledge). There is a formal meal on this occasion. Then there is a meeting between both sets of parents in one or other house: the son's or the daughter's, it doesn't matter which.' It is at this point that the settlement is made. This is a critical negotiation and to obviate some of the difficulties a local lawyer in Belmonte is consulted and a settlement drawn up on paper.

The costs of a wedding can be considerable, even though guests may bring food and drink as contributions. Traditionally, apart from the payment for the service itself, the celebrations included two feasts: one after the service and a second one in the evening with dancing which included *gaiteros* and now may include the rental of the disco in Boinas. 'You can't ask everyone to the feasts, but people have the right to come afterwards,' commented one villager. In 1978 costs were estimated in relation to the current value of a *ternero* or saleable bullock, each family on average contributing the equivalent of one *ternero*. As most households did not expect to sell more than two *terneros* in a year, this meant that a wedding cost the equivalent of half a year's income.[36]

'The faces we wanted to see just couldn't come,' was the sad comment of the bride of a January wedding which had been overshadowed by a snowstorm. Only one guest had managed to come from outside the village, and that was not the priest. 'We were waiting up by the *capilla* for him. He never came. So there was no marriage!' She seemed to have no regrets about the formalities, only that so few were able to come to the feast, which went ahead with dancing to a *gaitero* who happened to be visiting the village when the blizzard struck.

To what extent 'marriages' take place outside the jurisdiction of the church is not something villagers discuss. After the civil war all young couples had to have their banns read in church, as failure to do so resulted in a fine. It was also both a church and a state requirement that they should be confirmed before being married and the requisite documents had to be signed to verify the legality of a marriage. Since 1978, however, a law has been passed legalising civil marriages.

Married life

Though there are responsibilities there are also advantages for a woman *en casa*. She has to spend more time in and about the house than a man, and those with whom she is working will be her own family. But as an in-married spouse, especially if she comes from another village, she is more at the behest of her husband's relatives and particularly his mother (see Chapter 6). The difficulties and misunderstandings that can arise between a young wife and her mother-in-law are the butt of many a joke. But whereas within her own village a young wife may seek guidance and advice from her family, if she marries out she lacks the moral support of her own relatives against those of her husband's house, particularly should the mother-in-law relationship go amiss. Female suicide sometimes occurs for such reasons of estrangement.

The relationship between mother-in-law and daughter-in-law is still a critical one and remains of fundamental importance to the well-being and effectiveness of a house within the community. It is not a subject, however, which villagers are at all comfortable to comment on: 'This is something we do not usually talk about as nothing is to be gained by it,' observed one man. Then as if by way of an example he spoke of a neighbour whom he described as 'evil'. 'She was nice to outsiders [other villagers], but behaved badly within her family towards her daughter-in-law. She would refuse to feed her. She would give her nothing.' Eventually, the mother-in-law left to live in an old people's home in Oviedo. Clearly this was thought to be a terrible fate in a village where the elderly are always part of the family and cared for until death, for he added with some vehemence, 'And she deserved it!'

Men and women who marry into the village retain their links with their old domiciles providing they are not too distant. While still young and active they will return frequently to assist their families, particularly at harvest time and during the *matanza*. These loyalties and emotional ties can be very taxing, for no sooner have they completed their obligations in their adopted households than they depart to help out in their old village. As they grow older, however, and need to support and care for their own growing families, these links loosen. Once their parents have died there may only be casual visits or meetings at local fairs and markets. This is not an easy transition, not so much because they fail to adjust, as because they will always be regarded as outsiders. 'They are not like us!' was the comment of one old Alcedan.

Alcedans would not usually marry into *vaqueiro* villages, finding it difficult to adapt to the ways of these traditional herders; although conversely *vaqueiro* men and women have often married into more settled communities. There are a number of former *vaqueiros* and their descendants among the present population of Alcedo.

Second marriage is unusual in the event of the early death of one of the partners. 'If you have been married once you shouldn't feel like marrying again. The memory of your first husband is with you always.' The lady who said this was herself a spinster. However, if a young wife loses her husband, as was not uncommon at the time of the civil war, she cannot be expected to maintain a house and its possessions on her own. One woman's husband became ill during the fighting in the village in the war; it was not possible to find a doctor and he died. 'She had a lot of land—a lot of *escanda*, after the war,' said the same lady, in mitigation of her earlier statement. 'What could she do? With all that work and several children to bring up and only herself to do it. She would just get sick.'

In such cases villagers consider it correct for a woman to marry her former husband's brother. And in spite of the saying *apartado con poco amor* (separate with little love) which one villager quoted, she immediately added that a husband's brother would have kinder feelings towards his brother's children than others would. As for the demise of a wife and the prospect of a stepmother for her children, one villager quoted the old conundrum: 'Which is better: a bad mother or a good stepmother?'

Emigration

'The crow always returns to the rock where he was born you know!' A man from a village in the valley below Alcedo had just greeted me in English with an unmistakable Australian accent. My question about his reasons for being in the village had prompted this response. He told me that he had lived for fourteen years in Australia and that by working on oil pipelines he had managed to save up enough capital to invest in a garage business in Oviedo. He was one of a family of five children, all of whom had left the village and four of whom had gone to Australia. Although emigration had increased over the past two to three decades, it was surprising to hear of an entire family of siblings leaving their parents to fend for themselves.

It was said in Alcedo that when individuals emigrated they would often return, even to live in the village, but that when whole families departed they would never come back. In the early part of the twentieth century it was mostly individuals who emigrated and it is only from about the early 1960s that whole families have done so. This may have partly been due to the political climate after the civil war, and Asturias' relative isolation from economic developments in the rest of Spain during the post-war period. Also some men found it difficult to readjust to village life after being away for years during the period of fighting. However, perhaps most significant was the gradual transfer from sheep rearing to cattle raising and the greater need for meadow land, of which some villagers owned very little, having till then relied on grazing their flocks on common land.

Over the ten years from 1978–88 the exodus seems to have slowed down and the greatly reduced village population appeared to be stabilising. The reasons for this may be found in the more favourable political climate in Asturias after the re-establishment of democratic government and a parallel upturn in the general social and economic ambience. With the village population standing at less than a fifth of its estimated former figure, sufficient land has been released through inheritance, purchase or rental for those remaining to establish an essentially cattle raising economy. These factors, coupled with financial incentives to hill farmers funded by the central government, have made village life not only economically viable, but more acceptable by modern standards to the younger generation. The construction of new roads, the introduction of mains electricity, and the arrival of other amenities such as the telephone in Boinas, provide a viable alternative to city life with its lures and drawbacks.

Although villagers maintain that there was just insufficient food for all the young people in each household during the first two decades of the twentieth century, there was also another factor which obliged them to depart. This was the very real fear of conscription during the many years of the Spanish Moroccan war from 1909–1927. 'A whole generation left the village at this time,' commented one old man. 'They all left for Cuba or the Argentine to escape military service in North Africa which they all dreaded. In those days it could be for five years. They were afraid of disease. It killed many.' The villager, then in his eighty-fifth year, went on to tell the following story about his early life:

'I came from Castano, a village which lay between Belmonte and Somiedo. I went to the Argentine when I was sixteen. It was a long ship voyage—no land for many days. In San Paulo the blacks were still slaves. I saw some in chains and so many poor people. I went south to Montevideo. There they were all white and well dressed. The Argentinian *llanos* (prairies) were beautiful. You could go for days and never see a hill. Then there was the Andes. There were many Italians there, but unlike us Spanish, they stayed there. They never went back to Italy as it was a very poor country. The English were everywhere. They ran everything. They were very clever. The meat was very cheap. They had an underground in Buenos Aires and yet when years later I went to Madrid they were still using mules to pull public transport. I never went to school or was taught to read or write, but I learned to read numbers. I needed to do that for my work. I returned when I was twenty-three. I had trouble with my papers in Santander. They said they were false and I was taken into a building and interviewed. But it turned out all right—when we paid ninety or a hundred *duros* we were allowed to go.

'I came to this village then and married.' the old man continued. 'My wife was *hija en casa*. But then the *guardia civil* [police] came to the village looking for young men to enlist for the Moroccan war. I was full of fear. I was shaking with fear,' and the old man demonstrated this by shaking his hands and body, for it was still a vivid memory to him. 'I hid. Then I went off into the fields with the cows. Some of us hid in our houses by putting the shutters up. They were looking everywhere for recruits. That was the time of Primo de Rivera, you know [the Spanish dictator, 1923-30]. Then I went to Cuba for five years. I went without my wife. There were many problems. It is not good to be separated from your wife for so long, but that is the way we used to do it then. Now you can go everywhere with your wife. There

Plate 19 The tractor cart

was much trouble—much unhappiness. I returned to the village, but then went to work in Madrid. For the year I was there we were using mule-drawn carriages as taxis. Then we changed to motors. I got to know Madrid very well. Just before the civil war I returned to the village. I have been here ever since.'

The old villager's account regarding his threefold emigration was perhaps unusual but not exceptional. Born in 1894, he would have gone to South America about 1910, returning in about 1917. He then went to Cuba from 1918 to 1924 and to Madrid from 1924 to 1936, making him forty-two when he finally returned to settle in the village. Although he never learned to read or write he nevertheless understood numbers and said that he was good at reading street maps, a necessity for any cab driver in Madrid. He also learned to sign his name, something that his wife never managed, for she was quite illiterate like most other woman villagers of her generation. Thus the couple were not only separated for eighteen years of their early married life, but quite unable to communicate with each other except through a literate third party. The old man was however perhaps fortunate in that, unlike all the other younger men of the village, he was not called up for service in the civil war.

There was usually a very good reason why village women or *mozas* emigrated. This was because their parents were unable to give them dowries, and without a dowry they could not get married. This was a particular problem after the civil war when villagers were virtually destitute. For the younger women their best prospect lay in emigrating. As one village lady put it, 'Girls who emigrated without dowries have ended up rich. Those who stayed behind without dowries are far worse off.' They remained as spinsters, she added. But as such at least they could remain in the village and continue to live in their parental home. She described one house in the village whose youngest daughter became *hija en casa* after both her elder sisters left for the Argentine when only eighteen. They were joined there by a younger brother. A married cousin of the family who lived there had written to their parents suggested that the two girls should come out, and they lived in his household until they found jobs. One of the sisters worked in a hospital and later married; the other sent 'lots of money back to her parents in the village. The other one sent nothing, then later sent some—but by then the family did not need it.'

It was not only *mozas* who emigrated, however, and one old lady spoke of her reasons for going to the Argentine in the 1920s. She was married with one child when it was decided by her parents that she join her mother's brother in Buenos Aires. Her mother would look after the child in the village and her husband would look after the land in her absence. They had recently arranged to buy two meadows from neighbours and needed the money to pay for them: she was the obvious person to raise the money. She worked as a domestic servant for a wealthy family, which she said was a nice job but very hard work. After three years she returned to the village, having sent home sufficient funds to pay for the meadows. The memory of her journey some fifty-five years earlier still remained vivid to her.

'I was twenty-three when I left. I went by mule to Tineo and from there by bus all the way to Corunna from where the ship sailed. It was the first time I had ever travelled in a motor vehicle. The journey took twenty-four hours. I had to stand all the way. The bus was very full. It had been hired by a man and his family under whose protection I was placed. I asked for a seat but the man said, "Who will give up their seat for you?" He was sitting himself with his family. I had to pay this man. He was a robber! He hired the coach and got us all to pay and then filled it so full that many of us could not sit down. He cheated us. Lots of people, like myself, were travelling under his protection.'

Although these villagers were technically emigrating it depended on circumstance whether they remained in their adoptive country or subsequently returned. Many married and settled in the new country, some returning to visit, others not. Some went with the intention of raising funds so that a woman could endow herself and find a husband, or a man make himself eligible to marry an *hija en casa*; married people might go to raise funds to support their families. For men, conscription undoubtedly played a part in their decision to emigrate during the early decades of the twentieth century. At that time both Argentina and Cuba were comparatively wealthy with expanding economies and salaries were generous compared to those in Spain (see Kenny 1961b). After the civil war the countries most favoured for emigration by villagers were Australia and Mexico. More recently European countries such as Germany, France and Belgium and since the 1960s Spain itself, have been the favoured venues.

Whereas at the turn of the century emigration was seen as a natural outlet for houses with too many mouths to feed, or as a means of raising funds, it is now regarded more as a threat, not only to the continued existence of individual houses, but to the village itself. Now that families are much smaller than in the past the departure of just one sibling, let alone all of them, can spell disaster for a house; and it is a matter of time before the whole community ceases to be viable as a self-sustaining unit.

Villagers say that the young depart because they do not like to work the land, while the young say that there is no longer any 'gaiety and jubilation' in the village, partly due to the decreasing numbers of the *mozo* group. Older villagers say that compulsory military service is an unsettling experience for the *mozos*, as indeed is the need for children to leave the village during the week to attend school in Belmonte. All of these factors are seen as a threat to the future of the village and while in the past the young might have vied with each other to be *en casa*, now they have to be persuaded to stay. If they do not then the rest of the family may also have to emigrate. The introduction of state pensions has enabled some of the elderly to continue even if all their children have left, supplementing their pensions by selling off stock and renting or selling possessions to neighbours. Ultimately, however, they too will have to join the younger members of their families, whether in Asturias or elsewhere in Spain and for them this can be a very sad exodus. Some may never have been away from the village in all their lives except during the civil war, and to be confronted with city life in old age is traumatic.

One old lady in her mid-eighties was leaving for Oviedo with her son and daughter-in-law, their *en casa* son, his unmarried brother and his wife and their two children. The old lady's husband had died some years previously and she was resigned to her *en casa* grandson's decision. 'I am old. I can no longer walk well. I can't even fetch the cows. I am *no vale* [not worth anything]!' She had never been to Belmonte, let alone Oviedo where she would now have to live.

'I have never been away from here in all my life and I do not want to go and I am very sad to have to now, but it is the need of the family. It is their decision and I am content to go along with it.' Like other households who had departed, pride prevented the admission that their land was no longer viable for the needs of a growing family. Instead they maintained it was because of the children's education, a need the older generation had become well aware of during earlier emigrations when their skills had proved limited in the wider world.

Initially, men leaving the village may find employment as labourers on building sites or in other manual occupations. Others become taxi drivers or hall porters in residential apartments. If they have sufficient capital from the sale of land they may purchase guest houses. One occupation taken up by many of the earlier migrants was work in slaughterhouses. Villagers' skills in tending animals, slaying and preparing them for consumption were frequently sought after. Others, especially those who emigrated overseas, have through self education and dedication, or by fortunate chance and circumstance, become businessmen, doctors and lawyers, and at least one entered the church, unusual enough to be remarked upon by villagers. Women on leaving the village may obtain work in department stores, or as servants or assistants to professional people, while those emigrating abroad have often married into wealthy families.

Many return after nearly a lifetime away, like the old man who I met in Belmonte, who had spent most of his adult life in Texas and had returned, as he put it: 'to claim my pension, live out my years and die here.' The incentive of an assured state pension in Spain has precipitated the return of a number of exiles in their old age. Others come back on fleeting visits. Some, with smart cars and beautifully dressed, stand out in sharp contrast to their village relatives. Their old affections for the village, however, and a sense of nostalgia for the past and its continuing hold on their lives, is very apparent. Visits from long lost relatives are perhaps more common in the age of jet travel than they once were. Come summer, however, during the season of haymaking and family gatherings and festivals, such return visits still generate intense emotion.

For some it is like a pilgrimage to re-establish their roots and to visit places they remember from their youth: some particular meadow, a pathway through the chestnut woods, a view of Manteca or the *capilla* above the village where they were confirmed. For others it is just to breathe the air and drink the spring water, or to visit the old house where they were born, now disused and desolate.

One elderly spinster heard a rumour that her brother, who had left for the

Argentine as a *mozo* forty years ago, had just been seen in a bar in Oviedo. The next day someone told her he was in the village shop. She found it hard to believe: 'It was like reaching for the moon,' she said. They had never communicated in all those years and for her he was just a memory of her youth. He had his hat pulled down over his face, perhaps wishing to remain anonymous. 'He said he wanted to go walking where he used to go—a special place that he had always remembered.' Then rather prosaically she said, 'When he was young he had beautiful wavy black hair parted on one side,' and she made a motion with her hand to show how it was. 'Now he only had four or five wispy white hairs—and he was too fat!' He told her he had not brought his wife with him but that next time he would. 'I do not think he ever will,' she added.

Although it is apparent that for the young there is some social stigma associated with being merely a villager, an attitude which has some bearing on their opting out of this way of living, the older generation have no such qualms. One lady visited a middle-aged relative, a former close neighbour, at an address in Oviedo. She was 'shocked' to find her cousin answering the door all dressed up in 'a sort of white uniform'. She was clearly a servant or receptionist for a doctor or lawyer. 'And to think,' she added, 'she was head of her own household here!'

Town life for the young is always equated with money and an easy life, the village with a certain penury. 'I suppose we don't really need very much money here,' commented one old lady. A man said he liked living in the village, 'Because I am strong and I love to work. Work makes me happy!' A young *mozo* who thought he might like to go to Mexico, despite being expected to become *hijo en casa*, later had second thoughts. He listed the various advantages of village life which included the air, the spring water, the hard work, which he found compatible, and the food. 'Here we eat our own food, our own bread which our mothers have baked, and the meat you eat you have grown and cared for yourself—it is different!'

Plate 20 Maize chains hanging from *granero* veranda

Chapter 10

Ageing and passing

Villagers tend to live long and active lives, many to a great age. When we arrived an old lady in the next village to Alcedo had just passed away at the age of a hundred and three. She was described as being tall, straight-backed and very active till the end. It was fairly common in Alcedo for villagers to live well into their eighties. When asked how they accounted for this longevity, they would usually put it down to three main causes: the food they ate, the water they drank and the emotional satisfaction gained from a life of regular and sustained work.

The food most highly regarded and nutritious in their view was meat from animals nurtured by themselves and prepared in their own manner. Next came bread, particularly bread made from *escanda* wheat. Vegetables were also important, and of these *berza*, winter cabbage, was the staple most frequently mentioned. As for water, there was no comparison with the springs on the slopes of Manteca, and the higher the spring, the purer the water. Conversations frequently alluded to the water from just outside the village, the water from the fountain, and the water which had recently and only partially successfully been piped to most houses in the village. These different sources, although drinkable, were more often used for washing purposes and for watering animals. For water to be truly beneficial it had to come from a spring, straight out of the ground at its source. Great emphasis was always placed on this. A frequent last request of the very elderly, particularly women, just prior to death, was to have water brought to them from the 'purest' spring, of which several were known to villagers.

Food and water were not considered in a purely physical context, as being just healthy and nutritious and therefore good for you. They had qualities that went beyond the mundane, for to villagers what is natural comes from nature and is thus conceived of as having an essence of spirituality. If animals are well kept and wheat carefully nurtured, they not only provide good meat and sustaining bread but their essence is passed on and becomes part of the recipient. In this sense the *matanza* is more than an event in the calendar or an economic necessity: it is also a form of religious enactment, as is the careful *escanda* picking and the associated *banquetes* and picnics. A villager would say that the essence of the animal and of the germ of spelt wheat will become part of him and are necessary for life; that his careful nurturing implies a spiritual association with the land and its progeny. As other cultivated plants give off their essence, water likewise gives man its qualities, its innate purity: it too is imbued with religious and sanctifying elements.

The third factor to which villagers attribute longevity is the more prosaic concept of hard labour, without which there would be no food. It is only through a lifetime of work, the discipline and the day-to-day regularity of it throughout each year's seasonal cycle, that the land and its progeny become an expression of man himself as he grows older. The well-kept fields, *tierras*, woodlands and animals give meaning to life. In a sense the land is sacred and if a man dedicates his life to its care he will receive its blessing, though not in another life beyond the grave. As one sceptical villager commented: 'Who knows what happens after death? No one has come back to tell us!'

In 1978, out of a total population of approximately a hundred, there were two men and six women in the village who had exceeded the age of eighty. Three of the women were in their mid-eighties and two of them were still relatively active, going out each day and often all day, gathering fallen branches for fuel which they would secure in bundles and carry back on their heads, or watching over cattle in the fields throughout the day.

Whether such a high percentage of octogenarians is also characteristic of those who emigrate from the village is impossible to know. Those who had returned, however, frequently commented on this matter, attributing their age not to a lifetime's discipline of labour but rather to good food and water and, above all, the clear mountain air, something which villagers consider of little account.

A frequently expressed belief is that November and March are the months when the elderly are most at risk. These are the months during which they say most people die, especially November, quite openly expressing their mortality as analogous to nature. November heralds the onset of winter with its cold winds and snow and is equated with the metaphor of sadness and falling leaves. Conversely March is associated with new growth and rising sap, which is analogous to blood in the body. If the blood does not course through the veins or have 'force' like the sap which rises in plants in spring, the person is known to be dying. In reality, of the six deaths I recorded over the ten year span from 1978-88, two of them being in a nearby village, only one occurred in November.

Another strongly held belief concerns the cause of death. This seems to have a bearing on animal anatomy, about which villagers can claim considerable knowledge, and concerns the digestive process. In order to keep this functioning properly and avoid a perceived life-threatening situation, they adhere to certain abstentions after eating a meal or even between meals. It is important not to eat between set meals and villagers maintained this custom quite rigorously. No one would offer us food outside meal times and no one would accept food from us when visiting. Even children would decline sweets and other food inducements from our children, unless offered at a specified meal. The washing and cutting of hair, taking a bath and even wetting the feet immediately subsequent to a repast were considered most unwise. As one elderly villager commented, 'You can die if you take a bath after eating, or cut your hair,' adding as an afterthought, 'it cuts your digestive tract'. This attitude was confirmed on various occasions by many people, including the young. On one occasion a man protested on seeing my wife giving our two children a hip bath when he learned that they had just recently eaten.

Two unexpected deaths occurred in the next village to Alcedo while we were there. Both were of men in their sixties and both were considered to be self-inflicted because the individuals did not adhere to the customary practice. One, a popular figure who liked his food, partook of a *banquete* in a neighbour's house. The food he had eaten was carefully described by the narrator of this event. He then ate a second meal on returning to his own house and almost immediately expired. The second man, a popular *gaitero*, died 'with an apple in his throat', again just after having eaten a meal. Both these deaths were clearly attributed by the narrator to the breaking of this food prohibition.

Apart from natural causes of death, such as old age, villagers considered typhus, and particularly what they called *camus* (or *cambares* in *bable*), a form of amoebic dysentery, as having been a major cause of death in the past, particularly among children. Acute haemorrhaging at the time of parturition was also considered to have been the cause of deaths among women. Death among children however is now rare. During the ten year period from 1978-88 two children, both in their teens and good friends to my own children, tragically died in the village. One, a girl, died of cancer of the stomach. The other, a boy always considered frail, died of a cerebral disorder, according to villagers probably meningitis.

Other causes of death have been attributed in recent times to lightning, bears and wolves, though these accounts are unsubstantiated. Snakes are however a confirmed cause of death and of these the small asp (*Vipera aspis*) is considered the most dangerous: villagers maintain its bite can prove fatal within two hours. Death by violence is extremely rare since the civil war. No murder has ever taken place in the memory of villagers, though these are occasionally reported in the regional press.

Attitudes towards death

> *La tierra nos cría y la tierra nos come.*

When an Alcedan quoted this saying, 'the earth feeds us and the earth eats us', in response to my question concerning death and the afterlife, he was not just expressing his own personal view. Most villagers thought the same. Perhaps to a certain degree scepticism is a characteristic of rural Spaniards, but in the Asturian uplands, and certainly in Alcedo, there were few who would vouch for an afterlife, let alone the existence of a finite God. John Campbell (1964: 322), in his classic study of pastoralists in northwestern Greece, wrote that he never met a Sarakatsanos who doubted the existence of God. Much closer, William Douglass's assessment of the Murelagans and indeed that of all Basques as 'manifest[ing] unquestioning adherence to Catholic doctrine' (1969: 209), could not apply to the great majority of Alcedans whom I knew well enough to ask such a question. If I discussed such matters with the young or middle-aged I could perhaps expect a flippant response, but with the elderly or those approaching death I thought I might find a more considered one. Perhaps I lack the sensitivity to appreciate the subtleties of the Asturian dialect, but it was my experience that I seldom came across a villager who did not doubt the existence of God in an orthodox sense. There were exceptions, but the majority, and there were many I discussed this with, expressed a totally negative view. It was not even thought that there might be some omnipotent presence over the world. Such theological contemplation, as distinct from their thoughts on *naturaleza* (cf. p 211) just did not seem to concern people in their daily lives, even in their twilight years or facing death.

Such exceptions as there were seemed to be mainly among the few Alcedan villagers of *vaqueiro* descent (which concurs with Cátedra Tomás' analysis (1992)), and by implication two *gaiteros*, one of whom came from a neighbouring village. On the occasion of his death I had remarked that it was 'sad', to which a middle-aged Alcedan responded a little ironically, 'No! It is not sad. They have called him. He was not a worker!' On my asking who 'they' were, the villager inclined his head skywards in a slightly deprecating way, saying, 'They—God. Up in the sky!' I was still not sure what he meant by 'they', but assumed it was a reference to angels, the Holy Trinity, or perhaps other bagpipers who had gone before him. I remarked on another well-known *gaitero* from Cangas who was very elderly and might soon pass on, though he had played recently at a festival in the village. The response was that he would be all right and that 'he will just go on playing for ever'. Perhaps this was no more than a humourous aside on this bagpiper's peculiar but engaging propensity for sustained playing. Perhaps it was intended to acknowledge the perceived elevated status of the *gaitero*, for in a villager's view he does not have to work. This might imply a social distinction between believers and non-believers: that *gaiteros*, priests and other persons of status outside the village were destined for a life hereafter, but not the poor working villager. It would also imply a similar status for the *vaqueiro*, a view sharply in contrast to the frequently stated relationship between *vaqueiros* and the *aldeanos* or *xaldos* (a term used by *vaqueiros* to describe villagers). In a conversation with a middle-aged villager concerning bereavement and sudden death, she commented, with a shrug of her shoulders, 'It comes when God calls you.' Whether her remark reflected her own beliefs, or was directed at me as someone of supposed status, I was not entirely certain. Most comments concerning death and the afterlife were of a more personal and commonplace nature, clichés that might be heard anywhere, but at the same time they evoked a certain fatalism. Some of these, ranging from the more prosaic to the more poetic, were as follows:

'Life is short! You have to appreciate people when they are alive. It's too late when they are dead.'

'We have to live our life on earth. No one can tell us about life after death.'

'Then they will shut my eyes—when I pass over'.

If little reference was made to the afterlife, conversely there was no lack of comment, particularly by the elderly, concerning apparitions foretelling death. Frequent reference was made to phantoms, described as *sombras* (shades or shadows), as portents of a person's death. If people who emigrated did not return to the village in their lifetime, they might return in some form or essence after death. One old man likened crows to the context of dead spirits when he commented that 'they seem to live for ever'. However, other villagers tended to dismiss any notion of spirit forms or phantoms and maintained that such notions were encouraged by the church. They would allude to certain practices in the past when priests were alleged to have deliberately faked spirit manifestations. This was done, according to some accounts, by people dressing up in shrouds and acting out the role of a deceased relative or neighbour to frighten someone into attending mass.[37]

Death was not without its humour. All villagers had a certain superstitious dread of an unfortunate bird which they referred to as *racha*. This was because it was always heard to call at the time of a death in the village. An elderly village lady imitated its call as *acaba! acaba!* ('finishes'). Another lady commented in answer to my question, 'Ghosts or spirits? We don't believe in those things any more. It comes from ignorance. In the old days there was a bird called a *rallu*.[38] Whenever he called *cara! cara!* in the night and people heard it, it would upset them, as it meant that someone was going to die.'

One man told the story, a well-known one in Alcedo, about his grandfather who on a clear moonlit night went out with his muzzle-loader on hearing a *rallu* bird calling near the *capilla*. He managed to shoot it and with evident elation announced on his return to the house that he had saved the whole village from death: that now no more people would die! A younger villager rather spoiled the story by saying that this particular bird would always call out at night if it was in the vicinity. In the grandfather's day, he said, villagers just did not go out of their houses after dark and certainly not at around midnight. The only time they were likely to do so, rather than being fast asleep in their beds, would be at the time of *relaciónes* or burial wakes. These wakes, he rationalised, would usually break up about that time: hence the superstition!

Abongo, on the top of the watershed above Alcedo, was once a *vaqueiro* village. The inhabitants were thought locally to be former Moslems from the time of the *reconquista*. Until at least the end of the nineteenth century, these villagers were never allowed into the sanctuary of the church in Quintana. They always had to sit at the back of the nave because the church did not regard them as being proper Christians. They were also, according to the village account, obliged to wear one black and one white sock to distinguish them from others. They were normally allowed to bury their dead in the *parroquia* cemetery. However, at one time a *vaqueiro* brought back two women from Madrid, with whom he lived in the village. When one of them died the parish priest refused to bury her, apparently because he considered the relationship had been sinful. According to the village account the *vaqueiro* offered the priest a large sum of money to have her buried, at which no less than five priests came to carry out the rites, presumably all expecting to be paid. When the burial was completed the *vaqueiro* understandably did not wish to pay the sum agreed to all of them, to which one of the priests was alleged to have retorted, 'Why? Did we not bury her deep enough for you?'

Sometimes villagers' sense of humour was macabre. They related a story about a villager in the parish who had emigrated to Madrid, where he was joined by his ageing mother. She became very ill and her last request was that she should be allowed to return to her village and be buried in the parish cemetery. To grant her wish her son put her body in the boot of his car and drove north. On the way he stopped for petrol and something to eat, and when he returned to the car park he found that his vehicle was no longer there: it had been stolen. The villagers maintained that neither the car nor his mother's body was ever recovered. When I heard this story I was uncertain as to where it had come from, as no names or house affiliations were mentioned. Nevertheless I heard the story on two occasions, and the comments which followed its telling. Women listeners maintained that the man's intentions were honourable. The men, being more cynical, thought that his reason for bringing his mother back was that a burial service in the village would be much cheaper than one in Madrid.

No one born and nurtured in the village would want to die anywhere else. That would be like a form of permanent exile and against nature. It happened during the civil war and it happens nowadays when people are taken ill and have to go to hospital. Should a person die there their relatives will claim the body back for burial in the parish church cemetery in Quintana. 'Sometimes, however,' commented one villager, 'relatives do not know of the death, or the person has no near relatives who can claim back the body.

'When they go below—you know what I mean—going down below?' There are two belows, he added, as he went on to answer his own question, 'One is where relatives can come and reclaim your body and take you back to your house.' He then went on the explain that the other is where the body goes if there are no close relatives. That is where the body is used by students for their experiments. 'They have to learn you know,' he added. Clearly, to this man the thought of a person having no relatives to take him back to the village was abhorrent. To return home to the village, preferably before death, meant redemption, rather than having the last sacraments given in hospital. As for being used for experiments, a corpse to be dissected and then discarded: that was entirely unnatural. Not even a slaughtered animal in the village would be treated in that way.

There is another form of death which villagers feel goes completely against nature and that is suicide. The house that we lived in for our first year in the village was initially treated with circumspection by villagers, not because we lived there but, as we learned eventually, because it was a house of tragedy. That may have been why it was called Casa Mata which might very loosely be translated as Death House. Only one person had stayed since the events which I will describe, and that was a visiting priest for a brief few days. It was the events which had happened in that house some six years previously which still caused the villagers so much concern, and which seemed to haunt them even when passing along the cart track above the house on the way to their fields beyond.

Two brothers and the wife of one of them had lived for many years in the house. The married couple were handsome though rather sombre, if the faded photograph in its ornate frame, which still hung in the main room, was a good likeness. The man in the photograph was the elder brother who had inherited the house and was *en casa*. He had been badly injured as a boy in the village by an exploding grenade during the civil war and had died in 1970 in middle age as a result of his injuries. Within a few months his wife also died. They had no children and although the house and its land reverted to a near relative in the village, the brother could continue to live there and work the land.

Immediately after the wife's funeral her relatives came to the house and, having sent off the brother-in-law on some errand in the village, set about collecting her things. 'They just grabbed everything that they thought had belonged to her, even money which belonged to her brother-in-law and they left before he returned.' Although they may have had a right to take back her inheritance, such a right is not normally exercised, especially under such circumstances and after so many years had elapsed since the marriage. What the villagers disapproved of was the manner in which it was done and its happening simultaneously with the wife's burial.

Shortly after this event the brother, now living on his own in the house, tried unsuccessfully to commit suicide by hanging himself from a beam in the porch. A neighbour passing by at that very moment quickly cut him down and saved him. There seemed no reason for this action. He was always well looked after and neighbours frequently gave him food and asked him to a *fila* in their houses. He could work the land and he had some money which his sister-in-law's relatives had missed. However, he maintained he was bored. A close neighbour took him to see a doctor who pronounced him fit and well. No sooner did he return than he promptly went to the orchard below the house and hung himself from a tree where no one would notice, this time successfully.

A priest, a man of unusually liberal mind and admired by villagers, buried him in the parish cemetery with appropriate ceremony, despite his demise being viewed as a cardinal sin by the church. It was however the nature of this triple tragedy that disturbed villagers. It had all happened so quickly to their erstwhile good neighbours. Many always refused an invitation to enter the house, particularly the elderly, preferring to sit in the porch outside. It was as if the house was haunted by malign spirits that had brought such ill-fortune and a final act of self-destruction. I never heard of any other case of suicide in the village, or indeed in the parish. It may have been that it was something no one wished to talk about, but no one could remember it ever happening before.[39]

The wake

Villagers called a wake *relaciones* or the relating of stories. It was they said 'a custom from the past', its purpose being to keep company with the body of a recently deceased person. They considered this vigil to be quite separate and distinct from the rites surrounding church burial practice.

Only two wakes took place during our time in the village: one for an elderly lady and the second for a man in his early seventies, who for the purposes of the following account will be called Lisario. Despite his age he always seemed in the peak of good health. Straight backed and over six feet tall, he cut a debonair figure. With a ruggedly handsome face he was a quick-witted, humourous and intelligent bachelor. Although some villagers seemed somewhat ambiguous in their assessment of his character, the young adored him. He would pass by our house every day with a friendly greeting, a towering figure in his wooden clogs, clutching his shepherd's crook and herding his small flock of a dozen or so sheep. Invariably he was followed by his faithful mastiff, a huge dog which pined so much and became so difficult to manage after his death that it had to be shot.

Lisario, like others who were unlikely to inherit, emigrated in the 1920s to Cuba, where he became a professional cook. Returning to the village in the early 1930s, he was called up to fight for the Republican cause in the civil war. Subsequently he settled in Alcedo with his *en casa* niece and her husband from near Tineo, and lived in their house with their children tending their *tierras*, fields and orchards and his sheep. He was admired as a raconteur of stories and *refranes*. Every Asturian is that, but he had an exceptional gift, a fact which has a bearing on the account which follows.

Late one afternoon there was some shouting in the village. This was followed by the sight of a party of men rapidly climbing the steep path up the ridge to the south. Some half an hour later they could be seen descending and carrying a body between them. It was Lisario, suddenly struck down with what villagers called thrombosis, while tending his sheep. Once in his house he regained consciousness. A villager immediately rode down to the valley on muleback to the nearest telephone in Boinas to contact a doctor in Belmonte. He arrived some time later and prescribed some medicine. Lisario remained conscious for a further two weeks and although he hardly spoke, many neighbours came to sit by his bedside. Then one morning he died.

A villager immediately set off to notify the priest and to arrange for the funeral, which should customarily be held at 4 pm on the day following the death. As soon as this was confirmed, riders set out from the village to notify Lisario's relations and friends in nearby and more distant villages, so that they might attend. Earlier in the afternoon there had been a succession of visitors which had continued on into the early evening. The dead person should never be left alone. As one villager observed, 'It is a sort of collective responsibility for all of us. We share the grief of the family.'

By the time this visiting commenced the body of the deceased had been properly dressed and prepared by the women in the main bedroom of the house. It was laid out on the bed ready for those women who might wish to see it. Men, unless they are very close family, rarely view the corpse. For the occasion Lisario was wearing his best suit with his beret placed at an angle on his head in the manner he liked. Just beside the bed lay the coffin, into which he would be placed the following morning prior to the journey to the church.

The *relaciones* commenced about ten in the evening. Within half an hour the men, about thirty-five in all from different houses, had congregated in the main room of the house. After greeting one another they seated themselves in a semi-circle under a single ceiling light, on benches and straight-backed wooden chairs. At first they spoke in lowered tones to each other and a few remained silent throughout the proceedings. No women were present during the early part of the wake. They congregated in the kitchen area to converse among themselves.

With the exception of an elderly man from Quintana and one other, all the men present came from the village and every house was represented. At first two or three elderly men held the conversation while others listened, but as more arrived conversations broke out among three or four groups and no one person held forth on his own. From the outset the talk tended to centre on reminiscences of the civil war and its aftermath. Two of those present had been together in a Nationalist prisoner of war camp after the Republican northern army had been forced to capitulate. One of them spoke of the physical damage and human trauma which were all too evident in the village on his return after his early release and of the recriminations and vengeance which followed.

'There were more deaths after the war than there were during it,' commented one elderly villager. 'If I had an order to execute someone, I would do it,' said another man, adding, 'If it is an order, then you have to carry it out, regardless of your own personal feelings.' 'The last thing I would ever do,' interjected a third, 'and the worst, would be to take another man's life. I have never had to do it.'

Then other villagers spoke of acts of bravery: of the man who sat down with the soldiers who were about to execute him and offered them all cigarettes, 'as he would have no further need of them, after they had carried out their orders'. Another spoke of a certain captain who, knowing his fate, punctually drove his own vehicle down to his own prearranged execution by firing squad. Yet another spoke of a soldier who refused to carry out an order to shoot a friend of his accused of betrayal and had himself to suffer the consequences.

These anecdotes went on until about midnight. There were some extremely humourous asides on mundane matters, many concerning Lisario himself, who was a renowned practical joker; and although there were brief silences, the conversation was frequently punctuated with laughter. There were tales about those who who fought on the 'wrong' side in the civil war, and those who were forced to do so without any alternative. However, no one emphasised the horrors and all stories were told in a somewhat wry and resigned manner, seeking out the humour of these awful events. Few of the accounts concerned the village itself or indeed the parish, but tended to be set in the region of Belmonte or elsewhere. More local acts of revenge, such as the beatings to death I had heard spoken of by elderly villagers, were not discussed. Clearly these were matters better forgotten and not the sort of thing Lisario would have wished to be recounted at his wake. There was a strong element of romantic idealism in all the conversations of that evening, perhaps in the mode in which Lisario saw life about him while he lived.

At midnight precisely all the women entered from the kitchen. There were eleven of them and the room now seemed crowded. The men's conversation ceased abruptly. None of them vacated their seats and so the women stood about until a long bench was brought in for them to sit on. Apart from Lisario's niece, a lady in her forties, and her daughter, both of whom lived in the house, all the other women were neighbours. The youngest, a girl still at school, recited in the ensuing silence from a Rosary book of devotions which she held in her lap. The so-called 'Fifteen Mysteries of the Virgin', a few of which she read out, were greeted with a hushed salutation by a few of the women, but with silence by the men, as she paused at the end of each reading. Apart from the girl herself, who carried a rosary for counting prayers, I saw no one else with one. Some of the women crossed themselves, as did one of the elderly men, at the end of the recitation.

After this brief interlude the women brought in a bottle of brandy and a bottle of Asturian *anís* with three small glasses. All those present were offered a drink, but only about five of the men accepted, the glasses being passed among them. Two of the women also drank. Some further desultory talking followed while the niece took Lisario's nephew, who had come from a distance to join the wake, in to see his uncle. No one else throughout the evening went into the room where Lisario lay. Shortly before 1 am the men started leaving and soon only a few of the women remained for the night's vigil with the corpse. As I left, one young villager turned to me and said, 'That is just the way Lisario would have liked it—he always enjoyed telling and listening to good stories!'

The burial mass

> Polvo eras, polvo serás,
> En polvo te convertirás.

> Dust you were, dust you will be,
> Dust you will become.

The following afternoon at about 3 pm people started assembling in the narrow cobbled lane outside Lisario's house. There were not only Alcedans there, but others from nearby villages, many of whom had walked up from the valley below.

Some had come by car from further afield, including two officials from the Belmonte branch of the Banco del Norte. It was the very end of August. Rain had threatened earlier, but for the present it was just rather dull, overcast and quite warm. All the men wore dark clothes: some were in suits with white open-necked shirts and a few wore ties. Women mainly wore black dresses and some had black kerchiefs over their hair. By 3.30 pm a dark mass of upwards of two hundred and fifty people was gathered outside the house, awaiting the arrival of the priest.

They continued to wait patiently. The service was scheduled to start at 4 pm in the parish church in Quintana, but after nearly half an hour had passed the priest had still not arrived. Some people started to depart, walking down the old pathway, the *camino sagrado*, to the church in the valley. They thought the priest had been detained on his way from Belmonte or that he had decided not to come up to the village, as in the case of the old lady's burial some weeks previously.

Eventually he did arrive at 4 pm, and instead of the coffin being carried down the pathway on men's shoulders in the customary way, it was immediately loaded into the back of a Renault van. At least a dozen vehicles were jammed nose to tail in the narrow lane, but after some confusion and manoeuvring the procession of cars set off down the newly macadamised road to the church, while the walkers took the traditional route.

Eight pall bearers, all from the village except for Lisario's nephew, carried the coffin down the central aisle, placing it on a bench in front of the altar. By contrast with the coffin, which was covered in wreaths and posies, and the priest, who had donned magnificent vestments of scarlet and gold, the church itself seemed uncared for with its stark and functional interior unadorned with candles or even flowers. With the exception of the pall bearers, the bankers and a few elderly men who had removed their berets, the congregation of about one hundred and fifty people was entirely made up of women. Although there was a large space for standing within the church the vast majority of men, as was their custom, chose to remain outside. Throughout the service there was a constant loud murmur of voices as they grouped and regrouped to discuss events, greeting those they had not seen since the last burial service.

At the old lady's service some weeks previously the priest had begun by chastising the local congregation: 'Why do you only come to funerals? Why do you not come to mass more often? It is important to come more often. Death comes to us all. What else is there in life if we do not have God? You should be more attendant to the church!' This was not repeated during Lisario's service, perhaps because there were several officials from outside the parish present who would not relish being lectured about their attendance at church. With that omission his address was similar to his previous one. He spoke of the recently inaugurated pope: how he came from a poor working family and had spent much of his life looking after the depressed, the deformed and the backward. Having watched the crowds at St Peter's on television, adding that he had only watched for a few minutes for that was all he had time for, he marvelled at the multitude of people. Why did they come? Because they were Catholics. He did not mention Lisario's name, but went on to speak of the brevity of life. 'There is one thing that is certain and that is death,' he continued. 'We should all try to live good lives. No one is perfect and we all make mistakes. We all sin. If we say we don't then we lie, for no one lives without sin.'

The collection basket was passed round and this time the priest felt it was necessary to explain the cause for which money was being collected. Villagers however, as on previous occasions, remained sceptical: they felt it was part of the priest's payment for holding the mass. Some put money in the basket, some did not. Some crossed themselves at the end of prayers and some knelt for these and some did not. A few of the women went up for communion after the sermon, but there was a rush for the door after he gave the blessing and he was left alone, the last to leave, a strangely isolated figure.

Some two months later a new parish priest held a memorial service for Lisario in the small *capilla* in the village. It was well attended by about thirty villagers. His name was mentioned and it was a more personal affair as the well-intentioned priest wished to make more intimate contact with the villagers than his predecessor.

The interment

The graveyard just to the east of the church was a very small one. Triangular in shape, two of its sides were enclosed by a low stone wall, while to the south was a high wall, over 2 m high and 10 m in length, comprising a honeycomb of concrete *nichos*. There were about two hundred of these recesses, each one large enough to contain a a full-sized coffin. This structure rendered such a small cemetery sufficient for the needs of the whole parish, numbering some four hundred people. Before it was built in the early 1960s, bodies were buried in the ground.

At the end of the nineteenth century, when there would have been in excess of two thousand people living in the parish, one can only assume that the great majority of the dead were buried elsewhere; yet no one had any knowledge of other burial grounds. All maintained that the parish dead had always been buried in the cemetery. Based on a life expectancy of seventy, and excluding high mortality among the very young, the small cemetery would have had to sustain on average thirty burials a year. Such numbers would have covered every available space in the ground within two years. It is possible for bone remains to be removed after some five to seven years once the corpse has disintegrated, but not after two years.

One villager said that the *nichos* had been built because 'People don't like finding bones when they dig.' Another observed that for a grave to be dug it costs about three thousand pesetas, and that now with the *nichos* it was far less expensive. Those who dug the graves in the past would probably have been villagers, even the deceased's close kin to save on costs. It seems doubtful that there would have been professional grave-diggers within such a community. Either way it could not have ben a pleasant job, for they would have continually been digging up old skeletons. However, as one villager commented, 'They are just bones. They [used to] just keep digging up the same plots.' There seems to have been no problem in his view as he went on to explain that the body does not last long in the ground: 'not many years', adding that after fifteen years all that remains is 'a few bones: a skull, the pelvis and some limb bones.' He was very matter-of-fact about it.

Although only about a third of the *nichos* had been utilised at the time of Lisario's burial, it was still considered by villagers that after seven years the sealed *nichos* would be reopened and the bones removed to an ossuary, one of the *nichos* being used for this purpose. Some of the slabs which sealed the cavities had names and dates on them; others were without any designation. There remained a number of old gravestones, some still standing, others toppled over and scattered about the small yard, no longer marking the place of any remains. It was obvious that the cemetery was not cared for. Just prior to the old lady's burial someone, possibly a member of her family, had cut back the mass of nettles, dock leaves and brambles which had proliferated and almost obliterated the yard, even growing over the top of the high wall at the back. Cemeteries are usually considered sanctified ground, but this one seemed to have no such connotation or associated sentiment. To villagers this anomaly did not seem to require any explanation, although one Asturian in Belmonte expressed his views quite forcibly on the recently inaugurated system of *nichos* in the town: 'Before people were buried in the ground and that was that. Now they are put into *nichos* for some seven years or so. Then the bones are taken out and placed in an ossuary, everyone mixed up with everyone else.' Then as if in protest at the whole idea, he added: 'It is better that the dead are cremated rather than for that to happen!'

After Lisario's coffin had been carried out of the church, it was taken to the cemetery and laid on the ground amongst the cut ends of brambles and nettles. Some thirty people were standing around it; the rest of the congregation was outside in the roadway or starting to leave. The priest blessed the coffin, then departed himself. The coffin lay on the ground for some time; someone had removed the floral tributes. A young girl from Oviedo broke down and cried and there were tears in the eyes of Lisario's nephew. No one else betrayed any emotion, despite the undoubtedly strong feelings of many people there.

A villager backed up his car to the gateway and, taking some cement from a bag and some water from a container, he mixed them on the ground nearby. While he was doing this some of the men lifted the coffin up to one of the highest *nichos*. It would not go in so they placed it on the ground again. The coffin was quite an elaborate one with floral designs carved on the lid and trim around the sides. The latter was hindering its progress into the cavity and so it was stripped off. The end slab was then placed in position, cemented in and sealed. A few people lingered for a minute or so before the cemetery was vacated and the iron gate closed, and within an hour villagers were busying themselves with the evening round of their daily work

About two weeks after these events, Julio from Quintana, Lisario's great friend and fellow card-player who had spoken eloquently of him at his wake, suddenly died as the result of a heart attack. Villagers maintained it was because he had eaten between meals. If Lisario's funeral had been unusual in that it was attended by officials from Belmonte, Julio's was exceptional, no less than four priests being present. Two came from Belmonte, one of whom was the priest at Lisario's funeral. Another was an old friend of Julio's family who had travelled up from Madrid. This was the much admired Don Alfonso who, according to villagers, came at his own expense. The fourth priest was Julio's own brother, described as a 'rogue'. Even if villagers were laconic about this event it suggested some solidarity in the local church at a time when its influence seemed once again to be waning.

Many of the more elderly women in the village always wore black: shoes, stockings, dress, jersey and kerchief. They called it a *tener el seco*, which could have multiple renderings but here may be taken to mean 'to be plain'. 'A widow always wears black after the death of her husband, or she is not very serious minded,' was the comment of one elderly lady. A young, recently married woman concurred with this view only with some reservation: 'Things are changing. Now some widows remarry,' implying that should this happen they would cease to be in mourning and stop wearing black. Custom however prevails and she went on to affirm that mourning apparel was expected among women for two years in the case of the death of either parent, one year (or sometimes two) for a brother or sister and six months in the case of either grandparent. She did not mention in-laws. For men there was no specific stipulation except to wear dark clothes at funerals. For a mature woman, after a death in her immediate family it was simpler and less expensive just to continue to wear black for the rest of her life, as did most of the elderly women in the village.

The actual cost of a funeral is considerable but not excessive, the major expense being the coffin. These are normally made by a carpenter in Belmonte. In 1978 the average cost for a plain coffin made from a softwood such as pine was in the region of two thousand pesetas. If, as in the case of Lisario's, it had some moulded trimmings and flower engraving on the lid, then it would cost more. Five hundred pesetas covered the cost of the van to take the coffin to the church. Thus with the relatively minor expense of a wake, for drinks are seldom imbibed, the total may not exceed three thousand pesetas. However, unpredictable expenses relate to the church. In the past this may have included digging the grave if this was not undertaken by neighbours: a further three thousand pesetas, though much less now that *nichos* have been built. Then there is the charge levied by the parish priest for taking a burial service. 'Some charge and others do not,' was the comment of one elderly villager, 'some priests are politicians and robbers! They are paid but they still do it. Some have even asked for payment the day before the service.' These requests for payments were usually in the order of two thousand pesetas. The old man then included the collection money in his estimate, which he thought to be on average about a thousand pesetas, as a sort of group payment for the services of the priest. This was despite the fact that the priest at Lisario's funeral had specifically said that the collection would go towards a charity. Thus depending on the attitude of the resident parish priest, the costs for a funeral and burial could vary between three and five thousand pesetas. This would represent the cost of a good ewe at the current market price.

Allegations regarding charging for the service and presumptions regarding the proceeds of the collection are based solely on the evidence of villagers; they are stated here because of their relevance to the countryman's attitude towards the local church. Whether this is prejudice on villagers' part, or whether such things actually happen, is impossible to verify. One or two former priests are credited by villagers as being sincere, even generous. Thus they are not judgmental of the church at large, but more concerned with particular priests who have exercised considerable influence over their daily lives. Priests are not well paid and unless they have private means, the costs incurred just to travel to various parishes to conduct services are not inconsiderable. Also, from the priest's point of view, villagers are no longer regarded as poor, as they might have been in the past. Some indeed are quite well off in relative terms, and the cost of a ewe would not seem excessive to the priest for the price of a funeral.

Depending on the time of day of a person's death, it can be as little as thirty-six hours between his demise and his coffin being sealed into the *nicho*; certainly no more than forty-eight hours are allowed to lapse before the body is interred. This can cause distress if relatives living at a distance are unable to attend the funeral. Conversely, when villagers attend funerals of their relatives in nearby towns, several days may elapse between notification of the death and the date set for the funeral, which allows the bereaved to arrange their affairs and make arrangements to travel in a dignified manner.

A possible reason for this haste may lie in the preparation of the body after death. The relatively sophisticated urban funerary techniques for preserving the body are out of the question in a village environment where, particularly in the summer heat, a corpse can deteriorate rapidly; therefore speed must be of the essence if unnecessary embarrassment is to be avoided.

Despite the apparent urgency, however, within the village context custom prevails and is adhered to with care and dignity. No household in the village, regardless of personal feelings about the deceased, even if lifelong enmity had been involved, would ever fail to pay its respects by sending one or more members to the wake. This is also seen as a social obligation beyond the confines of the village. One elderly man's cousin who lived near Oviedo had just died and the old man wanted to go to his wake. He knew however that the deceased's wife hated him and he was therefore afraid to go. He consulted two male neighbours about his concern and they advised him that regardless of his personal feelings he should respect the passing of his relative. He accepted their advice and went.

Once the body passes out of the jurisdiction of the village, there seems to be greater ambiguity. This is firstly in the manner in which the church service is conducted, by both the priest and the congregation of villagers; and secondly, and more importantly, in relation to the cemetery itself, the final resting place of the deceased, with its unexpected outward impression of disrespect and neglect for the dead.

Perhaps villagers feel it is the church's responsibility to maintain the cemetery, but with their limited jurisdiction and funding the priests' apparent abrogation is understandable. In such circumstances why should not villagers themselves care for the burial ground? The answer may be due to the impracticality of maintaining any communal action among scattered villages; but it is more likely to be connected with attitudes towards church orthodoxy, which vary from ambivalence to disbelief. Hence both church and cemetery may be viewed as outside villagers' traditional sphere. It would seem that an understanding of natural religion and orthodoxy (see Chapter 12) is intrinsic to concepts about death, burial and a perceived afterlife, and the apparent long term neglect of the graveyard is indicative of this.

It may be suggested that on purely practical grounds farming communities do not have time to concern themselves with the tidiness of a graveyard, and that the sacred aspect of that ground is less important than the arduous daily cycle of their lives. But if this is the case, why is the wake, which is equally onerous, granted such sanctity? Possibly the Alcedans had their own cemetery at one time, but no one knew of such a place, unless burial on the fringes of the village of refugees shot during the civil war was indicative of some former custom which might have extended to burial in proximity to houses. If this were the case then the apparent ambivalence between what might conceptually be described as 'inside' and 'outside', the apparent discontinuity as represented by the *camino sagrado* between customary practices around death within the village and the ceremony associated with the church, represent distinct categories.

Before the road was macadamised, the only way to the church was via the *camino sagrado*. There was no question of a van abbreviating the last journey and thereby bringing the church conceptually closer to the village. The path goes first through the lower fields and woodlands of the village, which represent the inside. It then passes through transitional land belonging to the neighbouring village of Quintana, and on to what in village terms represents church land: the parish church itself and the cemetery. It is here that the outside is dominant, the corpse being transferred into the keeping of orthodoxy, that realm which is the antithesis of the natural world, the *naturaleza* of villagers' philosophy, those 'heathen' and 'pagan' ideas attributed to them by one Catholic priest.

Conversely and more mundanely it may be suggested that the cemetery is merely a reflection of the man-nature ethic of villagers. No animal is warranted more at its *matanza* than to provide man with good and necessary eating, no matter how much respect and affection it may have received in its lifetime. If man is regarded as part of nature too, why should he not become like the animals when death intervenes? They are not buried in sacred ground. So why should special care be lavished on a graveyard? Human remains are after all 'just bones' and death is part of the natural process of nature. Care of a cemetery will not somehow preserve the dead, and villagers might consider it sentimental. Just as the most favoured and respected oxen of the past are but a recollection, so villagers may regard collective recall of the dead in social memory as more important than their physical remains. They are thus preserved for as long as there are people to remember. If they are worthy they become the stuff of village history and ultimately myth, the very basis of tradition. Far better, some might say, than some transient memorial signifying skeletal remains in a Catholic cemetery. If the corpse remains outside, the memory of a once living person is embalmed within village consciousness. A villager might well ask: is that not sufficient?

Chapter 11

Civil war

For eight hundred years the crusade against the Moors had been the central theme of Spanish history: they still continued to be the hereditary enemy—the only enemy, in fact, against which the Spanish armies ever fought. Their savagery in war was well known ... Yet they were now being brought to fight in Asturias, that one sacred corner of Spain where the Crescent had never flown.[40]

'I was twenty-seven at the time,' recounted one elderly villager. 'My battalion, a Republican one, was in the Pyrenees. It was winter and we were caught in a blizzard. We had no food for four days. We stole some tins of jam from the enemy and ate this. But cold jam is not very good for the stomach in those conditions. We were in snow up to our chests and had to keep moving about. Those who slept got frostbite in their fingers and feet. I didn't suffer, but half the battalion had to go to hospital afterwards with exposure problems. No one was fighting. The enemy [the Nationalists] were just as cold as ourselves. Many of us had to have our fingers and toes amputated. On the fifth day enough food arrived for several meals—but we ate it all in one go.'

For villagers war and military service had been a concern for as long as they could remember. Some said that even the Napoleonic war had not left them unaffected, maintaining there was a tradition of occupation and fighting in the precincts of the village. This seems to have some basis in fact as one elderly man said that when he was a young boy his father had dug up an old lance and a small cannon in one of his *tierras*. The older members of the village could recall their fathers being involved in the Cuban-Spanish war, which ended in defeat for the Spanish in 1895. At the turn of the twentieth century military service could be for five years. Some of the older generation of villagers were themselves caught up in service in North Africa and the Moroccan war.

'It was not because of too many mouths to feed and hunger in the home,' commented one man, 'but more because we did not wish to be called up—being afraid of service in North Africa and disease—that many of us emigrated.' So in a sense there was nothing new about the fear of involvement in war.

Villagers were not directly implicated in the 1934 uprising in Asturias, for this mainly concerned the mining communities in the east; but when general civil war broke out in 1936 they were involved: not just the men of military age, but everyone in the village. The events of 1937 and the subsequent years of deprivation were therefore no hearsay to the older generation. It was a subject on which everyone over the age of forty-five had personal recollections, while the younger generation could recount stories told by their elders with a vividness which might almost suggest they had witnessed these events themselves. Most of the village men were enlisted to the Republican cause at the outbreak of hostilities. Some, who did not return to the village until several years later, only learned what had happened during their absence from wives, parents or children who had remained behind. A number of villagers, either because of forgetfulness or reticence, preferred to remain silent even after forty years had passed.

A whole generation of men, their ages ranging from sixteen to over forty at the outbreak of war, were involved in various campaigns in northern Spain from Galicia to the Pyrenees. When the Republican cause collapsed in Asturias in 1937, a few found their way back to the village. A few more, according to hearsay, later enrolled in the Blue Division which fought alongside the German army in Russia. The majority, however, either remained interned or were forced to join the Nationalists and endure further campaigning in other parts of Spain. These men were unable to return to the village until between seven and ten years after their original departure.

Few of these men had any idea of the trauma of warfare which their village had sustained, or of its aftermath, until they returned, for they had little means of communicating with their families. Very few of them could write and even if they could it was unlikely that letters would be delivered in a war zone. They returned to stories of deprivation and atrocity, the complete abandonment of the village over a period of the hostilities and its partial devastation. The consequences were all too obvious: their huge flocks of sheep ravaged, their byres empty of cattle and their formerly immaculate *tierras* unkempt. There were no oxen to plough the fields, carry manure or bring in the hay. Their neighbours labouring in the fields were carrying burdens on their backs and heads, rather as if the domestication of animals had yet to happen. It took years for the villagers to restore a semblance of normality and the manner of living to which they had been accustomed since before the eighteenth century.

Less immediately obvious were the social scars: the still deep divisions in relationships, not just between villages in the region but within the village itself, between houses and even within families. In some ways the return of the soldiers was a balm to these community frictions and enmities arising from alleged betrayals, counter-accusations and an aftermath of revenge. The majority of these enlisted men, though mainly apolitical, were obliged to fight on both sides during the war, and for those who survived this, division had become almost an irrelevance. They saw the way ahead as one of recreating a village community, restructuring a sort of unity. Isolated villages such as theirs could not have any realistic future unless old scores were, if not forgotten, at least put in perspective to ensure the survival of the community. In the late 1970s the village was still known for this sense of unity, even as far away as the district capital Belmonte, though deep antagonisms and aversions remained beneath the surface.

The experiences of emigration, war and its aftermath lent the more elderly villagers a conscious and sharpened sense of history through their collective memory of past events. These were discussed interminably during gatherings, in casual conversations, and at wakes such as that described in Chapter 10. This communal self-awareness has implications in attitudes and relationships which, though difficult to determine, are of primary importance in understanding village life. Alcedo was not by any means lost in a period of rural bliss and unchanging patterns of work and observance passed down through the centuries. Indeed, no medieval village community in Europe, riven by similar experiences of labour and servitude, feudal and church dominion, and subjected to all the vagaries of strife and war, would have been any different. History as recorded in individual and collective memory is vital to an understanding a community and the way it perceives itself.

A strategic village

'It is in a very good strategic position,' one young villager explained. 'There is a low pass above Abongo [which connects two valley systems] overlooking the Rio Cauxa valley, with mountains on either side. It was a corridor and Alcedo lies in the middle and each peak of the Sierra Manteca was converted into a Republican redoubt.' Villagers said that even in the 1920s 'people' came to look at the Sierra de Manteca. They suspected that these visits were for some military purpose, but were not sure. Undoubtedly the Sierra, with its peaks up to 1500 m high running in an approximately north-south direction, overlooks large areas of this western part of Asturias. It also overlooks much of the Narcea river system, perhaps best known for its trout and salmon and where, after the war, Franco himself was a visitor during the salmon season.

Whether the Republicans, or others who may have advocated an independent Asturias, saw the mountain as an excellent strategic position in the wider context of the province, I do not know. To command the heights in any country may give a defending force an advantage over an attacking one, and certainly Pelayo in his mountain redoubt in the Picos de Europa further east used such a position to his advantage over the Moorish invaders in the thirteenth century. Another successful defence occurred during the civil war, according to village accounts, when a Moorish battalion of some eight hundred men tried to take a very precipitous peak some 5 km to the north of Alcedo but were forced to withdraw.

There is a logic in such a strategy, but it does require good communications and supply lines. Most of the high mountain villages in the area were inhabited by *vaqueiro* pastoralists who, according to local knowledge, would depart south in early spring to graze their flocks in the plains of León, leaving the villages empty until their return in late autumn. Alcedo however, with its primarily agricultural economy, was an exception. It was also much the largest mountain village in the area at that time. Other large villages and small towns in the region were all at a lower altitude and closer to the main valley systems which might be controlled by an invading force. It was perhaps for this reason that Alcedo, as a supply line and source of food, became a central pivot for the Republicans' defence after they had lost control of urban areas and the main valley systems to the Nationalists in the western part of the province.

There are a number of accounts of the war waged in Asturias from August 1936 until the capitulation in October 1937, but none as far as I am aware concerns events in the area immediately to the west of Belmonte. However, these were of great concern to the population of the region and more particularly to villages like Alcedo, which at the time was still a populous and well integrated community of some forty households. In rural terms it was relatively affluent, with cattle, large herds of sheep and a highly evolved system of pasturage and garden cultivation, representing a virtually self-sufficient subsistence economy.

The following reconstruction of events in Alcedo between the autumns of 1936 and 1937 is mainly based on the recollections of three of four elderly women villagers. A few very elderly men, who had been too old to be called up, and a number of villagers who were children at the time, were also consulted. Thus my information is selective and fragmentary, each person tending to remember only that part which he or she had witnessed or heard of at first hand. There was no village historian to place the various actions and counteractions together into any sequence, nor would anyone have wished to do this. This collective memory, of supreme importance to the community, has therefore been like a puzzle which I have tried to piece together.

At the outset of war it was inevitable that there would be divisions of opinion as to the rights and wrongs of the contesting sides in the developing conflict. Some villagers had previously fought for Spain's overseas dominions, or had relatives connected with administration or industry, or espoused a church commitment, and might therefore be inclined to the Nationalist cause. Others for various reasons were committed to the Republican movement and possibly an independent Asturias. But for the great majority who had no strong feelings or commitments either way, there was no wish to become involved. They wanted nothing more than to be left alone in peace to care for the land they had inherited. It was Alcedo's situation in the landscape and its obvious strategic relevance which caused their lives to be disrupted, forcing them to take sides, even within families. No one could remain neutral. Divisions, distrust and lasting enmities prevailed.

'It was terrible. There was not enough to eat. Village was against village and brother against brother,' was how one eighty-five-year-old described it, while another said that it was a nightmare: 'Father against son—I just want to forget it,' and she had nothing more to say.

Thousands of similar small communities all over Spain must have suffered devastating effects of the civil war, and Guernica became a symbol of that suffering.[41] Alcedans were affected no less and perhaps more than most and the war's aftermath remains in their memories and story-telling. The elderly are prone to romanticise their youth, but all the evidence suggests that the war marked an abrupt change from an old way of life which they never quite managed to re-establish.

'After the war everything changed from the life we had before—there was no joy!' was the way one old lady described it. She chose the word 'joy' after some hesitation to encompass her recollections of village ambience when she had been a *moza* before the outbreak of hostilities, when there had been seventy young people like her participating in festivals and dancing and recitations. Many of these occasions took place on a flat grassy area just to the north of the village named the *pasquinero*, meaning a place of satire and lampooning. This was therefore a place redolent of village conviviality and joy, and was still being used for certain celebrations in the late 1970s. Yet ironically, it was the very place where some of the bloodiest engagements in the region occurred between the opposing sides, as they tried to gain control of the high ground it commanded overlooking the village and the surrounding area. From all accounts the *pasquinero* became almost a fixation, with constant 'to-ing and fro-ing' of the opposing sides throughout a year of fighting.

In the personal accounts which follow the opposing forces will be referred to by different names, sometimes with derogatory connotations. These may betray the narrator's own affiliations, but more often they are used simply because these terms became incorporated, both locally and nationally, into the general vernacular to describe and differentiate between the two sides in the conflict.

A sequential reconstruction

From the outset of civil war Asturias was one of the key provinces for the Republican movement because of its mining and heavy industry concerns centred close to the capital, Oviedo. Spanish nationalists viewed it as a hotbed of Republicanism, particularly in the light of the 1934 uprising of Asturian miners, cruelly and cynically crushed by foreign mercenaries. Galicia to the west, the birthplace of Franco, was predominantly Nationalist in sentiment and the Republican cause there was quickly snuffed out. By early August 1936 Galician battalions had already invaded the westernmost districts of Asturias. By 8 August they had advanced on and taken the large fishing port of Luarca. By the 22 August they had entered Cangas de Narcea, lying some 50 km by road to the west, but as the crow flies over a series of deep north-south valley systems, a mere 20 km from the Abongo pass above Alcedo. It was during the last week of August that Alcedo heard its first artillery exchange. The Nationalists had taken up positions on the Alto de Reigada, a low mountain just to the west, overlooking the village. They started shelling Republican positions on the western slopes of the Sierra de Manteca to the east of Alcedo.

The intense bombardment caused all the inhabitants of Abongo, which was in the direct line of fire between the two forces, to evacuate the village. Most of them descended to the villages in the Cauxa valley below, but a few sought relatives to stay with in Alcedo. A short time later some of them returned briefly, only to find that all their animals had been slaughtered, allegedly by the Republicans. After that no one returned until after the conflict.

'Our village was caught in the firing,' related one woman who had been a young girl in Abongo at the time. 'We were ordered to evacuate the village at midnight.' The reason for this, she explained, was not so much their safety as a concern that some of the villagers might pass on information about the Republican positions on Manteca. 'When we left we were only allowed to take our milking cows and the heads of wheat which were in our baskets.' This meant that the wheat had only just been picked and had not yet been winnowed or milled into flour. 'We went firstly to Bagega and then on to Quintana. There we were told by the [Republican] soldiers that the villagers had to look after us and to let us have fields to graze our cows in. We were put into the houses of the families who had gone off to join the Nationalists. During the summer of 1937 we were allowed up to our fields near Abongo to pasture our cows and the [Nationalist] soldiers didn't shoot at us.' She explained again that they had been allowed to take their *escanda* with them the previous autumn, but that they were not able to plant the new crop in the early spring. 'Anyway,' she continued, 'we had nothing left to plant. We had to use it all for bread and then we had very little to eat, but we had a roof over our heads! Then later in October [1937] when we returned to our village it was like a wilderness. The grass was as high about the houses as in the fields!'

Abongo never really recovered from the war. Too many people never returned, many settling in the villages to which they had been evacuated. In 1978, although all the houses were still standing, for despite its position in the line of fire, Abongo had been virtually untouched by the fighting, it was almost like a ghost village with no more than four or five elderly inhabitants.

In co-ordination with a general Republican counter-offensive against the advancing Nationalist forces in the Somiedo region of western Asturias, an attack was mounted on the Nationalist positions on the Alto de Riegada during the first few days of September 1936. A villager who had been a boy at the time described the action in the following terms:

'A company or so of Nationalists, about forty-five men in all, had positions on Riegada. They had mortars and field cannon with them.' It was this detachment of Nationalist soldiers which had been exchanging fire with the Republicans since their arrival during the last week of August. 'From there,' the man continued, 'they had a good view of all the surrounding country to the north and towards Tineo to the west. The Reds [Republicans] had Manteca at that time. One night at about 3 am the Reds made a surprise attack on the position. They climbed up to the top from this side, which is fairly steep, and took the position, killing all the defendants.' The Nationalists apparently included civil guards, militia and Navarra brigade troops. The narrator made no mention of the Galician troops, *los gallegos* as they were known, who were engaged further to the north at the time. He then indicated that the Republican position was attacked by the Moors, but this in fact did not occur until some ten months later in the summer of 1937.

'Many Nationalists were killed,' he continued, 'and that night we, here in the village, could hear them [the Republicans] singing from the top of the mountain. The next day we went up there with our ox-carts and we brought down the bodies, eight at a time, in each cart. We put all the bread we could find in the trouser legs of the dead men.' It is not clear why this was necessary as at the time the village had not suffered any direct attack, and there should not have been any shortage of bread, unless the Republican troops had been using up their supplies. All the bodies were taken down to Boinas for burial either there or in Quintana. The narrator added that within days the Nationalist soldiers regrouped, or were reinforced, and retook the position. It seems therefore that a number of the defenders must have retreated, and that they were not all killed as previously indicated.

Until this time Alcedo itself does not seem to have been directly affected by any fighting, although the Republican soldiers were in and about the village. About three weeks after the regaining of Alto de Riegada by the Nationalists, towards the end of September 1936, the Republicans established positions close to the village and overlooking it on the steeply inclining ridge just to the south. In the process of digging trenches in a large hayfield called *pro baxo* or lower field, a huge boulder was dislodged. It rolled down the hillside not far above the village, where it lies today beside a cart track near a cow barn which still shows evidence of a direct hit by a mortar bomb. Although nowadays Alcedo itself shows little evidence of the conflict, a number of outbuildings were rather proudly shown me with the tell-tale pockmarks villagers had not bothered to repair. It was about this time, in October, according to villagers' accounts, that the Nationalists mounted an offensive.

'We stayed in our kitchens that night to shelter from the bombs,' said one elderly lady, adding that the kitchen areas with their huge brick bread ovens afforded the best protection from mortar attacks. However, they did not stay there for long when the fighting intensified. 'We were a Republican stronghold [by then] and the Nationalists came over the top from the direction of Abongo before dawn. It was very frightening. We all ran down in our nightclothes towards the valley beneath the village. We hid in the chestnut woods, behind the trunks and in the branches. We stayed there all the following day and night.'

Despite the trenches above the village, the Republicans were not ready for this attack. At the time they had not prepared positions on the *pasquinero*, which was later considered to be the best defensive position, and coming under such sustained attack they were almost surrounded before they hastily retreated, abandoning the village. They immediately mounted a counter-attack, in which bitter hand-to-hand fighting took place, trenches being re-occupied and then retaken again by the opposing sides. It seemed, according to one narrator, that the Republicans were gaining the upper hand, when they ran out of ammunition and finally had to withdraw. From then on, for approximately four months until the following February, the Nationalists retained essential control of the village and the surrounding area, though subjected to sporadic attack.

During this time the Nationalist Galician columns had taken several of the main urban areas to the north in their advance on Oviedo, and were operating in the Narcea valley to the north of Belmonte. The Republicans were meanwhile retaining control in the southern section around So:niedo, bordering on the province of León. Although Republican positions on Manteca were cut off from their lines of communication through the village, and their food supplies, they would probably have been able to maintain the lines to the south. On 23 November Republican forces managed to cut the lines of communication of the advancing Nationalist columns at Grado in the north, but these were soon re-established.

These advances and retreats, attacks and counter-attacks were characteristic of the fighting over most of Asturias at this time, much of it concentrating on the central section of the province, particularly Oviedo, the mining-industrial belt and the port of Gijón to the north. As for the village itself, from all accounts it seems to have had a period of relative calm during the winter months, with only sporadic and relatively ineffectual sniping and mortar attack.

'The Nationalists called us back to the village and said that we could stay there again,' commented one old lady, adding that some of the villagers known to be Nationalist sympathisers had temporarily left Alcedo during the previous Republican occupation, for fear of reprisals. 'The Republicans would tell us to go,' she continued. 'Once the soldiers told us that we could come back to the village. They knew the women would want to bake their bread. So they allowed us to stay for a week, then ordered us away again and we had to leave all our bread behind—for them!

'The Nationalists set up a sort of pharmacy. It was a room in my house. A doctor would come up here to attend the wounded. We got bread and sugar in return for this. The Nationalists had their positions on the *pasquinero*. There was a bitter fight. It was very cruel—an attack by the *contrarios* [Republicans]. But the Nationalists gave us things—they were better.'

'When the soldiers came,' another lady commented, 'we would hide in our houses. We shut the doors and closed the window shutters and were silent. This was when the Nationalists were looking for *contrarios*. We couldn't make a sound. Our house was made of cement [most village houses were made from stone and wattle and mud]. The bullets went through the roof, but not through the walls. We kept away from the windows. We could hear them passing by outside thinking that the houses were deserted.'

Another woman, clearly with Republican sympathies, had the following to say about this time in the village: 'When the *fascistas* came we all went out to hide in the fields or wherever we could. Sometimes we hid in our own *cuadros* beneath the houses. That was how Pablo Ramirez's wife was killed. We were terrified. Then we left. Some of us went to Abongo, others went to Quintana, to Boinas and to La Vega [all villages in the valley] to join relatives who lived there. They used to throw bombs [grenades] into the *cuadros* when they thought there were Republicans inside. It is marvellous now compared to then!'

'We tried to hide things during the war,' said another elderly woman. 'We put them in various places in our houses. But the soldiers came from villages too and they knew where to look! We even tried to hide things in the ground—but they found these too!'

'I had a crucifix,' another old woman recalled, 'I sewed it into a mattress, but when I returned after a year away, I found it smashed on the floor in the house. But I put some valuables inside a basket, including my plates and cutlery for *banquetes*, and buried it beneath a pile of manure in a very dark corner of the cowshed and that was not found. But everything else was taken!'

It was not until February 1937 that the Republicans made a concerted offensive to recapture the village and the Nationalists' positions. At this time there were about eighty Nationalists, approximately company strength, dug in on the *pasquinero*. The Republican offensive came from all sides in a massed attack. As they came through the village, they lobbed hand grenades into the barns and houses of those suspected of Nationalist sympathies. One villager had his barn blown up in this way, killing his few remaining cows.

'One woman was standing just inside her house' related an old villager, explaining that it was now the village shop. 'She was holding her baby. A soldier lobbed a grenade in, killing her instantly, but the baby survived.' They did this, according to the narrator, because her father-in-law was a *derecho* (Nationalist). Another villager, terrified by the noise, ran out of his house and was hit by shrapnel in his stomach, from which he subsequently died.

Meanwhile the main battle centred on the *pasquinero*. Bayonets were used to take the trenches and force out the defenders; the outlines of these trenches can still be seen today. There was terrible carnage. The old barn beside the *pasquinero* was, not for the first time nor the last, used for the dead. As one old villager described it:

'There was terrible fighting here—the *pasquinero* barn was literally filled with dead bodies. There were so many of them they were all burned rather than being buried. Other villages in this area were hardly troubled. Here however, it was first one side then the other—and we were punished by both.'

The remnant of the Nationalist defenders withdrew to the southwest towards Abongo and Riegada, but not before the commander of the Republican force was shot dead by a sniper from the window niche in the *capilla*, which both sides used as a redoubt. 'Yes! The bullet went right through a notebook he had in his chest pocket. It had money inside. It went right through and killed him. The Republicans had their own money you know, but it wasn't worth anything. They [his comrades] brought his body down from the *capilla* and left it outside our house on the pathway.'

The old lady who related this last incident seemed to have remarkably precise recall after more than forty years. Her account, however, was not unlike the many others which clearly lived in the memory, as if the event had occurred the previous day. Whether the body was left outside the narrator's house because it was used as a pharmacy by the Nationalists, or because responsibility for the death was placed on a house which had supported the Nationalists, she could not say. Affiliations, however, were known in the village: denunciations took place and there were revenge killings, though no one would admit that such a thing could have happened in Alcedo.

It was about this time that three civilians coming from Belmonte were caught by the Republicans trying to cross over their lines to reach the Nationalists. There were two women and a man. They were shot and buried in the *pasquinero*. 'One of the women was exhumed some months later,' said the old man who had witnessed this incident. 'She was in perfect condition—as if she was still alive. Her hair and features were almost normal. They took her away in a box [coffin] with a glass front to some place near Oviedo.' The old man's recollection was very precise in its detail of this sad incident, which still clearly moved him.

The Moors

By February 1937 many villagers had left, and many more were leaving to join relatives in the valley or further afield. Obviously they had found that trying to live under these conditions, with the constant threat of attack, bombardment and violence, was just too much. Most tried to take their few remaining cows and sheep with them, but everything else had to be abandoned. Some may have left at this time fearing persecution, or even execution, as a result of denunciations or suspicions of conniving with the Nationalists during their occupation. The villagers really found themselves in an impossible situation, and the few who persisted in staying, or who returned after a brief absence, were soon to be subjected to an even more terrifying disruption to their lives.

From February through to the end of July 1937, apart from occasional shelling and sniping, the Republicans held the village and the *pasquinero* and the surrounding area. By early July the Nationalist forces had wrested the Somiedo region from the Republicans, and by mid-August they were poised to take Belmonte, the last major Republican redoubt in the region. In early August, however, a Nationalist battalion of Moorish troops moved on to the Alto de Riegada overlooking the village, and then commenced to advance on Alcedo.

'Riegada was black with horses and men,' was how one old villager described the scene. 'It was like a huge black mass,' agreed another. 'They wore baggy trousers with wide bottoms and sandals. They came over the top from the ridge between Abongo and Riegada. We all fled when we saw them. They killed any man they saw and many in the villages below us.'

'They wore white turbans and baggy white trousers and puttees on their lower legs,' was another description. 'They cared for no one. They killed anyone on sight, soldiers, men, women, anyone. They had no respect for women or cattle. They believed that if they were killed in battle they would go to heaven.'

'They were like animals,' was a further comment. 'They killed all the men they could find, raped the women, stole all the animals and terrified everyone. Many took to hiding in caves and rock shelters, but the Moors hunted them down with their dogs. I was standing on my doorstep. They were going to kill me, then they left me alone.' This, the narrator explained, was because an officer told them not to, presumably because he was a known Nationalist sympathiser. It would seem however that he was fortunate, for according to other accounts everyone was subjected to violence, regardless of allegiance, even children.

'Franco shouldn't have done that,' the old man continued, alluding to the Nationalists' habit of of sending in their Moorish troops to carry out a scorched earth policy and then disclaiming responsibility for their barbarities. 'They were brought over by Franco for the victory celebrations you know. He was surrounded by them in his open car. They were all mounted on beautiful horses. They could have turned on him too.'

Another villager maintained that the Moors had a grudge against the Spanish because they had once been conquered by them, a reference to the *reconquista*. 'They broke into houses and smashed everything that they didn't want,' he continued, 'but they didn't burn the houses here as they did in some other villages.' The Moors set up their camp just below the village for a short while before moving on. During that time they ransacked the village for everything that they could find and particularly food. 'They just took the maize cobs and built fires in the *tierras* below the village. They put the cobs in the fire and ate them, all burnt just as they came out—terrible people!' Evidently there were still some Alcedans around who were in a position to observe Moorish culinary habits.

One person summarised the various invaders' tendencies in the following terms: 'The Nationalists took the cattle belonging to those they suspected of having Republican sympathies; but the Republicans also took cattle. They would slaughter them outside Casa Genero, in the centre of the village. They also stole cattle from elsewhere during the night. But the Moors took the sheep. There were no cattle left in the village by the time they came. They would roast them on a fire and eat them half raw. Villagers managed to sow *escanda* in isolated places, and baked bread and kept it in places where it wouldn't be found. Others came to the village to work for nothing, just for something to eat. Nationalists and Republicans were no better or worse than each other, but the Moors were animals—they were savages!'

For much of the thirteen-month period of occupation by one or other side in the conflict, the women were afraid to go into their gardens, let alone their *tierras*, to cultivate or collect food, for fear of being shot. As one eighty-year-old put it: 'We mainly ate *berza* and drank milk—as long as we still had cows. There was little or no salt. We just couldn't get to our gardens to cultivate.'

Yet presumably it was to the advantage of the occupying force to enable villagers to continue to work their cultivations, as this would ensure a supply of bread and vegetables. This seems to have been the case with other village communities in Spain where there were occupying forces in their vicinity, though there is relatively little information on this period in the literature. There do however seem to be differences when comparisons are made. Most communities were united in their allegiances or better able to make compromises (see for example Freeman 1970: 23-25). They do not seem to have been so consistently occupied, or subjected to so many periods of violent conflict, or to have to cope with alternate forces of occupation, or be under continuous sniper fire by the side not in occupation at the time. However there is the possibility that communities have chosen to forget these times, or are still wary of making comments on these matters, even after more than half a century has passed.

Although I never heard any report of a villager actually dying from starvation, there were frequent allusions to extreme hunger. As one old lady put it: 'There was very little food. There were few potatoes as they were taken by the soldiers. Sheep and goats were stolen. They even took the chestnuts—we were not allowed to gather them for ourselves.' It seems that the worst time of deprivation, for those few who had remained in or near the village, was during the Moorish occupation from August till mid-September 1937, when from all accounts any form of exchange was out of the question.

In about mid-September the Moorish troops moved northwards to the other side of the Cauxa valley, an area until then relatively unaffected by the conflict, where there were still pockets of Republican resistance. A villager, who had been about fourteen at the time, had herded sheep there during the Moorish occupation when Alcedo was abandoned.

'The Moors moved into the Ferradel area one night and killed many people—women and children as well—but they met resistance from the Reds and I think they were all killed.' There are however variable accounts regarding this last heroic act of resistance and it is possible that not all the Moors were killed on this occasion. What seems to be corroborated by all accounts is an attack by the Moors on La Roxada. This was confirmed by a villager who was in the vicinity at the time.

'A battalion of Moors marched on the peak above Ferradal called Roxada. Only three Republicans were defending it. They were in a good position at the top of the peak. They had machine guns and many grenades. They waited until the Moors were well exposed and then just machine-gunned them down and then threw their grenades. Those who survived retreated and left the mountain.'

This was the last action of the war in the region. About three weeks later the

Asturian Republican cause ceased. If this story has any basis in fact, which I think it probably must have, it was a remarkable victory over the odds and happened, ironically, just when the Republicans of the north were finally defeated. In a strange dissimilitude, but under precisely these conditions, Pelayo changed the course of Spanish history from his Asturian mountaintop retreat through the *reconquista*. If I have any doubt as to the story's veracity, it centres on the suffering these Moorish troops had inflicted on the local populace and how in their apparent annihilation a form of justice was wrought. Thus the therapy of myth creates a rhetorical coherence to all our lives.

A refugee's story

At one time or another all the villagers were refugees: some for only a few months, others for a year or more. Where they went and how they managed to exist is all part of the collective history of the village. Sooner or later most of the women and children who survived, returned. The following account is by a woman who left the village at the outbreak of hostilities when the Republicans were still in control, prior to the attack by the Nationalists in September 1936. Her husband had already been drafted into the army and her travels were undertaken with her seventy-year-old mother and her three children aged eight, three and one and a half. It should be remembered, and it was continuously asserted, that at this time very few women had travelled far from the village and certainly not as far as Belmonte. Even in the late 1970s there were some older women who had never had any call to go beyond the parish boundary. For the men it was different.

'When the Reds first came there were only three able-bodied men left in the village. [This was at a time when the village population would normally have still exceeded three hundred]. After about two weeks the Reds wanted us to leave the village. So the women formed a council. They asked me to be their spokeswoman. [This she said was because she spoke better Spanish than the other village women]. I approached the Captain who was in charge to ask him if we could be allowed to stay. He was very sympathetic to begin with and listened to me. But then all the women started shouting and saying that they would not leave their houses. The soldiers then came and beat many of us with their rifle butts and stripped some of us naked. The officer did not prevent this. The shouting and screaming could be heard from far away.

'Many of us women went down with our children to pass the night in the millhouse in the valley as we were terrified. I tried to intervene but the soldiers kept telling us that the Moors were coming. [In fact the Nationalist militias were coming. The Moors did not come until a year later]. The soldiers were putting all our cows out of the *cuadros*. We stayed two nights in the mill and the soldiers came. One of them wept when he saw us. He said his mother came from a village like ours. There were also women from Abongo with us there in the mill and they also had their children. They put the cattle out because they thought the Moors were coming and they would come to less harm. When I left mine they were in a meadow. I never saw them again. We left our houses with nothing, only the clothes we were wearing at the time.

'The next thing I remember is that we were all fleeing. We were running down the valley alongside the river, I with my mother and my three children, towards Boinas in the valley. I was carrying my youngest child to protect him from the shooting—anyway he was too young to run. Bombs were hitting the ground and rock splinters were flying everywhere. [This would have been the first Nationalist attack on the village]. We made our way to Los Estacos [a village in the next valley to the east] and stayed there in a house which belonged to some relatives. But there were already eight more people living there and no man to help, and they could only look after their nearest relatives which did not include us. After a week or so they said we would have to leave. But my mother had a good friend in the village so we went there, and they welcomed us with open arms. We helped them by picking *escanda* [this would have been in September].

'I went down to Belmonte [a Republican stronghold] and through the help of a lady in the local government offices, who had tears in her eyes when she heard our story, I managed to get some rations, like oil, meat, sugar, salt and vouchers and other things. I brought these back in a big basket to Los Estacos.

'Then the fighting came to Los Estacos and we left for Belmonte. We stayed in a house that belonged to people who had emigrated. People were very friendly. They brought us blankets and straw to sleep on. While there we were offered a house which belonged to a Nationalist family which had fled. But it had already been damaged and I didn't want to be held responsible for it should they return. So I refused.

'At this time my mother wanted very much to return to Alcedo. She mentioned this to the mistress of the Republican mayor, and she told the mayor who was angry about it. I had to explain that it was just an old woman talking who did not understand the implications of her wish [Alcedo being at that time held by the Nationalists]. I was very alarmed at the mayor's attitude and I decided to leave and go on to Mieldes where my husband was born and where his relatives still lived. We started to walk up the Pigueño valley, but we stopped over with two old spinsters who were sheltering in a *cabaña* [field barn]. They had some food which they shared with us. A Red official found us there and took us up to his command post where there were a number of soldiers. He was very suspicious of us because my mother said once again that she wanted to go back to Alcedo. But the officer in charge was sympathetic towards us. Some of the soldiers knew Alcedo and were friendly and they gave us some food. One recognised my profile as being like that of my sister, whom he knew. We were allowed to go on, in the company of the official, to Mieldes where we stayed until we were able to return to Alcedo after the fighting was over [in October 1937].'

The soldier's tale

This brief account is related partly by the former soldier himself and partly by his father. It is an example of father and son being in different political camps during the war. At the outset the son was a convinced Republican; the father was a convinced Nationalist and admirer of Franco who felt that Spain would not recover from the dictator's recent death in 1975. The son's account was as follows:

'At the beginning of the war men came up to the village to enlist all of us young men, that is those between the ages of eighteen and forty. All the men in this village joined up with the Republicans. We were all Republicans at the beginning. I went everywhere. I was in Valencia in the south at one time, in León at another and even in Portugal. I was wounded in the fighting.

' I never killed anyone, at least not to my knowledge, as we were always firing at a distance. Sometimes my comrades were obliged to become part of impromptu execution squads. They used to say, "one to tie, one to shoot, one to dig the grave". Many prisoners were shot on both sides. On one occasion near Zaragoza, a large number of us were captured and shot by the Nationalists. I managed to hide under a pile of wood. They were the old floorboards of some house. I managed to escape. But all those with me were shot. We were all prisoners. It was a crime—but it went on a lot.

'At one point we were really dying of hunger. We came across a cart full of melons going to market. While some of us talked to the vendor, a boy, others took the melons. Eventually we took all the melons while the boy was crying for his mother. On another occasion we came upon a house at night. The wife came to the door thinking we were Nationalists. When she saw us she shouted to her husband, '*Los gorros!*' [The *gorro* was a cap used by Republicans.] Her husband fled from the house and up the hill at the back—and left her all alone!'

The ex-soldier, a very tall, gentle and taciturn man, never explained how he was wounded, or why it came about that he changed sides, becoming a Nationalist in the latter part of the war. This was left to his father who recounted these happenings in the following manner:

'Miguel was wounded. He was badly wounded by a smoke [or flare] bomb which he was carrying. It blew up on his chest. We heard no news of him for a long time. We thought he was dead. He was on the other side of the Nationalist lines beyond Oviedo.' This was the time when Oviedo, the capital, was virtually surrounded by the Nationalists, which effectively cut the Asturian Republican resistance in two. 'A priest saved him. He was a relation and a friend of someone who lived in Quintana [the village just below Alcedo]. He managed to get Miguel to a hospital. Then he personally brought Miguel all the way back here to the village, because he was afraid that he would never get through on his own.' This was a very brave thing to do as a number of priests were shot in Asturias by Republicans who suspected them of Nationalist sympathies.

'Miguel was nursed back to health here in the village by my wife and his terrible wounds healed.' He still bears the scars across his face and chest. 'When however he was better he was once again called up, this time by the Nationalists. They came up here to take him.' This would have been in late 1937 when the village was no longer occupied. 'He then had to serve the Nationalist cause for many months.'

It would seem that the ex-soldier did not benefit from changing sides. Nor did any of the other villagers, who suffered a similar fate. As he later commented: 'The Nationalists got pensions after the war and their wounded got compensation too. But we Republicans got nothing. We were on the wrong side. Now it is better. We all get pensions!'

The aftermath

Miguel's experience was not peculiar. Most villagers found themselves in a similar position, as did this elderly man when he spoke briefly of his war experiences:

'I was away from the village for forty-nine months in all. I was with the Reds for nine months. Then I was captured and was put in a concentration camp. After that I was placed in a labour battalion. Finally, I spent two years with the fascists.' He was perhaps lucky being away for only four years; others were absent for as many as ten. Several villagers maintained that a number of men never returned, although I never came across a family which admitted to having lost a member in this way. Perhaps it was better forgotten.

Resumption of normal life in the village was not easy. There were no draught animals; gardens and *tierras* were in an abandoned state with no seeds or tubers to initiate replanting. Above all there were at first no able-bodied men to work the land; and when they did start returning there was a constant fear of reprisal. Some villagers maintained that the Moors returned after the war, but this was a very small delegation, as explained by one woman whose husband had been the village *vigilante* at the time of their visit. She said that she gave them some food and drink, adding that she was very frightened by them. Their mission seemed to have been a passive one, but on further enquiry at another village, a young man who had heard of this return was very direct in his response:

'It was not the Moors who came back but the Falangists [Nationalists] who after the war came through the villages asking for Reds and then shot them. Earlier in the war,' he added, 'the Reds searched out Nationalist families and shot them. Thus, this was a reprisal.'

Even in 1978, over forty years on, some people were careful about what they said and seldom mentioned anything in the hearing of other villagers about their experiences during and after the war. Others were, however, more open. One old man who, unusually for Alcedo, had been a miner, was quite forthright in his views:

'We had fear with Franco and there were many informers. They would come to the village and then report on you. Within your own family it could happen. No!

we had fear. A mouse couldn't move. It was all dry [here he indicated his mouth]. Our mouths were sewn for forty years. We couldn't open our mouths or we would be hung or tied up—and then two shots. What kind of person is that? When a mouse cannot move? We couldn't strike or anything like that. The police would come immediately. He [Franco] hated his own mother, you know, and his brother. He was a dictator—like Salazar.'

It was noticeable that when the first free elections came in 1978, many of the older people were reluctant to vote. For some of them the last time anyone had done so was in 1936. Since that time there had been some local elections, but as one villager explained: 'It was an open vote or ballot. It was not a secret one as now with an elected government. It was therefore known to others whether you were voting to the left or the right. The army knew. Your neighbours knew. People were shot for expressing left wing sympathies. It is for this reason that many will leave a blank paper, even if they go to vote. Particularly the elderly who remember all this. They are still afraid. Many were denounced by neighbours and shot. Many people were killed in the village[s] during the civil war—many!'

Some took revenge into their own hands and, lacking guns, they would tie a man's hands in front of him and beat him to death with clubs and sticks. Many were said to have died in this way. No one however was named, nor was it ever even indicated that any Alcedan villager had been put to death in this way. As one elderly woman said:

'There were many things I knew about my neighbours: their attitudes and things they did, but we never spoke of these things to anyone. Others did in order to settle old scores, as a result there were many killed, not only during the war but afterwards through vengeance. By and large, however, people here stuck together, and there was very little of that sort of thing. There was so much hunger we all had to help one another. There was little time to settle old scores.'

After the war when they started working the *tierras* again, they would find old shell casings and bits of metal everywhere. Grenades, Mauser shells, bullets and even mortar bombs, some unexploded, are still being dug up. As there were no animals at that time everything, from the hay harvest in autumn to the winter manure for the fields and *tierras*, had to be carried by hand. Even the frequent moving of earth up the slopes of the *tierras* had to be done with baskets on their backs. They had little time to engage in recriminations and in a sense they had all already suffered too much. They just wanted to forget and to help each other to survive: an ethos which still prevails.

Then there was the plight of the refugees. As one villager described it: 'Miners with their families, children and all, would come to the village begging for food. Many would go to work in the fields to help where they could. They would arrive in winter without shoes, just barefoot in the snow.' All the mines were closed at the time and they had no work, but the villagers had very little to give.

'There was really very little to eat and food could not be bought until about the

1950s,' said another villager. 'There was no salt, sugar, oil or tobacco. We were able to grow things of course, but a quota had to be given to the local government in Belmonte. There was terrible hunger everywhere. Miners had to work without food. Their children came to the village to beg. Many died of hunger. Miners who were relations or friends stayed in the village with us at times. People would kill for food—they were that desperate.'

Then there was the position of the church. It has been said that many Catholic priests lost their lives in Asturias during the war and many churches were burned and archives destroyed deliberately. Not all priests were Nationalists by inclination, but villagers tended to associate them with the right wing of Spanish politics. As one person, though too young to have been a witness, described it: 'After the war the priests tried to enforce religion in the villages. They had a lot of authority. They were, in a sense, agents of the government and people around here did not like that. Now it is better and religion and politics do not go so much together and people do not mind the church so much. Things are changing a little.'

As another villager put it, summarising the changes which had taken place since the post war period: 'In those days after the war we were like animals—like mules. We had to carry everything on our backs. Now we have animals to do the work for us and we live much better than we did then.'

Plate 21 Field barns or *cabañas*

Chapter 12

Natural religion

They [the priests] want us villagers to go and live in the sky while they look after the earth.

The majority of Alcedans are sceptics concerning established religion. The church, and more particularly the priesthood, is frequently the butt of colloquialisms and asides. There are those who, though not devout Christians in a strict sense, are nevertheless sympathetic to the church; and a few may be true believers. Their belief however is tempered by the awareness that religion is also politics. To be in accord with the church, in the eyes of most villagers and particularly the older generation, is to be associated with the right and the Nationalist cause during the civil war. However, their scepticism is balanced with realism, and the orthodox *rites de passage* are still mainly observed. Most babies are baptised and children confirmed, because formerly a couple could not be married without this certification, civil marriage being a recent introduction; and at death the church celebrates the last rites for all.

Before the civil war the church had a strong representation in the mountain villages in this region of Asturias. Alcedo itself was one village in a parish of eight similar communities with its main church and resident priest in Quintana. During the civil war this system, with the various parishes in the area centred on the regional capital of Belmonte, was disrupted. Church property was confiscated or desecrated; registers, rolls and archives were destroyed; and in some cases churches were burned, including the church in Belmonte which was virtually razed to the ground, a new one being built some two decades later. The priests themselves for the most part left to seek sanctuary in Nationalist-held areas of the country. After the war the old system was to some extent re-established, reinforced in some cases with the backing of the *guardia* (police), a fact bitterly remembered by many of the older generation. However it never held sway as in the past, partly perhaps because the attempt at enforcement alienated villagers. More recently, the old parishes in the region were for the most part dissolved in favour of a centralised system in Belmonte from where priests visited their respective districts. Improved roads and transport, church economics and fewer young men taking up religious orders were contributory factors in these changes. In addition the move toward centralising education in Belmonte as a result of the declining rural population meant that the young were more immediately accessible for some form of religious instruction.

This was the situation in the late 1970s when five priests were in residence in Belmonte. Since 1989, owing perhaps to the younger generation of priests preferring to work in deprived urban areas, the Belmonte precinct has been the responsibility of one sole priest, who oversees the whole of the upper Pigueño valley with the assistance of an elderly colleague. It could be said that the church's role has greatly diminished; however the villages themselves, over which the church had jurisdiction, have been depopulated dramatically and some no longer exist. The attitudes towards the church of many of the older villagers are influenced by its dominant position in their lives before the civil war, its demise during the war and its subsequent attempts to re-establish itself in the region. The younger people do not see the church in the same way, but tend to view it as part of the new modernism associated with the post-Francoist socialist government. In losing much of its former influence, the church has perhaps gained some acceptance among those most opposed to it: the older generation of villagers who once had to cope with the impositions it placed on their lives.

Underlying this orthodox relationship, there remains a strong if tenuous substratum of concepts, ideas and beliefs in part influenced by the church and in part by a naturalistic philosophy. This was passed down over the generations from a time when orthodoxy held little sway in these remote regions, and was still apparent, particularly among the elderly, in the late 1970s. These beliefs and philosophical ideas, essentially heretical to the established church, formed a bedrock of spirituality associated with various natural phenomena. They concerned trees, water, plants and animals and were intimately related to health and illness, bodily cycles and curing. Associated with these ideas and lending them texture and stability were the rhythms of the natural world: the seasons and the cycles of seeding, growth and harvesting of crops.

However, like the orthodox religion in which these traditional philosophical ideas found a counterbalance and an opposition to sustain them, natural religion is also becoming a thing of the past. The introduction of mechanical techniques for farming and transport, the cautious use of chemical fertilisers, the replacement of internal reciprocity with money-based market exchange and not least the advent of television and telecommunications, are all taking effect. This is particularly so among the young, many of whom now regard these earlier ways of thinking as merely archaic and quaint. The sections which follow all have a bearing on what older Alcedans regard as important in their philosophy of *naturaleza*: the old beliefs.

Green and water, bread and moon

The power of green, its *fuerza* or force, is frequently alluded to. As one villager explained: 'You cannot give recently procured green vegetables, fresh grasses, or anything of that nature to a cow just after calving. Not for the first few days anyway, as it is very strong and is very bad for them'. The green leaves of maize are also considered to be very strong. This is the reason they are stooked in the *tierras* and left for two to three weeks, so that the leaves discolour. Villagers consider that even handling the maize stalks after cutting can cause illness or infection, particularly to children. Some equate this strength to the colour, others to the dampness, of the leaves.

Sheets and all other white textile items, such as tablecloths or handkerchiefs, are placed temporarily on green grass so that the green and the dew draw out all the stains and make the linen white before it is dried. A menstruating woman should not go near any green plants or grasses. Even the branches of broom used as fuel for the baking ovens and green vegetables in the garden are avoided, including potatoes as they have green leaves. She may collect a few leaves of winter cabbage, but only from those plants on the outside edge of the garden as it is inadvisable to walk towards its centre. It is not the plant which is in any danger or can be damaged by this proximity, but the menstruating woman, who may become ill.

Water can have both beneficial and detrimental effects. In Chapter 10 I have referred to some of its beneficial attributes when for instance spring water is requested by those about to die; it is also credited with remedial qualities. If a person is not feeling well, explained one villager, or suffering from some illness, water, especially when taken from its source, can be very beneficial: 'It gives you a good appetite'. It is important however to drink it from the source. It is possible to bottle it and bring it down to the village, but 'if taken that way it is not quite the same'. Emigrants returning to the village after half a lifetime away will seek out these springs to drink the water they remember from their youth. The higher the source of the water the better; the springs issuing from Manteca especially contain great *fuerza*, and are said to be life-giving and even spiritual in essence.

However water from nearer the village, if used externally, can like 'green' be most harmful, particularly if a person is not well. 'When you have a cold or are ill,' said one village lady, 'you should not get your hands wet, or your face, let alone your body. You cannot wash clothes or anything like that. You just have to remain dirty.' Another woman said that you can wash your face, but no more. Equally villagers firmly believe that you should never take a bath after a meal, which they say can kill you. 'Our bodies are like wood,' said an old lady. 'Wood likes the sun. Water is bad for it, or rather too much water. It rots it away!' This body and wood analogy is often used, particularly with reference to water.

Maize makes good bread: solid and sufficient. Rye also makes good bread and was once widely used, but it does not rise well. *Escanda*, however, makes the best bread. It is nutritious, lasts a long time, tastes better than maize or rye bread, and when baked rises well.

Just as hay from south-easterly facing fields creates strong calves, so *escanda* is believed to create healthy babies. In fact, villagers' perceptions go well beyond this merely transformational concept and for them breadmaking has overt metaphysical connotations. In the 1970s when they still grew *escanda* the whole process, from the careful picking of the heads by hand to the burning, winnowing and milling retained an almost reverential aspect. Indeed, the actual breadmaking process—the preparation of the dough, the adding of yeast, the wrapping of the dough in blankets to rise in special wooden troughs—all these processes were considered analogous to the conception, birth and growth of a child. The completed loaves coming from the various household bread ovens were described as *mozos*.

While the sun is considered to be beneficial to growth, seeding takes place preferably in the period of the *luna menguante* (the waning moon), as does the slaughter of animals. It is said by villagers that at other times the meat is not so good, the skin of the animal cannot be removed with such facility, and the salt will not penetrate so well when the curing process takes place.

Wood, the seasons and blood

Alcedans frequently make allusions to wood. Understandably they have a fundamental and wide knowledge of trees and the wood they produce. Their durability, flexibility and other qualities are known to all. They maintain for instance that chestnut wood, incorporated in buildings hundreds of years old, has greater durability than oak.[42] Until recently everything villagers used in their various rural pursuits, from agricultural tools and yokes to ploughs and carts, were made of wood. Not all of these were made from chestnut, but it was the preferred wood for everything from clogs to the proverbial *graneros*. Although there were specialists in particular crafts, such as the making of the Roman ard and the wooden cart, and the village blacksmith forged the metalwork for billhooks, axes, forks, shovels, scythes and sickle blades, the men crafted their own shafts and handles for these items. They also made hoops for harvesting chestnuts, hay-rakes with fire-hardened teeth and supple yew wood shafts, small wooden flutes and a variety of other products in daily use. All of these were finely made and the men would take pride in their display, often placing their tools in extended racks or hanging them from wall fixtures outside their houses ready for daily use and resembling some museum exhibition of rural craftsmanship.

Trees and their various qualities and utilities would frequently come up in conversation, perhaps more for the anthropologist's benefit than the villagers' own. Their frustration however was manifest when they spoke of the desecration of magnificent chestnut, oak and walnut groves cut down by absentee owners raising capital for their new urban interests. These people seemed to have forgotten the old tradition of respect and reverence for the tree. There were the jokes and innuendoes about wood itself, some of which had erotic overtones and which could only be fully appreciated by being conversant with the graining, knotting, colouring and other characteristics of different types of wood.

Village landscapes in most parts of mountainous western Asturias have their characteristic *tierras*, gardens and clusterings of dwellings with proximal extensive woodlands. Some of these woodlands may be natural forest covering vast tracts of mountainside and valley, while others—the stands of walnut and chestnut and the orchards of fruit trees—may be cultivated and cared for by generations of villagers.

Bordering the fields and meadows are the stone-walled and well-maintained hedges and the pollarded willow, poplar and ash, the cuttings of which are fed to animals before the *matanza*. Whenever other work permits the farmer will maintain his property, so that the visual effect of the locality is one of neatness and order.

There is always a time of year or a period within the month when it is considered better to cut and prepare the products of wood. June is the best month for making small wooden whistles and flutes. Sticks and cudgels are made when the wood has reached a certain maturity and at a particular phase of the moon. A basketmaker can only construct his baskets from hazelwood and willow during the late autumn and winter when there is less sap.[43] There is a time when ash wood is at its best for making clogs; for grafting fresh chestnut branches on to the older trees; for cutting the bracken for the winter bedding; and for collecting broom for fuel. It is important to be able to bind the broom into bundles for carrying and this is always done during the waning moon. At any other time the broom will snap when being used to tie the bundle, but during the waning moon 'it is always supple,' a younger villager assured me. 'At that time it is just like string and it never breaks.'

Knowledge about trees, plants and shrubs and their association with seasons and moon phases is part of a practical and metaphysical association with the individual's health and well-being. There is a symbiotic analogy between the human body and the plant life around it. As one old villager put it, 'The trees are sad when the leaves fall, because they are like us. They come to life, they grow, and then they die like us. They have spirit like people.'

'We are like the plants of the earth,' was the rather more prosaic comment of another elderly man. 'The animals are like us too, like plants of the earth. Men are like nature. When the sap slows in the trees, so the blood slows in our bodies. When it begins to run again in the spring, so it does with us.' This old man went on to comment that in summer he got up at 4 am, well before dawn, and worked all through the daylight hours until about 9 pm. He said he did not concern himself overly about food, but ate normally. In winter, however, he got up sometimes at eight or nine in the morning, went to bed early and ate more than in summer. 'This,' he added, 'is because the blood is sluggish and needs food to fortify it. In summer it is running fast and there is less need.'

It is the transition of plant life through the yearly cycle which, by analogy, influences the well-being, both physiological and psychological, of a villager. This may be partly explained by their concept of the relationship between sap and blood. If asked to explain this philosophical, even religious, conception of life villagers will rationalise these feelings and ideas to the calendar year and pinpoint particular months regarded as in some way 'critical'. It is not so much the dead season of winter, or the living season of summer, but the transitional periods between these states of nature which are important.

March is considered the most dangerous month for the elderly, when everything including humans, plants and animals is at its weakest. So it seemed in March 1979, for nearly the whole village went down with various ailments in the course of the month. It was noticeable at the time that very little work was being done in the fields, and that the village remained quiet. The animals were being fed, but little else happened. I enquired about this and my observations seemed to be confirmed by a villager.

'Yes, most of the village is down with fever. It is the time of year for this. It happens every year. It is the time of year when the bad blood has to go out of your body. It always happens—every year', he repeated, adding: 'You have to change your blood and get new blood for the spring. You get rid of the old and you are renewed. The whole body is renewed.' He then added that it was the same in November, but not so bad then. 'Now [March] is the bad time. It is also a bad time to kill animals.' On being asked why this should be, he replied that he did not know, adding: 'But no one does it—in the abattoirs, yes—but not here.'

Despite this comparison, others felt that November was the time of death, not just for plant life but, as one villager put it: 'the time of human death'. As indicated in Chapter 10 there seemed little evidence that this was actually the case, yet the belief was prevalent among the older generation. An old lady said, 'When the leaves fall it is a bad time for the elderly,' and she went on, like others, to draw an analogy between the blood in the body and the sap ceasing to run in trees. There is also some connection here between the death of humans and that of animals at the *matanza*.

Villagers consider that blood in the human body, like that of animals and sap in nature, is 'sluggish' from November to March. They refer to it as 'cool'. Conversely in summer it is considered to run fast and is called 'hot'. A woman who was feeling her age spoke of her 'blood growing cold', even in the summer months. Another elderly lady commented, 'The blood begins to get cold in October.' A middle-aged woman corroborated this connection between well-being and blood: 'It is better in summer because the blood circulates better.' Another villager who spoke of the need to fortify the blood with 'strong food' was alluding to meat which is considered the strongest form of nutrition. After the winter killing there is always an abundance of meat. Meat therefore, and the blood incorporated into the sausages made at the time of the *matanza*, are conceived as fortifying the body by the addition of animal blood through the winter.

December is not the coldest month; January and February are colder, and in terms of the meat preservation it is possible to have warmish weather, even flies which can contaminate the meat, in December. As indicated previously, the period of the waning moon is preferred which spans and therefore disregards the orthodox Christian celebrations, and it might be impractical owing to freezing and inclement conditions to have it later. However, the timing of this rite does coincide with the critical period when the body, because of 'sluggish blood', needs strong food to survive the winter. This coincidence seems to bear out the primacy of blood in villagers' beliefs.

When walking among his trees in a chestnut wood a villager spoke of grafting, an old tradition which his father had taught him. It helped, he said, to retain the shape of the tree by allowing old non-nut-bearing branches to be replaced by new ones. In this way the trees remained healthy and bore good chestnuts. The pruning is done in the spring when the sap is running and he used the word *sangre* or blood for sap rather than *savia*, its botanical name. When I asked him why, he replied, 'Because trees are like people. They have their blood too.' And again like others, drawing on the analogy, he added, 'they grow, flower and die—just like us!' I asked him if these conceptions about *fuerza* and blood in humans and their analogous associations with trees and other plants and animals were widespread in Spain or peculiar to Asturias. He maintained that he was not aware of these ideas beyond the confines of the village. However, as the same sentiments were expressed by in-married villagers, it would seem that these associations must be common in the region.

A young *mozo* told me that he had been chided by a visiting *padre* for not attending his 'talks' in the village, or coming to mass. He replied that he believed in *naturaleza* or natural philosophy, like many other villagers, rather than church teaching. The priest asked him to explain these ideas, some of which have been touched upon in this chapter. He said that the priest became visibly upset and quite dismissive, implied that he was talking nonsense and immediately terminated the conversation.

Magical leaves

The evil eye is someone who does not wish you well.

There was an old lady in Abongo who used to smell so much of laurel in her clothes that we villagers would tease her. We would say when we met her, 'the witches won't be able to get to you!'

I have referred in Chapter 8 to the use of *nogal* (walnut) and *fresno* (ash) leaves being placed on barns and other outbuildings when still wet with the dew about the time of San Juan. In former times nearly every building in the village, including the fountain, would have sprigs of these leaves in prominent positions: they were placed under the eaves and along the balcony rails of *graneros*, over the entrance ways to the sheep and cow barns and even over house doors. In the last instance they could have been placed at night by a romantically inclined *mozo* for the young *moza* who lived there, to be discovered in the morning 'unsigned', rather like a Valentine card. However, sprays of leaves also signified more mundane matters such as protection of the animals within a building. If for instance a cow was not yielding milk, or was sick, a household might suspect that a neighbour had cast a spell on it and the placing of the spray would be both beneficial and a protective talisman against such a possibility. It might also be put there as a protection against the bad luck of some untoward accident, such as cattle rolling down a steeply inclined meadow or damaging one another with their horns, or being struck by lightning. By the late 1970s it was still possible to see walnut leaves placed on some buildings, where they might remain for weeks.

The custom of giving cattle ash leaves to eat, usually prior to the *matanza*, was also still continuing at this time. Considered to be nourishing and beneficial, they also gave a distinctive flavour to the meat. This custom coincided with the pollarding of hedgerows in late autumn after the hay harvest and the collecting of bracken. Villagers also felt that by eating ash leaves the cattle were to some extent protected against various ailments, which did not exclude the ill intentions of neighbours in whatever form they might take.

Ash trees are however deciduous and the foliage which contains most *fuerza* and which is utilised in a magical context for human benefit is from the evergreens, most notably the 'sacred' laurel or bay-laurel (*Laurus nobilis*). The evergreen laurel is still considered among the most potent of magical plants, and even more so if 'blessed'. Like bread, water and wood, laurel sprays were also blessed. Villagers would take bundles of the sprigs to the church in Quintana during the week before Easter. This is no longer done, but the general consensus was that these blessings took place on Palm Sunday for laurel, followed by wood, bread and water on the Thursday, Friday and Saturday respectively before Easter. If a villager had no laurel on his own holding then a neighbour would give him some to be blessed. This would be used frequently in the house and in the holdings, where each field and *tierra* should in theory be blessed with sprigs (see also Uría Riu 1976: 219).

This field blessing, though discontinued by the 1970s, was once practised by every household and considered a very important rite. The laurel sprig was sprayed with or dipped in blessed water and was then shaken at the 'entrance' of each of the *tierras* and meadows. A sprig of laurel would then be placed in the ground in the centre of each holding. As some houses might have twenty or more meadows scattered as much as three kilometres apart, and as many as a hundred different holdings in all, it seems doubtful that each would be blessed, but this is how it was described. As each one was sprayed there was a brief recitation:

> *Apartar sapos y ratas,*
> *Y toda la munición,*
> *Que allí les vaya el agua*
> *De la bendición.*
>
> Let the holy water
> Despatch toads and rats
> And all the rest.

The use of laurel in the house seems to have been just as important as its use in field blessing. It could for instance be placed on an open fire or in the kitchen stove and burnt, the smoke being thought to afford protection against lightning. It was also customary to 'pass' a newborn baby over sacred laurel to protect the child from a number of possible misfortunes. It was considered propitious against *bichos* which included biting insects, spiders, rats and more particularly snakes, especially the feared asp. Babies were thought to be particularly vulnerable during the summer haymaking when they were left in the shade in their basket cradles. Although garlic would also be placed beside them as protection, to have been 'passed' over the laurel was an added precaution.

'We used to hang our clothes over the open kitchen fire so that smoke from burning laurel leaves would scent them,' commented one old villager, who went on to say that if clothes were put away, dried leaves would be placed between the folds. Others considered scent less important than the protection laurel afforded against numerous misfortunes and accidents and although one lady commented, 'We don't believe in that sort of thing any more,' others maintained its efficacy against supposed witchcraft. A more phlegmatic old villager however maintained that there was a rather prosaic rationale behind the custom: 'We used to heat laurel leaves to put in the children's clothes—it is like using an iron which kills small insects in the cloth.' This he maintained is why laurel is still used today.

There was always a noticeable reserve among villagers about making personal remarks to or about children and we never heard compliments or deprecations being expressed about another household's children. No one would openly say that a certain child was intelligent, beautiful or handsome, let alone stupid or ugly. Children are considered extremely vulnerable to others and if an ill-judged remark was made by anyone, even if of a complimentary nature, it could easily be misconstrued.

Some of the older villagers, usually women, maintained that at some time in the past they themselves had been subjected to some form of *brujería* or witchcraft (cf. Lisón Tolosana 1979 on Galician *brujería*). In a case concerning a boundary dispute in the *tierras* a woman was accused, not of moving a boundary stone, but of extending her cultivation beyond it. A heated argument broke out and the wife of the man who made the accusation was later subjected to 'sour looks and grimaces' by the accused, whose face was quite contorted as she made as if to bite her.

'A chill went through me,' related the wife, 'and my legs and arms felt sore and when I got home I found I was covered in little bruises.' She said that she felt she had been bitten all over her body. It was only later when she sought an explanation from her husband that she learned of the violent argument with the woman who had caused her so much discomfort.

I have referred above to a newborn child being 'passed' over laurel as a protection against misfortunes, included among which may be envy. If for instance a young child is behaving strangely, it may be suspected that someone wishes it ill. 'You can feel it but you can never be sure,' was the comment of one villager. Should the child become seriously ill through suspected *envidia* or envy, she went on to explain, you can cure it by placing a cross of laurel sprigs on the floor and then, inserting dried laurel leaves between the intersections, burning them. At the same time, holding the child in your arms, you move it over the burning leaves in the sign of the cross while saying certain incantations. There are specialists called *curiosas* (who may also be midwives) who know these recitations and make concoctions from laurel leaves which are also considered effective. The women who practise this so-called *brujería* apparently know a number of methods of counteracting *envidia*. 'But,' the elderly lady added, 'you have to believe in it for it to be effective.'

Many villagers say that the fear of *envidia* and the practice of *brujería* tended to disappear after the time of the civil war, even though we found evidence that they were still taken seriously by some villagers in the late 1970s. This suggested decline in the use of magical means to counteract perceived ill-doing is analogous to the villagers' changing views towards orthodox religious practice since that time. It might therefore seem from the evidence that the early imposition of Christianity may have been grafted on to traditional beliefs about the efficacy of magical methods, which gained greater force by this conjunction and orthodox benediction.

Curers

Indigenous pharmaceutical knowledge based on local plants is extensive and known to most villagers, particularly women, among whom the experts known as *curiosas* specialise in matters of general health. Men tend to have more knowledge on osteological and musculatory matters and defer to the knowledge of particular savants known as *curanderos*. There is a proximity between the curing of animals and the curing of people and villagers' understanding of animal ailments and anatomy is fairly profound. Few European farmers still retain this essentially practical oral knowledge held by their medieval ancestors; it is no longer necessary as their animals are now butchered far from the farm and modern veterinary services are available in most places in the event of sickness. However, the Alcedans were still slaughtering their own animals during the *matanza* in the late 1980s, and until recently the village was too isolated to benefit from veterinary assistance, the fees being beyond the reach of most inhabitants.

Although times are now changing the knowledge associated with the curing of animals, from the treatment of minor maladies to the setting of broken bones, has continued among mountain villagers. The practice of bone mending and curing muscular disorders is still a very important part of a *curandero*'s knowledge.[44] In fact animal curers and those who practise as village 'doctors' are usually the same people, their knowledge in one field contributing to the other. Many of the cures used on people, including incantations, are also applicable to animals. While cures may be applied by men in the case of animals, knowledge of remedial plants and herbs is usually sought from women.

Animals are not prone to the range of ailments that humans tend to suffer from, but it is remarkable how many things can go wrong and which a *curandero* may be called upon to tend. In the late 1970s there were still several well-known *curanderos* in the region. None came from Alcedo that I was aware of, although several men within the village were respected for their knowledge. Animals like humans are liable to *brujería* and *envidia*, and these cases have to be treated in ways not dissimilar to those applicable to people. A *curandero*, unlike medical doctors, does not accept monetary payment for his services; he may however expect and be given a gift. Sometimes his services may be reciprocated by the beneficiary helping him with his haymaking, *escanda* picking, potato harvesting or some other labouring assistance, for all *curanderos* are also farmers and have their own possessions to keep up.

The *curandero* is however a specialist. For minor ailments a villager will usually carry out a cure on his own or with the advice of neighbours. A common example, which illustrates the proximity of human and animal curing, is the use of *nogal* or walnut leaves as a very propitious disinfectant. For a person with an open wound, two or three leaves are placed in a container of boiling water and when cooled, the leaves may be applied directly or the 'water' is applied to the wound. This treatment is often used where professional medical advice and antibiotics have failed. For a large animal such as a mule or cow a handful of leaves will be needed for the same purpose. On one occasion a donkey was butted in the rump by a cow, its horn actually penetrating the donkey's anus and causing severe laceration and heavy bleeding. A *curiosa* in the village advised *nogal* leaves in boiling water and after a day's continuous treatment its owner reported, 'The donkey was obviously relieved by the treatment and allowed us to apply the remedy without hindrance. It was soon restored to full health.'

A young villager suffering from severe chest pain consulted a Belmonte doctor who, on ascertaining it was not a heart condition, had little advice to offer. The villager sought out a *curandero* who applied some potions to his chest and bound it up; within a few days the pain had dispersed.

Although the *curiosa* is still in some demand in the villages, the *curandero* is losing out to modern developments. With access by the new road and the increasing sale of calves providing more financial stability, villagers can now pay a veterinary surgeon's fee. When cattle accidently roll down hillsides, instead of calling on a *curandero* to repair the damage a farmer can now call up the local butcher who will pay for the carcass. Equally nowadays the local midwife or *comadrona*, like the *curandero*, is also becoming redundant within her village role, owing to the dramatic decline in the birth rate and modern communications which enable most expectant mothers to be taken to maternity wards for parturition. There is however considerable overlap of the midwife's role and that of the *curiosa* (see Chapter 7). Although the former might view her work as being of a more practical nature and more closely related to modern medical practice, she is also likely to have some knowledge about the efficacy of plants and herbs, which is the peculiar calling of the *curiosa*.

Villagers maintain that the *curiosa* has a role even today in the village and she still commands respect for her abilities and her considerable knowledge of the utility of specific plants for particular ailments. She knows the type of leaf, root, or flower required for each diagnosis and the methods of preparing them for curative purposes, including the time when they should be collected and the methods of application. She also knows the various recitations, orations and incantations specific to particular remedies. The applied remedy however is insufficient without the patient's belief in the perspicacity of the *curiosa* and a certain magical element in the process of curing.

Another aspect of the work of a *curiosa* lies in helping women who might have real or imaginary ailments supposedly resulting from *envidia*. This involvement in psychosomatic curing requires the *curiosa* to act as a go-between, that is between the supposed recipient of *envidia* and the person accused of it. This requires considerable tact, but an aspect of witchcraft may also be involved, something of which the *curiosa* herself may in certain circumstances be accused. This has been an area of undoubted sensitivity among villagers in the past.

The potions a *curiosa* may prepare can be used for a wide range of maladies. Some of the plants, especially certain flowers, should be obtained with the dew of San Juan on them (see Chapter 8). This will give them enhanced force and large quantities are gathered around the time of the summer solstice to last all year. Apart from external ailments such as burns, rashes, swellings and sores a *curiosa* can also treat throat and chest complaints, back pain, rheumatism and various internal afflications such as stomach pain, rupture, hernia, jaundice and liver problems. Among other ailments two are described which do not occur in the normal pharmacopoeia. Villagers refer to these as 'dropping stomach' and *nervios*, a form of nervous disorder. The former malady seems to be peculiar to the area and is described as 'swelling around the lower rib cage'. Local medical practitioners have no remedy for this and tend to send patients with these symptoms to the nearest *curiosa*. *Nervios* seems to affect women rather than men and its symptoms are tension, depression and insomnia. For this yellow flowers of *tilo* (the linden or lime tree) are picked in July and preserved. Taken with water they are regarded as particularly effective. Villagers maintain that people, including pharmacologists, come from a distance to collect plants from the area of Manteca, especially the yellow marigold (*calendula*) and camomile flower (*manzanilla*). This may be due more to the reputation of the local *curiosas* than to any innate quality of the local flora.

Chapter 13

Clerics and villagers

Priest: I do not believe there is anyone here who has deliberately
killed a man.
Villager: I've killed men!
Priest: Perhaps, but during the civil war.
Villager: Well, I have killed men—and so has the church.

(interrupted sermon, 1978)

This is a land of mountains, chestnut woods and bears!

(sermon, 1979)

The innuendo of the calculated remark of a visiting priest was not lost on villagers. He had no need to emphasise 'bears'. They had after all been called 'peasants', 'savages' and various other names by men of the cloth. In fact they did not mind being called bears, which with its political overtones was a rather flattering epithet. There were sadly few left in the wild and they had become something of a rarity, but villagers professed a certain admiration for these bumbling but mighty denizens of the forests. By and large Alcedans are pragmatists on matters concerning the church: a pragmatism tinged with scepticism and occasional cynicism. Most villagers would perhaps regard themselves as as being Christian agnostics. An often quoted refrain, not peculiar to Asturias but well known to villagers, may partially elucidate this:

En el cielo manda Dios,
En el palacio la reina,
Y en este mundo, señores,
El que mas dinero tenga.

In the sky God commands,
In the palace the queen,
And in this world, gentlemen,
It is he who has the most money!

For themselves Asturians have a more cryptic self appraisal which goes as follows:

Asturiano, loco, vano y mal cristiano!

The Asturian is mad, vain and a bad Christian!

Concerning San Antonio

I saw an old lady returning to the village one evening laden with a huge bundle of sticks which she had been collecting all afternoon. Her slight frame bowed down with her load, she suddenly caught sight of the *capilla* through a gap in the hedgerow above her. A momentary look of consternation passed over her face and then, almost fearfully it seemed, she removed her right hand from the precariously balanced load and quickly, almost surreptitiously, crossed herself, muttered and continued on her way. I had seen villagers cross themselves, but rarely and only in church, and I was struck by this moment of devotion. So I asked a villager why his compatriots so seldom made the sign of the cross, even in the *capilla* during mass.

'Oh! that is what the priests do,' and he laughed. 'Do you know what we say about that here? Well, we say it represents the priest's wishful thoughts.' And then, going through the motions himself, he made the sign of the cross, moving his right hand to his head and then to his stomach and then to his left and his right arm while he intoned, 'I think here—how I may provide for this—without using this—or that.'

When I remarked on the lack of processions in the village compared to those I had witnessed in Cangas and elsewhere on festival days, a young villager commented that these were never held any more. 'The young priest at the time did not like having them,' he said, referring to some years previously. 'Not here in this village anyway. He thought that the procession incorporated some aspects of the old beliefs.' He did not explain what he meant by 'old beliefs', but added, 'Anyway, the people here who took part in those events preferred San Antonio to Christ. So they were stopped because of that too!'

In fact it is San Vicente, not San Antonio, who is the patron saint of the village and his effigy stands in the *capilla*. An important festival of a secular nature takes place in the village under his name, and in village recollection has been moved three times: originally a winter festival, it is now held in August. There is also San Martín, the patron saint of the *matanza*, but neither saint, unlike San Antonio, had any hold on village sentiment.

That sentiment specifically relates to a small group of elderly village women. To these few, who included the lady I had seen crossing herself, San Antonio was more important than Christ or the Holy Trinity or indeed to the Virgin Mary, central to the Marian cult prevailing in many other parts of Spain. He seems to be pre-eminent among this group not only because he is the patron saint of animals (and, it seems, like San Sebastián, of travellers also) but because of his efficacy in local traditions bearing on the occult and curing. So closely is he allied to this aspect of village belief that when I asked a middle-aged man about this attachment to the saint he just laughed, saying, 'Some believe in *brujería*—I don't!' It is perhaps therefore no wonder that the church frowns on this connection.

'My mother, who was a *curiosa*, used to help people who came to see her by reciting the oration to San Antonio.' The very elderly lady who recalled this added that she had learned the oration too and that it had been passed down from her mother's female forebears. 'I once prayed to San Antonio,' she continued, 'for my husband, who was going on a long train journey. There was a terrible accident and his coach was the only one that was not damaged. He was unhurt. Before going on any journey I would always pray to San Antonio, even on short car journeys. We would also pray to him to make us safe from wolves. Once I had gone to Tineo with my donkey. On the way back I was supposed to meet up with two men, but they were delayed eating their supper. Then I realised a pair of wolves were following me. I couldn't see them. It was too dark by then. I just knew they were there.' On being asked how she knew this as it was so dark, she replied, 'Because their bones cracked—like dried wood. They came very close to me. So I recited the oration to San Antonio. I know it was because of this that they didn't eat me!' Then she muttered the oration in *bable* (the Asturian dialect) to herself and it was only later that another old lady gave us a slightly more comprehensible version which was as follows:

> *San Antonio de Padua en Goya natiste.*
> *Tu padre fue ajustiado, el brebario perdio.*
> *El hijo de Dios lo hayo, tres veces yo llamo.*
> *Mira a qui tu brebario, lo perdido dea ayado.*[45]

The old lady introduced the oration by referring to it as *un contrario San Antonio* (St Anthony was a Republican!) and uttered an *avemaría* at the beginning and the end of the recitation. She said that she always repeats this oration when she has lost something about the house. She has taught it to her son and her grandchildren and says it for her grandchildren whenever they are travelling.

'Before the war we used to celebrate on San Antonio's day,' an elderly villager recalled. 'We all used to go down to the parish church. We would take with us all sorts of food including sweet cakes and bread and various meats: ham, bacon, *morcilla* and *chorizo* sausages and even a *ternero*. The father of the last mayor of La Vega (a village in the valley) used to act as the master of ceremonies. There would be dancing to *gaiteros* and perhaps a *tambor*. The *mozas* would form *corros* [circles] of four and more and the men would ask to join. The girls could refuse. If a man was allowed, he would join by linking fingers [the little finger]. Sometimes another man might ask to dance next to her and she should not refuse, or she could be slapped. This could result in blows being exchanged between her boyfriend and the outsider. Sometimes very large *corros* were formed and everyone would join in. The girls would give the boys food and the boys would give them wine or cider. Then the *ternero* would be auctioned by the master of ceremonies. There would be much bartering and it would be sold to the highest bidder. He would have a year to pay off the money he owed, in time for the next festival of San Antonio. The money raised by barter would go towards paying the band of *gaiteros* and and for the wine and some would go to the church. We had a fund of money we could put aside which would help towards the festival. But then the priests said they wanted all the money to go towards the church and the festival was stopped. No one took any more interest in it.'

At 5.30 pm on Monday 18 June 1979 the priest rang the single bell on the *capilla* for the mass of San Antonio. It was quite well attended. There were eighteen in the congregation, consisting of two old men, a younger man, seven women (mainly elderly) and seven children. One of the women and a young boy took communion. The curate, a new one to the village and the diocese, which may explain the unusual attendance, sang the responses with a clear voice. In his address he spoke of a new saint just created, Maximiliano María Kolbe, of whom it is doubtful whether any of the congregation had ever heard. It was a very sober service and afterwards, outside the *capilla*, the curate spoke kindly to the young boy, who had been recently confirmed. Earlier in the day the priest had held a service in the parish church. It had not been well attended, in sharp contrast to San Antonio festivals of the past. That evening a small group of *mozos* from the village went down to a disco recently opened in Boinas. There were no other celebrations and when I asked an old lady why this was so, on what should have been an important day for the village, she replied, 'In the old days we used to go to mass in Quintana on San Antonio's day. Afterwards we would all sit on the green outside the church and eat our *meriendas*. Then there would be a *fiesta* afterwards and there would be *gaiteros* and we would dance. Now it is just a case of going to the disco and paying money!'

Alcedo is not the only community in the area with an attachment to San Antonio; others, including the communities around Cangas, also view him as their patron saint. Whether, as in the case of the midsummer 'dew of San Juan' (see Chapter 8) there is an association between the festival date of San Antonio (13 June) and pagan celebrations of the summer solstice is mere conjecture, but this is a coincidence. The saint nevertheless was accredited with powers which were put to practical use by village *curiosas*, in their role not merely as curers, but also as seers. This practice still continues, despite the humourous scepticism of villagers such as the narrator of the following account:

'There was an old lady who used to live in Mieldes (a nearby village) who, it was said, could tell where people's animals were if they were lost or if wolves had taken them. She could also put a blessing on animals, so that they would be safe. To do this she would pray to San Antonio. People used to come from all over the region to see her, from Cangas, from Belmonte, even from Tineo and of course from this village also. We would ask about the whereabouts of our animals (mostly sheep at the time) if they were lost, or if they had been taken by wolves. We would ask her for protection for our flocks, and she would pray to San Antonio.' It seems, however, that she could help others but not herself, as the narrator slyly noted, 'She would make sure that her own sheep were brought in before nightfall and if any were missing she would not ask San Antonio to protect them. She would send her children out to look for them. She would even go out herself to bring them in immediately, and they would all have to go on looking for them until they found them, too!'

It seems that seers were occasionally men (who may be called *curioso*) and that San Antonio's influence was such that his name could also be invoked for unscrupulous purposes, exploiting villagers' gullibility. The story was told of one seer, 'not a man from this village' the narrator hastily added, who used to receive 'payments' in the name of San Antonio for consultations regarding lost property. Whether to enhance his own reputation or that of his patron San Antonio, he apparently occasionally arranged for the disappearance of animals so that he could later reveal their whereabouts. His duplicity however went further than that and his own nephew finally unmasked him when he suspected that some of the lost animals ended up at market. The seer not only benefited from the client but also the sale of his property!

Shrines

There are various shrines in the region. Perhaps the most notable of these is the one at the Acebo monastery near Cangas, where pilgrims gather on 28 September each year to climb up the hillside to the shrine: some on their hands and knees. Although it is an important *vaqueiro* shrine (see Cátedra Tomás 1992: 32) and for many who come from all over Spain and even further afield, no villager to my knowledge had ever been there.

One elderly lady had an attachment to the shrine of Monserrat near Barcelona. On one occasion when her husband was visiting relatives nearby, she asked him to make an offering there on her behalf for an illness from which she later recovered. Some villagers had been to the shrine of Covadonga, from where Pelayo turned back the Moors. This, however, is seen rather more as a national memorial than a specifically religious shrine.

There are also local shrines closer to Alcedo, which seem to have been a *bête noir* in the past for the more sceptical of male villagers. They would express complete disbelief that anyone could be so gullible as to think that offerings at shrines would make any difference to anything in their lives. Most men viewed such ideas as being complete humbug.

'It is only money for the priests,' commented one in tones of complete dismissal.

'How can the Virgin help? asked another.

'No!' said a third, 'they [the priests] don't give the money to the poor, or if they do it is very little—they eat it!'

'There is a shrine above Belmonte,' observed a fourth man, 'where some women from around here go to pay money to ensure that their sons don't come to any harm during their military service. The priests pay someone to go up there and move the figures in the shrine, so that the women think they are moving of their own accord. It is just a trick!'

Villagers were equally scathing regarding the origins of and dedications to particular saints at certain shrines and even *capillas* in the district.

'A priest would bury some object or relics in a field near to the village,' related
another sceptic. 'He would put salt on them and then cover them with earth. The
salt would attract sheep and cattle and villagers would wonder what was there and
notify the priest. He would come immediately and make his discovery by
unearthing the relics and he would dedicate a new shrine to them. Lots of people
would then come to the new shrine and he could make lots of money!'

Whether the narrator knew this apocryphal tale from experience or word of
mouth I do not know. He did however maintain that such events had happened
within the parish, though he did not say where. This reflects the willingness of
some to dismiss out of hand any apparently extraordinary event which might be
associated with representatives of the church.

'After the war,' recounted a young villager, who had been told about this by his
grandfather, 'when money was short and the priests were in need of it, they would
use various methods to get people to attend mass and then by means of the offerto-
ry charge them for attending. There was an example of this in Puente Castro', he
continued, 'when on one occasion a priest there hung up a pumpkin from a tree
with a candle inside it in which he had cut out a face. He did this at night in order
to frighten passing villagers, who the next day all went to to mass.'

'The church used to get a lot of money from people who wanted to go to heaven,
you know,' I was assured by one rather sardonic old man, who frequently
expressed radical views on politics.

'But those who died never returned did they?' was a frequently reiterated
phrase of male villagers. 'So we don't know, do we? If indeed they were successful
and got their money's worth!'

'At one time, you know,' the old man continued, 'people used to go around the
village dressed up as spirits or phantoms to frighten people. They would come at
night and claim they were their forebears and suchlike. People would be terrified
and go to mass and pay for absolution. But this was before the war. Later people
had guns—and if you threaten a phantom with a revolver he will soon reveal himself for what he is!'

To confirm that this was not just idle gossip I asked a young university student,
who knew the village well, whether such stories had any basis in fact. He replied in
the affirmative, giving me yet another example of these bizarre happenings.

'There was a case in one of the villages near to Alcedo, of a *padre* who actually
paid a woman to go out in a white shroud, made from sheeting. She used to stand
near a certain crossing of paths between villages. She was a local woman who knew
all about these villagers' lives and about their recently deceased relatives and of
their recent attendance, or lack of it, at mass. As each person walked by after dark
she would appear and call out to them, claiming to be a deceased relative or ances-
tor. She would ask them why they had not gone to mass for her [the apparition's]

sake and indeed for their own souls. The unfortunate passer-by, who was usually a woman, was understandably upset and frightened and would go to the curate and ask him for a special mass for the dead person—to rest their soul and her own, for which of course she would be charged by the curate.' The young man then confirmed that this sort of thing was quite common before the war, 'when people were more superstitious and susceptible to the supernatural. Nowadays, this sort of thing couldn't happen. People are far more phlegmatic!'

'Some of the older priests, not the younger ones, even now get people to pay for their services.' There were, continued the young man, various ways in which they could do this. 'There was a case near here at Nando. It is probably about the only village around here which still does not have electricity. There is a *palacio* there which it is said was built by a curate from the money he was given by local people. Now the land about there is nearly all abandoned. He used to lend money to villagers in temporary exchange for some of their land when they got into difficulties. Then he would ask for the money back the following year. Of course, people couldn't pay him immediately, so he took the land instead, which was often worth two or three times the value of the money he had lent them.'

As if this catalogue of misdeeds were not enough there were other accusations levelled at the priests by villagers, including that of hypocrisy. Abstention in matters of food and drink was always expected of the priesthood and they were not supposed to drink alcohol at all. Yet this was often a pretence for some priests, when invited to a *banquete*, would eat voraciously and drink quantities of wine and cider which some villagers could ill afford.

Villagers and priests

Villager: (an elderly man)	Father, I want to give you three hundred pesetas. Will you pray for me to San Antonio?
Priest: (good-humouredly)	Yes I can pray for you, but as for the money, I don't know where he lives, or his address, in order to send it to him!
Villager : (disconcertedly)	But I want the money to pay you for the mass, father!
Priest:	It would be better that you keep your money for something worthwhile, and instead just come to the mass yourself.

It might be thought from the litany of adverse accounts detailed in the previous pages that all priests conformed to the characterisation portrayed through village recollection. As the above dialogue indicates, however, this was far from the case.

In its telling, by a wise old villager amused by its implicit ironies, the priest's gentle rebuff to the wealthy villager's assumption is underlined by his mockery of villagers' credulity in their (heretical) belief in San Antonio. Nevertheless, there was cause for resentment for some of the impositions of the church and amongst these was the levying of fines concerning the breaking of the Sabbath. One elderly villager said that his father was once found by the local cleric working his *tierras* on a Sunday. There was nothing particularly unusual about that as everyone did it; as his father had said, how could they not work on Sundays when so much needed doing, not least in winter when the animals needed daily feeding? Yet some women in the village were concerned that outsiders might think they were not Christians if they worked on Sundays. As it was the old man persisted and the cleric summoned two policemen. Under threat of incarceration the old man paid his fines, after which villagers made sure they were not caught.

There seemed to be a very fine line between what the church regarded as a fine or *multa* and the *bula*, that is payment for dispensation. In the first case you paid for some wrong doing, in the second you were allowed to do wrong so long as you paid for it. One woman gave an example of this in terms of close marriages within the village, something which occurred not infrequently in these rather isolated close-knit communities. Anything in the order of first or second cousin marriage was 'forbidden'; however, special dispensation was possible.

'You have to pay for this dispensation,' she explained, 'and wait up to two or three months to get it. Then your marriage banns have to be read out three times on consecutive occasions in the parish church. You have to pay if you only have them read out twice, and more if only once. And if they are not read at all, if for some reason you wish it to remain a secret, then you have to pay even more. It can cost a lot of money. It is all business.'

Prior to the war a lot of meat was eaten between Carnival and Ash Wednesday. After that villagers were expected to abstain during the following forty days unless they obtained a *bula* which gave them permission to eat meat during Lent. This naturally ran counter to their belief of 'fortifying the blood' during this critical winter period. The *bula*, which in this case seems to have been a slip of paper given by the priest, required the head of each house to pay 16 pesetas, which after the war was raised to 20 pesetas, a not inconsiderable sum for impoverished villagers. They say that at the time Lent was observed by some of them, others paying for the *bula*. For the first decade after the war few villagers had any meat to eat anyway; nevertheless these impositions were deeply resented.

A lady from Luarca on the coast confirmed that her townspeople also once had to obtain these *bulas*, but that unlike the Alcedans they did not have to pay for them. She had been particularly shocked some twenty years earlier, when *bulas* were in force, to find a group of priests eating meat at a meal on a day of double enforcement: a Friday in Lent. When she asked them why they were breaking fast on so inauspicious a day, 'They just laughed and said "It doesn't count when you are travelling!" which is apparently true.' Shrugging her shoulders she added, 'Now it is different—no one fasts.'

In the village however, it was different: there it was either the *multa* or the *bula*, and either way you paid. If it was not for marriage dispensation, it was for Friday and Lenten dispensation or for non-observance of the Sabbath. This, villagers pointed out, was when the clerics had salaries from the state, for rightly or wrongly they were convinced all these 'fines' went into the pockets of the priests. There were also the taxes levied on pigs by the unpopular figure of the *vigilante*, who also kept an eye open for breaches of religious observance. This state of affairs continued to be enforced until about the mid 1960s .

Such matters, and many examples were cited, conjured up in villagers' minds a church more interested in money than in spiritual concerns. Even now, when people are better off and could afford to give something to a church in decline, they still resent these past injustices. In the late 1980s the sole remaining priest for the whole region decided to send out envelopes to each household with villagers' names on them, requesting that they send a donation to the church. It seemed innocuous enough and no demand was intended, just a request. Villagers however felt embarrassed and resentful, perhaps because they felt their faith would be tested by the amount they gave. A few complied, but the majority refused. For them past decades of impositions and enforcements were too much to be easily forgotten or forgiven, and the overworked but well-intentioned priest was saddened by the response.

Priests and villagers

First woman:	We villagers don't really believe in the story about San José [Joseph] and the Virgin Mary—do you?
Second woman:	Nor do we really believe in heaven or in hell!
First woman:	It would be better if curates were allowed to marry rather than show a bad example.
Moza:	Christ was not married and the curates are supposed to copy his example.
Second woman:	But Christ was still quite a young man when he died.

(conversation in the village, 1989)

God is for the *padres*—not for us.

(elderly male villager, 1979)

The story goes that a detachment of Republicans, caught up in the fighting near Llanos in eastern Asturias during the civil war, were desperately hungry. They had found some flour but had no means of baking it, so they collected all the effigies of saints from a nearby church to use as fuel. 'Now we will have holy bread!' was a soldier's laconic remark. In a village next to Alcedo which had no *capilla*, a priest arrived to conduct a service in a house. He noted that there was no figure of a saint in the room, whereupon a male villager called out, 'Bring us one—it will make good firewood.'

The contrast between the women's conversation quoted above and the general attitude of male villagers regarding orthodox religion may indicate that women were better disposed towards the church than men. Some women however could be equally uncharitable. In the words of one elderly lady concerning an unfortunate priest, who understandably did not remain in the parish for long, 'We don't like the priest. No one likes him in the village. It is not that we are not Christians, just that we do not like him—we don't like his face.' Another priest came and lived in the village for eight days, but as another lady explained, 'He wanted to make the men of the village very religious, but he had no success, so he called them all "savages" and "pagans"! But it didn't matter one way or the other.' On one occasion in 1979 some villagers deliberately removed the bell rope from the *capilla* so that the young visiting priest, who wanted to summon the people to mass, had to climb on to the roof to replace it.

A story frequently told was of a novice priest in Quintana whose sermon was interrupted by a roll of thunder. Being a countryman himself he realised that the hay drying in the field next to the church would be soaked, so he asked all the men in the congregation to rake it up and stook it while he and the women carried it into the shelter of the church porch. Unfortunately, instead of the word *llevar* (to carry) armfuls of hay, he used the more explicit *abrazar*, meaning to embrace. To the congregation his slip of the tongue made it sound as if he was sending the men out to work while he 'embraced' or made love to the women. His embarrassment at the congregation's barely suppressed hilarity, and the fact that this was said on a Sunday in church, added spice to a story which has stood the test of time.

Villagers never say that a baby looks like its mother. If any comment is made they will say it looks like the father, thus acknowledging the husband's parentage. If doubt should be cast on a child's genitor, the joke is always that it looks like the parish priest: a jest reflecting general scepticism concerning vows of celibacy. One villager laconically remarked that priests are men too! Providing discretion is maintained, the occasional lapse is unlikely to become common knowledge. However if a priest should openly flout the rules, there is potential for gossip and embarrassment for the clergy.

On one occasion, during the course of his sermon, a priest referred to himself as a celibate, emphasising the difference between his calling and that of his congregation. According to one villager the words he used were 'those of you who are fathers of sons' implying that this was something he could not be because of his vows. For villagers this initiated a debate as to the rights and wrongs of what he had said, for the whole parish knew he had taken a local woman as his mistress and had had two daughters by her. Some villagers maintained that he had not spoken a falsehood because he had no sons but only daughters. Others were not concerned about the breaking of his vows, which made him a human being like the rest of them. The unfortunate man subsequently obtained work for his mistress in the precinct in Belmonte, which proved too much for his colleagues and he had to depart.

Confession was another aspect of the church which villagers found difficult. This would take place at Easter, but people were very reluctant to confess. One elderly man recalled a time before the war when all the *mozos* who had recently been confirmed were expected to attend mass in the parish church. 'Afterwards we always used to have a *banquete* in the resident priest's house in Quintana where we would tell each other all the best confessions! Now we don't confess, not at Easter or at any time. It is all *tontería* [stupidity] anyway.'

Normally priests do not stay much longer than three or four years in rural dioceses, so we were glad on our return after ten years to find our former friend still resident in Belmonte. Circumstances however had changed and he was now the rather lonely overseer of dozens of small communities as well as Belmonte itself. The villagers remarked that they saw very little of him. He was a little disillusioned and only too painfully aware of the inevitable distancing from his various communities, let alone the families and individuals within them. Even ten years earlier following his arrival there had been misunderstandings. One day in March he had come to see us somewhat distraught because no one had attended a mass he had called in the *capilla*. He clearly suspected mischief until we pointed out to him that, as was frequently the case at that time of year, the whole village was down with influenza and other ailments. No doubt his colleagues had regaled him with stories of recalcitrant villagers, their obstinacy and suspicions and not least their strange ideas concerning the 'old beliefs'. To his credit he immediately went off to visit a number of houses to see if he could help or commiserate. Even then however, with several colleagues in the same diocese, it was not easy for him to keep in frequent contact with the more remote communities .

'Most priests don't like us villagers and we don't like them,' said one elderly lady. 'Don A., however, we loved very much. He was here for some years—about five in all. It must be nearly ten years now since he left. It was because of him that we eventually got the road. At that time we had no teacher in the school, so he came up from Boinas, where he lived, every day to teach. He could go into any house in the village and have a meal. He was always welcome!'

Another villager advised us not to trust the priests. 'Don't give them anything—they are thieves!' she hissed. Then after a pause she added, 'Don A. was different. He worked on the road himself, you know, just like us villagers, and all day long too! He gave two thousand *duros* towards the road himself, out of his own pocket. He arranged for its financing with the local authorities. If it were not for him we would not have a road now.' A younger villager, who had clearly been influenced by the priest's example when a young *mozo*, expressed his opinion more succinctly. 'He worked with us and just like us. He didn't ask for money. He knew how to do things and all about farming and he helped with his hands.'

Yet pranks, humour and gossip about the church were the staff of village life so long as the clerics still had a presence. We sensed a feeling of loss in 1988 when we were told that the priest we had known well hardly ever came to the village now because of his commitments to so many parishes. It was as if the opposing side in a game had suddenly disappeared. The church's apparent dismissal of the villagers' old beliefs was countered by theirs of the central tenet of clerical celibacy. In a sense the church provided an opposition for villagers which gave them a sort of unity. Once the church ceased to be such an obvious intrusion into their lives, they began to lose the sense of purpose in their own beliefs which that opposition had provided.

Holy Week and the old beliefs

> To judge the spiritual state of contemporary people from their actions is immensely difficult; in the past it is impossible (Southern 1970: 99).

It would appear that there has been a slow erosion of villagers' old values, brought about by a number of factors and not least the church itself. Yet the essence of meaning in their lives still centres on the conjunction and disjunction of orthodoxy and *naturaleza*. The demise of the church means that the old beliefs will be reduced to quaint folk stories, mere *tontería*, just like the customs of the Catholicism described above.

'After the civil war the priests tried to enforce religion in the villages. They had a lot of authority. They were, in a sense, agents of the government and the people did not like this. Nowadays, religion and politics do not go so much hand in hand and people do not mind religion so much. Things are changing a little and it is better again.'

This view, expressed by a lucid and thoughtful young villager, is interesting for several reasons. Firstly, the implicit sentiment is tolerant, far more so than some of the views expressed by an older generation of villagers who suffered under the authority he refers to. Secondly, it is hopeful and looking to the future rather than dwelling on the past. Thirdly, it seems to suggest that 'religion' is something slightly apart which, though important, is not endemic to the village. Fourthly, it suggests a difference between the pre- and post-war church, the latter being much more authoritarian and less sensitive to local values. This last distinction has a particular bearing on what follows concerning the rites associated with Holy Week and the issue of tolerance.

In 1979 there was no special celebration or festival during Holy Week except for a poorly attended mass in the parish church on Easter Day. This was curious as villagers, especially the older generation, had always made particular reference to the events surrounding Holy Week in the past. Clearly it had been a most important event for them and they all recalled the various blessings of laurel, water, wood and bread on different days; although confusion over the sequence of these events suggested this was something which had ceased happening quite a long time ago, possibly before the civil war.

One villager, on being asked about Holy Week, gave an interesting description of the different breads the women made, and still make, for Easter Day. Clearly the religious aspects of that day were not uppermost in his mind. A young *moza* thought there were blessings made on bread and water, but she was not sure, whimsically adding, 'You can get your car blessed by the *padres* you know—for nothing!'

Some elderly women thought that the last occasion that the Easter cycle took place must have been 'at least ten years ago'. Then one of them, after some consideration, said, 'My eldest daughter [then aged seventeen] never witnessed them [the blessings], so it must have been stopped before she was born.' Why had it stopped? Some thought it was because the then resident priest did not wish to continue with the rites, the implication being that he thought Easter Week was celebrated by villagers for the wrong reasons, associated with the old beliefs. Others thought it was because the priest wanted all the proceeds from the auctioning of the *ternero* for the San Antonio *fiesta* to go to the church or, as they maintained, to himself. Others had a more rational explanation: it happened when there ceased to be a resident priest in Quintana and it was decided that all the priests should live together in Belmonte. The general consensus was that the last time these events took place was probably about 1959. Whether these were elaborate festivities like those described by the older villagers for the time before the the civil war, I was unable to ascertain. Clearly, however, the authoritarian attitudes of the post-war church referred to above did not seem to apply in the case of the events surrounding Holy Week. The visiting priest in 1979 confessed that he was disappointed over the very small congregation which attended his Easter service. He seemed to know nothing about the former festivities surrounding Holy Week, so important in the recollections of villagers.

In writing of 'festivities' I am not referring specifically to the music and dancing, games, auctioning, drinking and jollity of the Easter Sunday gatherings, matters which the church seems to have had to stop. I am referring to activity over the whole week, with the gathering and preparation of things to be blessed, most notably laurel, and the baking of bread. I am also referring to the general conviviality which such events created: the walks to and from the parish church; the meetings with villagers from elsewhere during and after the services; and not least such events as the telling of confessions, to which I have referred. Clearly there was a mood of excitement generated around this week which remains in the collective memory.

It was perhaps the concentration of minds on the celebration of *naturaleza*, symbolised by the laurel, water, wood and bread, which epitomised for villagers both the magico-curative and life-sustaining aspects so central to the old beliefs. The fact that these aspects were given confirmation by the church's blessing was accepted and incorporated into orthodox ritual by a more liberally-minded and pragmatic church and clergy, something which perhaps the new order of post-war priests felt should be changed. For them, this was perhaps also all *tontería*. It had scant symbolic reference to the church's teaching and understanding of Easter week: Christ's entry into Jerusalem; the last supper and washing of feet; Christ's death and resurrection. It also incorporated St Anthony in many magico-curative aspects of the old beliefs to the detriment, near negation, of Christ. In the light of these matters, it is hardly surprising that a newly re-established post-war authoritarian Asturian church wanted change and a more rigorously aligned orthodoxy.

It is likely that similar symbolic referents were used in the same way in many rural communities throughout Iberia and that Alcedans were no different in this respect from any others. What I am however suggesting is slightly different and concerns the sentiments underlying these outward manifestations. Where in fact did the actual spiritual affiliations of villagers lie (*pace* Southern 1970)? It is perhaps presumptious to assume that any elucidation on this matter is possible. Nevertheless, the aforementioned descriptions based on villagers' perceptions of what constituted the old beliefs would suggest the existence of a remnant of a once more pervasive tradition which still retains a certain coherence and spiritual essence. It is perhaps for this reason also that in the religious context such epithets as 'savage' and 'pagan' have been part of the clerical vernacular in describing and addressing villagers. By compiling the recollections of some dozen or more elderly female villagers, the following is a general consensus concerning Holy Week benedictions prior to their cessation.

Villagers used to take laurel (or bay) leaf sprigs to the Palm Sunday service in the parish church in Quintana. Some might take only a few sprigs, others an armful. In some rural areas in the region whole cartloads of laurel might be taken to church. If a house had no laurel of its own on its holdings, which would be unusual, then other houses would give it some of theirs. This would be blessed by the priest during mass. How this was done was not clear. This now 'holy' laurel would then, as previously described, be placed in the centre and entrances of fields and *tierras*, often being sprayed with 'holy' water. Some of it would be kept until the following Easter to use for blessings and purifications and as burnt offerings against storms. Four days later, on Maundy Thursday, sticks of wood would be taken by the men to the church.

'There was a service in the church and there was a large object like a tree with many branches,' and the elderly lady splayed out the fingers on both her hands to demonstrate the candelabra's size. 'On this tree,' she continued, 'there were many candles, all of them lit. The *padre* recited prayers and every so often he would pause and put out a candle. As the last of the many candles was snuffed out, there was a noise of sticks being broken, and also the sound of pans being banged together. This,' she added, 'was later stopped by the *padres* themselves.'

An elderly man described his own experience of this rite, which he called *tenebras*. 'On Maundy Thursday we men would break sticks. We would kneel in a circle and as the last candle went out, the sticks of wood each of us was holding had to be broken.' One villager thought that bread was blessed on Friday of Holy Week (Good Friday), but others were adamant in saying that they took water to be blessed on that day. Some maintained that this was 'pure' water obtained from a spring above the village and taken in a bottle to the service. Another protested, 'No! It was just water from the fountain, water which had been lying about for days: very dirty water!' This water, once blessed, would be sprinkled on laurel leaves, used for curing purposes and even given to sick animals. Wood was carried down to the church for blessing according to some villagers on the Saturday of Holy Week. Each villager would carry a piece of firewood to the service and after the blessing they would each put their piece of wood in a pile and make a bonfire in the church porch. At midnight on that same day (Easter Eve) the church and *capilla* bells would be rung.

There was nearly unanimous agreement that bread was blessed on Easter Day. This was apparently *corriente* or standard bread loaves made from *escanda*, though some thought that this was the day on which they used to make sweet loaves, which they still do, and one lady pointed out that 'No one does anything at Easter now, except eat sweet bread!' This blessed bread was subsequently fed to the cows. 'They yield more milk that way!' was how another villager described it.

After the Easter service, the bread blessing, and the procession around the church which followed, the festival to which I have already referred would take place. 'You did not have to go to the service,' added one elderly lady, 'but we all attended the *fiesta* afterwards!' That of course may be another reason why these events ceased, villagers regarding the Easter Day festival as more important than the Easter mass.[46]

Chapter 14

A missing photograph

The inhabitants lived in certain ways, engaged in certain occupations, kept alive certain customs, just as they are shown doing in these pages ... I have instituted inquiries to correct tricks of memory, and striven against temptations to exaggerate, in order to preserve for my own satisfaction a fairly true record of a vanishing life.

Thomas Hardy[47]

It was in the early summer of 1979 some weeks prior to the hay harvesting that, together with a working party of villagers, I had spent a day repairing potholes, ditches, bunds and bridges on a cartroad giving access to the hayfields across the valley to the east of the village. It was communal work and several of the houses with oxen and carts had joined in, although the work itself only benefited the two or three houses which had their hayfields in the area. In the late afternoon we all started back towards the village in a procession of carts, wending our way over bracken-covered moorland and between stone-walled fields. Each cart, with its complement of picks, forks, shovels, rocks and earth for quick repairs to the track back to the village, was hauled by a pair of oxen with their yokes and leather-thonged head harness, and accompanied by its owner and other household members. As we rumbled along in close convoy villagers shouted to each other over the noise of grinding axles while encouraging their animals to keep up with the cart in front. We were still about a kilometre from the village when, passing through a forested area of chestnut and oak trees, we came to an open glade still bathed in late afternoon sunlight. I had climbed a moss-covered bank overlooking the track, just to get a view of the scene, when I noticed that the whole procession had halted within that space, and that all eyes were turned expectantly in my direction. I realised with a sinking feeling that they were waiting for me to take a photograph and that I had not brought my camera. This had not been from forgetfulness but rather because of my concern that I could be causing offence by taking pictures when I should be working like everyone else: participating and assimilating as is the wont of the anthropologist.

They all waited patiently for a minute or so and then, looking I thought somewhat crestfallen, their carts began to creak forward again into the gloom of the wood beyond. Not only had I missed a unique photograph: for where else in western Europe was it possible to see such a sight in our mechanical age? but on seeing their apparent disappointment I felt rather ashamed at having let my companions down. At the time they still took great pride in their traditional mode of life and their sense of cooperation and interdependence which that scene seemed to exemplify: for them perhaps as much as to myself.

I have regretted this moment ever since. No one owned a camera in the village. On special occasions such as christenings and marriages, a professional photographer would come up from Belmonte to take the pictures, or villagers would go to a local town to have a studio photograph taken which would then be carefully framed and placed in their house. Occasionally a villager might have his photograph taken by a visiting relative, perhaps from overseas, standing in front of his prized oxen, and this might adorn a side table in the dining area. On reflection it occurred to me that this was why they wanted a picture taken at that time: as a *recuerdo* of that particular moment, a moment that perhaps they knew would not be repeated.

I have dwelt somewhat on this event as it seems to me to epitomise the particular facets of a villager's life at the time on which I have concentrated in this book. There was the sense of a form of labour and cooperation and a technology that would have been recognisable over many past centuries of rural life. The village itself and the way of life at times seemed almost medieval, and sometimes I was conscious of a feeling of living in a sort of time warp. There was really nothing in that scene that might have placed it in the latter part of the twentieth century, except perhaps for one or two T-shirts. And then there was the glade and the surrounding forest, a reflection of belief in *naturaleza*, of trees such as the oak and the chestnut in full leaf exuding force in nature and by analogy man himself.

As if to confirm villagers' consciousness in the ideal of cooperation, an incident occurred before they reached the village. The lead carter, having dumped his cargo of stones and earth in one of a number of large pot-holes in the track, suddenly started off again before the others had completed their work. One of their number called out to him to stop and to wait for them. 'Let's all enter the village together!' he shouted. But the leader would have none of it. Even if the sentiment was there, he would break ranks and not be regimented. But most of that day had been spent by men from thirteen different houses combining to repair the cart tracks of only two or three of their number, so that they could bring in their harvested hay with greater facility. Thus not only was there an emphasis on family, but also inter-family relations, extending out to incorporate the whole village: *un pueblo muy unido*, as one Belmontian had put it. But beyond that was the wider sphere of the 'parish', a term somewhat derided by other Asturians. This denoted a wider sphere of cooperation and the influence of the church. It was symbolised in the minds of older villagers by a landscape of intricately networked footpaths, a manifestation of past inter-village communication and reciprocity now falling into disuse because of the increased mobility afforded by new roads. Emigration, civil war, military service and even the absorption of village schools into the regional centre of Belmonte, has brought distant places into the village ethos, causing villagers to think of themselves more as Asturians and bringing with it consciousness of a wider tradition of nationalism.

A story much appreciated by younger villagers, which perhaps represents this nascent sense of nationhood, concerns the bandying of friendly insults among young Asturian soldiers on national service and their more southerly colleagues, the latter calling the former *vikingos*, to which the former respond by naming Castilians *turcos*. If the latter is intended to imply an Islamic past, the former points to a marauding reputation engendered by the *reconquista*, even though Asturians regard themselves as Celts.

Technology was another aspect expressed by that group of carters in the glade: a technology which concerned the essential need to have an adequate hay harvest to feed the animals the following winter, and hence the need to repair the roads by which the haycarts would have to travel. Many of the nearby villages no longer scythed their hayfields, but utilised handheld motor mowers imported from Italy; but the Alcedo hayfields were too steeply inclined for the use of these machines. Thus geomorphology is a major factor in the villagers' relative inability to adapt to new technology. Their continuing use of oxen when motorised tractorcarts had become available was another aspect of their environment, tractors being impractical in many areas for the same reason as motor mowers, though some villagers had, despite this disadvantage, started to use them.

Tradition also played a part in this conservatism. Hill farmers in western Asturias have consistently declined having their holdings 'packaged' so as to create a more economically sustainable agriculture, preferring to maintain their inherited scattered holdings. They continued to use ards for ploughing for the practical reason that they did not turn too much soil in their *tierras*. They also preferred their bread to be made in the traditional way using *escanda*. Hence no sickles or scythes were used in obtaining this wheat, but the hand-picked heads had to be singed to allow them to be flailed. In recent years *escanda* has no longer been grown as bread is made from flour which can be purchased; and indeed some villagers now buy their bread. But all these different traditional modes of subsistence are of considerable interest to contemporary prehistorians.[48]

All this in a sense describes a paradigm of village life, but it does not precisely deal with Alcedans' own consciousness of what it means to be a villager.[49] Why for instance are they so proud when their relatives and former neighbours return to visit the village, which the majority frequently do? What is that precise ethos of villageness which compels people to return, not just to see their relatives again but to partake in that essence of place, time and memory which the village embodies? There seems to be less emphasis on death and the afterlife in their daily thoughts and preoccupations than has been ascribed to their *vaqueiro* neighbours.[50] Nor indeed does there seem to be any ideal, in the Nietzschean sense, of a well formulated mythology which constitutes some unitary cultural value, unless we include a continuing belief in the old Republic and politics of the left, or in the historical accounts of Pelayo known throughout Iberia but particularly to Asturians. More important perhaps at a local level is the wit of proverbial exchange (*refrán*) and the raconteur in recalling a past which embodies collective village memory and not least the drama of civil war. Beyond that, however, is the grouping of four material elements—water, bread, firewood and laurel—symbolising major facets of village existence which over time were assimilated into church ritual and characterised by the rites surrounding Holy Week.

In a sense, most villagers are sceptical pantheists. On the one hand they hold to their beliefs in the *curiosa*, in magical plants, in metaphorical associations between the seasons and the human body, blood and sap and in the sanctity of trees. On the other hand the old beliefs in *naturaleza* are subsumed into a pervading orthodoxism. Thus everything from plants and animals to the land itself is endowed with an essence of life which may be viewed by some as spiritual, a spirituality which may extend, not so much to a transcendence or omnipotence of God, but to a manifestation of God in everything; hence God and the universe are one.

Fernand Braudel (1992: 21) has written that 'the history of the mountains [in Europe] is chequered and difficult to trace ... Coming down from the mountain regions, where history is lost in the mist, man enters in the plains and towns, the domain of classified archives'. Anthropologists too rely on archives for their research, and if this account is lacking in a firmer basis of actual documentation but relies heavily on oral accounts and observation, that is because some of us are drawn by nature to the hills and the mountains beyond, and to that sense of timelessness which they and the resilient people who live amongst them evoke.

Notes

Chapter 1

1. (p8) Both the question of lack of documentation and the decline in the population of the village require some qualification. There is no historical demographic information on the community of Alcedo in the earliest official cadastre of Marqués de la Ensenada which commenced in 1748, nor is there any other early information in other documents which I examined in various archives in Oviedo, although I was unable to consult the Simancas archives. P. Madoz's *Diccionario-Geografico-Estadistico-Historico de España*, Tomo XIII p. 310 (Madrid, 1849) contains information of a general nature on the locality, but Alcedo is bracketed with Quintana, Boinas, La Vega, etc. with an overall figure of 450 houses with information on agricultural produce. The *Estadismo de la Diocesis de Oviedo* (Oviedo, 1894) in the Archivo Historia de la Provincia again contains no specific mention of Alcedo, and only the most recent censuses (see below) have information specific to the village. In the Deputación Provincial I examined material pertinent to the monastery of Lapedo: C. Floriano's *Colección Diplomatica del Monasterio de Belmonte* (Oviedo, 1960); and a fascinating old volume, *Tumbo de Monasterio de Belmonte* (1604), which details Lapedo *foros* including fifteenth century Boinas and Quintana, but not Alcedo.

    Villagers say that in the last decade of the nineteenth century there were 50 *casas* (a term used for both house and family) in Alcedo, 45 in the main village and a further five in Tabla. They estimated that each *casa* averaged ten members (families at the time averaged from six to twelve children with the majority in the upper range). This would include paternal or maternal grandparents (depending on whether a male or female sibling had inherited the possession), the parents plus unmarried siblings and the parents' children. Taking various factors into account, including infant and child mortality, this would suggest a population in the region of 500. By the mid-1940s the number of occupied houses had been reduced to 32, suggesting a population in the order of 300. In 1970 (*Censo de la Población de España de 1970*, Tomo IV, 33, Madrid 1973) the number of occupied houses is given as 26, with a population of 124 villagers. In 1978 there were 19 households, 17 of these in the main village and two in Tabla. The precise population figure then was 98 and the average family size had dropped to between three and five children. In 1988 the number of occupied houses had reduced to 16 with a total population of 86.

2. (p10) These young pre-marriage groups of both sexes were common to all villages in this part of Asturias and possibly beyond. They consisted of all the younger members of a community between the ages of 14 and 21, although sometimes much older, and were referred to respectively as *mozos* and *mozas*. The 1890 estimate, based on the older generations' parents' accounts, was that there were 50 young people in this grouping. The 1945 figure, according to the recollection of those who themselves formed part of this group, was between 30 and 32. I obtained figures for other periods also which tended to confirm these estimates, together with a figure of 10 for the late 1970s. Allowing for a relatively stable age-generation ratio and an upper age limit of 80 (and allowing for some females still unmarried in their early twenties, still regarded as *mozas*, and pre-*mozo* death figures being offset by post-*mozo* emigration), the figures only served to confirm my earlier information.

Chapter 2

3. (p16) It is difficult enough to map the shape and dimensions of field systems in relatively flat country. In the extremely rugged and precipitous Cantabrian mountains, it is a near impossibility. Thus aerial photography became an extremely important utility when it was introduced for the implementation of land survey work. However, when pictures from the air are compared with fields on the ground they bear little resemblance, unless the field has a comparatively flat or horizontal aspect facing the aerial lens. Nevertheless, although distortions arise and actual

area is difficult to assess, all the fields of an individual or community are accounted for.

4. (p17) In the following sections in this chapter I shall be confining myself mainly to the situation as it was in the late 1970s in relation to the use and evaluation of the tripartite field system at the time.

Chapter 3

5. (p30) The buyer writes in a notebook the sum he has paid, usually including the seller's name and village. Normally the money transactions are completed as soon as the animal is loaded, the buyer taking out a wad of notes from his pocket and paying the seller on the spot. Should the villager have a bank account then the buyer may pay him a cheque. Sometimes a note or IOU is written by the buyer should he have insufficient cash at the time. Most farmers prefer cash at the time of the transaction.

6. (p32) There was some uncertainty in the air as to what would be the outcome of the pending election and on the confirmation of the new constitution. These were understandable concerns, as Spain had not had free elections since before the civil war, more than 40 years previously. There was also the increasing threat of meat imports from France and the Argentine.

7. (p36) These bells varied greatly in dimension and price. Sheep had very small bells but cowbells ranged from 10-20 cm in diameter and were priced around 2,000 pesetas (approximately £12). They were essential in these often mist-enshrouded moorland pastures.

Chapter 4

8. (p48) Descriptions of this yearly ritual crucial to village life are few in the ethnography. Two exceptions (both from Portugal) are those by Beamish (1958) which confirms the cooperative nature of the *matanza*, several men being required to restrain the pig, and Lawrence's (1988) detailed sociological interpretation. In a wider context Thomas Hardy describes the practice in *Jude the Obscure*. However, it would seem that Hardy, like Pieter Brueghel, never actually witnessed the event he depicts: unless the pigs of previous centuries were more docile, or the multiple restraint exercised by Iberian villagers is merely a metaphor for male solidarity or an exorcising of guilt by numbers for the pigs' demise.

9. (p50) These *graneros* are of two types. There is the *hórreo* (also called *oro*, *horo* and *hoyo* in local dialects) which is the conventional square structure supported at the corners by four wooden, sometimes stone, stanchions. Secondly, there is the *panera* with six or eight stanchions, which is rectangular. Both types may have verandas on one side or completely surrounding them. They are frequently ornamented with small rose-shaped or other carvings on the external walls. Some are said to be hundreds of years old. Other names by which they are known in dialect or *bable* are *alhondiga*, *alfoli* and *troj*.

10. (p52) It is difficult to estimate the amount of meat consumed by one adult daily. It is likely that in some houses they eat far less than an Alcedan would maintain they do. Certainly when there are guests and during the haymaking, they appear to eat very well. On the estimated consumption of 0.5 kg a day, one person could consume 180 kg a year.

11. (p53) Wooden containers, made from solid oak or chestnut, were still being used in 1978, although some houses had begun to use containers made from concrete. Villagers who had obtained these manufactured containers maintained that less salt was wasted through seepage during the salting period and that they were therefore more efficient for preserving meat.

12. (p54) Contrary to this view, which may suggest that villagers never keep their meat for very long, was a much advertised auction house sale in England in the 1980s of a 60-year-old cured ham which was still apparently in prime condition.

Chapter 5

13. (p59) For most communal events throughout the year the women would draw up a rota so that all the younger wives of the active households would prepare certain allotted foods (including breads, sweet breads, cakes and *empanadas*). These would then be amassed in one chosen house for the final cooking and baking, in which all would participate. It was customary that their joint efforts, in which they took great pride, would then be carried in procession to the place of the feast or gathering, each wife carrying and displaying her own contribution.

14. (p64) These five houses are excluded for various reasons. They include houses occupied by elderly people whose offspring had all departed from the village, or who only returned at times of the year when they could assist with the hay harvest or other essential tasks; and houses involved in dual occupation within and without the village, which were therefore only partially committed to mutual exchange (cf. Iturra 1977 on mutual exchange in rural Galicia).

15. (p66) This aspect of creation or transformation may also be found in other women's work roles; however as I have indicated this is an inherent aspect of villagers' lives and its symbolic and physiological implications tend to be offset by an emphasis on the equality and interchangeability of work roles between the sexes, influenced perhaps more by political considerations than traditional values.

16. (p67) Every house in the village has its own huge circular and domed baking oven inside the house next to the kitchen. The complex preparation of the large quantities of dough, the careful heating of the oven with broom, the time taken and its symbolic connotations (see Chapter 12) are all central to the role and knowledge of a good village wife. She is appraised on her breadmaking abilities and her shrewdness in judging the large number of loaves required by the household over the ensuing two weeks before the next baking.

17. (p67) I am here referring to the peculiar local conditions in the sub-mountain region of western Asturias. In other parts of Asturias, particularly at lower altitudes, different conditions and forms of agriculture and dairy farming prevail, while at very high altitudes along the southern border with Castile, transhumant sheep and goat herding still prevails. (See Uría Riu 1976: 83 for map indicating migration route of *vaqueiro* villages near Alcedo; also Freeman 1979 for similar conditions in Santander.)

Chapter 6

18. (p70) There is in fact a preference among villagers to name children after their grandparents' generation: the first-born son after their paternal grandparent (FF); the first-born daughter after the father's mother (FM); the second-born son after the mother's father (MF) and so on, with subsequent differing combinations of these names.

19. (p71) Several houses are named after a person who lived there at some time in the past: Alvaro, Gonzal, Marcelo being named after men; Incarna, Sabina, Honesta after women. Others may be named by some physical characteristic: a house called Sierra is situated on a prominent ridge above the village. Names like Rubio, Mata and Genero are more obscure, though the last named, a particularly handsome house, is probably an abbreviation of *generoso* or *noble*.

20. (p71) House names are important throughout Iberia as a means of identification, particularly in rural areas. However, they seem to take on a certain significance and piquancy in this part of western Asturias, which perhaps dates back to an earlier tradition.

21. (p74) Some households could have up to four generations of women, from young daughters, an in-married daughter-in-law, a mother and unmarried aunt(s), a grandmother and even a great-grandmother all living under a single roof.

22. (p78) In explaining more specific relationships within the village the term *primo carnal* signified first

cousin, that is two people of either sex (cross and parallel cousins) with a common grandparent; *primo segundo* denoted second cousins with a common great-grandparent. Among the existing marriages in the village in the late 1970s, including those where only one partner remained, there were in all approximately 30 examples. Of these six were of the order of 'first cousin': one actual one with common grandparents, the other five 'removes' with one generational difference, that is the common parent is two generations back for the male and three generations back for the female. A further fifteen were of the order of second cousin of the same generation or of one partner being one generation removed from the common parent (usually on the female side). Nearly all the others, even those from outside the village (with one exception) were of third or fourth cousin relationships: actual or removes. One marriage was very close, between a man and his brother's or sister's daughter (it was difficult to establish which). For whatever reason, villagers say the marriage was not a success.

Chapter 7

23. (p85) There is considerable emphasis on a man's responsibility in not planting what villagers term the 'seed', if a couple should be *amigos de bailar* (lovers). Conversely a *moza* should understand the facts of life and not 'frolic', think too much about dancing or be 'starry-eyed'. On birth control, despite traditional methods such as *coitus interruptus*, and the more recent introduction of prophylactics, one elderly lady was quite emphatic: 'They should sleep separately if they do not want children.'

24. (p86) As I have indicated, despite careful supervision young *mozas* do get pregnant and it can happen that the father of a girl's child does not want to marry her. She will then have to bring up the child herself with the help of her house. 'After all you can't just throw it away!' was the comment of one old lady. It is also rare that another man will marry the girl after this happens. The girl herself may feel *vergüenza* (shame), but this is a condition generally accepted by others and even if disapproved of, there is no question of any form of social retaliation.

25. (p87) Whether the need to carry a birth certificate still applies I do not know, but certainly villagers felt it applied during the time of the Nationalist government. The baptism has to be officially registered in the local government offices in Belmonte, the district capital.

26. (p92) This is an abbreviation of a well known saying (*refrán*): *De este mundo/Quieres gozar/Tienes que oir/Ver y callar* (In this world, [if] you wish to be happy, it is better to hear, see and remain silent).

27. (p95) In theory, no form of religious teaching was allowed during the time of the Second Republic (1931-39). The narrator would, however, only have started his schooling after the Nationalist government was formed at the end of the civil war. It re-established religious teaching in all schools in Spain.

28. (p97) At the end of each term the teacher would set tests for the children. At the end of the year an examination, set out according to certain prescribed guidelines, would be given to the older children. If however a student wished to go on to take the then elementary baccalaureate he would have to continue studies outside the village in nearby centres such as Tineo, Belmonte or Oviedo. A few villagers have done this in recent years, though in the 1970s most would discontinue after the village school.

29. (p97) Except for public holidays when there would be no school, lessons would start at 10 am, allowing sufficient time for children to do their morning chores about the house and farm. There would be a lunch break from 1-2.30 pm and school would finish at 5.30 pm. There was no school on Saturdays or Sundays. Apart from a prayer at the beginning or end of each day and some singing, the rest of the day, apart from half hour breaks in the morning and afternoon, would be taken up with classes. These were arranged according to a set timetable.

30. (p98) The classroom itself consisted of one large space. There was no vestibule, just a door on the

north side to the right of which was a place for the children to put their shoes or clogs. On the left was a large cupboard in which were various school books and paraphernalia needed for the lessons. On the west side of the room there were various maps of Spain and Asturias depicting physiographical, topographical and environmental features. Next to these the children's artwork, mainly watercolour paintings and pencil drawings, was displayed, and a picture of the Virgin Mary. On the east side where two large windows looked out over the valley, the *tierras* and Manteca beyond, there was a framed colour photograph of King Carlos and Queen Sofía. At the farther end of the classroom, to the south, was the teacher's desk in the centre and on the left a table with an unusable television set on it. In the corner fixed to its pole a furled flag of Spain leaned against the wall. On the right was a large movable blackboard. Arranged in the central part of the the room, which was timber-floored, were the desks and chairs on either side of a central corridor.

Chapter 8

31. (p106) These *verdes* or greens are flattish grazing areas frequently found amongst the scrub, heather and rocky outcrops of both the *monte* uplands and the lower slopes of Manteca. Usually they are no larger than a golf green, with very lush short grass: ideal for gatherings of talkative shepherds.
32. (p119) The lady added that women who were having their period at the time would not go to the rye fields. Her husband was more guarded in his comments on this event: 'We used to play bowls on the day of the *fiesta*. Later that night the *mozos* would go walking together through the village and beyond.'
33. (p120) This apparently fixed date for Carnival in the refrain and its 'beginning of the year' description contrasts with the accepted pre-Lenten description of this event. The term used is also very similar to the local term *entrudo* in northern Portugal, which Pina-Cabral (1986: 137) suggests as coming from the Latin root *introitus*. As I have indicated, refrains may be local to the village and spontaneous, or variations on better known ones which may have been published (cf. Luciano Castañon, *Refranero Asturiano*, 1977; see also Fernandez 1976).
34. (p120) Although older villagers knew of this custom, it was not possible to ascertain whether it actually took place in Alcedo in the past. Certainly the surrounding geomorphology of the village would not allow a cart to be sent careering down a slope to reach, let alone enter, the next village in the valley below without a great deal of assistance from the *mozos* who instigated this prank. Although theoretically possible it was perhaps regarded more as a symbolic act than an actuality.
35. (p122) The speaker here is alluding to fasting during Lent, and the 'taking away of meat' from which the word Carnival (Latin *carnem levare*) is derived. Although fasting during Lent has been variously observed by the Christian church, actual abstention from eating meat for the eight week period up to Easter, which the church seems to have attempted to enforce on villagers immediately after the civil war, was particularly onerous to a people whose main staple during the winter months was meat. To alleviate this problem it was requisite for the head of the household to obtain a *bula*, literally a papal bull or seal, to allow his house to eat meat during Lent. For this piece of paper they paid 20 pesetas (some said 10 pesetas) to the local priest. Apparently most houses did this until the mid 1960s, when it was stopped. Until then however it was considered sinful not to obtain a *bula*. One villager was scathing about this: 'It was just a business deal for the priests!'

Chapter 9

36. (p135) The village shop owner, who by virtue of his interests would be obliged to ask all the villagers to his daughter's wedding feast, the same number coming from outside, estimated his potential costs as being 100,000 pesetas, or 200,000 pesetas for both families contributing

equally towards the costs. At the time (1978) this would give approximate figures of £700 and £1,400: the equivalent to the sale value of one good *ternero* each.

Chapter 10

37. (p149) It is perhaps worth noting that this alleged past practice of the priests was not peculiar to the village, or elsewhere in Asturias, for it is also reported from fifteenth century England where, 'if contemporary Protestant propagandists are to be believed, the Jesuits were not beyond faking the occasional apparition so as to prove the existence of Purgatory and convert impressionable females to the Roman Church' (Thomas 1971: 596).
38. (p149) In local (village) dialect this bird was called *rachu*. In Asturian dialect it is known as *rallu*. In Spanish it is called *chotacabras* or 'goatsucker'. It is the common nightjar (*Caprimulgus europaeus*), though the red-necked nightjar is a summer visitor to the area. It is a night bird and seeks moths and insects in flight. It is seldom seen in daylight when it remains crouched motionless along a tree-branch; almost invisible because of its remarkable camouflage of mottled feathering. Its appearance and habits may have engendered superstition, hence its Spanish name and local village belief.
39. (p151) For examples of suicide rates in the general region, but among *vaqueiros*, see Cátedra Tomás (1992). The figures for these former pastoralists seem remarkably high, and I do not think they are comparable to the *aldeanos*, the more agriculturally based villagers in western Asturias.

Chapter 11

40. (p162) This quotation (1990: 287-8) from Gerald Brenan's *The Spanish Labyrinth*, refers to the October 'Revolution' of 1934: the Asturian miners' rising, 'an epic which terrified the bourgeoisie and fired all the working classes of Spain (*ibid.*: 284). It was generally regarded as the first battle of the Spanish Civil War (1936-39). The miners were defeated by a combined army force which included the Foreign Legionaries (*Tercio*) and Moorish troops (*Regulares*), hastily dispatched from Morocco by General Franco. The description by villagers of the Moorish troops occupying Alcedo in August 1937 is not detailed anywhere to my knowledge (this includes searches of several contemporaneous Oviedo and Gijón newspapers of both political persuasions, including *El Noroeste, Región, La Prensa* and *El Comercio*). For other references to Moorish troops in Asturias at the time, see MacMaster 1990.
41. (p165) Guernica, lying between San Sebastián and Bilbao, was the meeting place of the old Basque Parliament, said to have traditionally been held under a venerable old oak tree. It was deliberately devastated on Franco's orders, by bombs of the German Air Force Condor Squadron (which later bombed the Asturian port of Gijón) on 26 April 1937. This act outraged international opinion at the time and has been depicted symbolically and immortalised in Picasso's famous painting.

Chapter 12

42. (p184) When I said that in Britain the oak (*Quercus robur, Quercus sessilifora*) was in past centuries generally preferred over the chestnut (*Castanea vesca*) for the construction of ships and in larger buildings, villagers suggested that the chestnut might be better adapted to the environment of the village, that is to the higher altitude and variable climate, than the oak and would therefore produce a more workable and durable timber. Symbolically however, as in Britain, the oak (*Quercus hispanica*) is the most important and revered tree in lowland Asturias, as in the Basque country. An example of this is the outpouring of popular grief

when the famous *corbayo* (Spanish *roble*) or 'El Carbayon' in Oviedo (illustrated in C. Rico-Avello's *El Bable y la Medicina*, Oviedo 1964) after standing for centuries in the centre of the capital had to be cut down at the end of the nineteenth century. (See also Fernandez 1998).

43. (p185) Hazel wood is usually used for basketmaking. It is heated over a fire and stripped and split into lengths. This can only be done during the autumn and winter months. In the spring and summer the *grasa* (*sangre* is also used to describe sap) is too active. Baskets vary in size and cost; a very large basket (for carrying *escanda*, hay or manure) may be 1,000 pesetas (or may be exchanged for food or labour). Alcedo had a basket and clog maker, but since his death villagers have obtained their baskets from a man in Abongo, who, when not working on his holdings, can make up to three or four baskets a day.

44. (p190) A role which was also attributed to the *curandero* was that of curing snake bite. Apart from the usual procedure of sucking out the poison, it was said that they used special stones, accredited with certain magical powers. which were said to be beneficial when placed on or near the bite.

Chapter 13

45. (p195) A tentative rendering of this into more comprehensible Spanish might read as follows:

> San Antonio de Padua en gloria naciste.
> Tu padre fue ajustiado, el breviario se perdió.
> El hijo de Diós lo halló, tres veces te llamó,
> Mire aquí tu breviario, lo perdido hallado.

A translation of this last rendering may read as follows:

> St. Anthony of Padua, you were born in glory.
> Your father was executed, the breviary was lost.
> The son of God found it, three times he called you,
> Look, here is your breviary, the lost is found.

The force of such prayers may lie in the personal rendering of a particular *curiosa*: the prayer then being peculiar to that person and symbolising her power. Their apparent obscurity may be due to their derivative nature and constant repetition with no means of substantiation with an orthodox rendering of a recognised prayer in the liturgy (cf. a more coherent *vaqueiro* example cited by Cátedra Tomás 1992: 44-45). St Anthony (the Great) was born in Lisbon, is patron saint of Portugal and died in Padua (see Attwater 1965). He is known for his good works as a fighter for the poor and is therefore common to many folk traditions throughout Europe. He is perhaps best known for finding things, and hence his importance to the village *curiosa* (see also Christian 1972).

46. (p207) The changes referred to earlier in this chapter, and estimates of when these Holy Week festivities ceased, may be related to the Second Vatican Council or Vatican II (1962-65), which was noted for various reforms, not least the introduction of the vernacular (Spanish) in place of Latin for the Mass. Such reforms may have been interpreted by local priests so that a more rigorous approach was taken towards not only the Easter Day festivities but also the consecrations which took place, especially of wood, laurel and bread (which according to orthodox practice should not have occurred on Friday if the villagers' recollections are correct). The breaking of sticks (referred to as *tenebras*, which should be 'tenebrae', for the three days prior

to Easter), is not part of contemporary practice. The bonfire within the cloister of the church in Quintana symbolises the fire lit by flint (surely a pagan rite?) which then is used to light the candles as still practised in Holy Week (pers. comm. Hélène La Rue).

Chapter 14

47. (p208) Quoted from Hardy's General Preface to the 1912 edition of *The Wessex Novels*.

48. (p210) Agricultural practices and related technology of some of these hill and mountain farming communities still found in more remote areas of northern Portugal and in the north-west of Spain, do have a bearing on archaeological research. Examples of this are the use of strip (lynchet) field systems; their cultivation using the Roman ard and oxen; the training of oxen; the use of spelt wheat and the practice of hand picking the heads, and their singeing to burn off the very tough *espigas* (spikes). The training of oxen to the plough and the time taken to do so, and the use of the ard on strip fields has been subject to contemporary research and reconstructions in, for instance, the Butser experiment (P.J. Reynolds, *Iron Age Farm*; London, British Museum, 1979). There is also the frequent finding of deposits of singed grain, which has puzzled researchers. Despite the lapse of centuries, even millennia, these examples of traditional methods might seem to have particular relevance for contemporary research.

49. (p210) Although I have carefully avoided any specific reference to cadastral information that might have economic implications, it may seem that I have infringed on village sensibilities on matters pertaining to their views on religious beliefs. I originally wrote this text assuming a village pseudonym, as has been customary in Mediterranean studies until recently. John Davis (1977) advocated greater openness in the matters of identity and disguise by anthropologists. This initiated some debate at the time (see Loizos 1992). Few studies, of the some hundred in the Mediterranean zone cited by Davis (1977: 163-6), actually named the area, let alone the specific community within which research had been undertaken, and this still largely appertains today for a number of reasons. My decision to identify the village, as I have indicated in the Preface, is because I did not wish to cause offence by not naming it, and because much of what I write, particularly that pertaining to villagers' recall of dispositions during a key episode in village history—the civil war—would be invalid if I did not. I also felt that so much time has passed since my field research, let alone many of the events described, that it would be obvious that this was not a description of contemporary life in Alcedo which, as I hope I have made clear, has changed radically in the intervening years.

50. (p210) It is rather attitudes regarding the afterlife, not mourning and death, which I wish to emphasise here as being distinct from those described for *vaqueiros*. I have argued that there appears to be a separation between the village sphere and that of the church in terms of the old beliefs and orthodoxy (Chapters 12 and 13). In fact, *vaqueiro* attitudes on their *velorios* (wakes) as detailed by Cátedra Tomás (1992: 209-213), seem very familiar, as one would expect, to those of Alcedans and to those described by Pina-Cabral (1986: 219-223) for rural northern Portugal, with the exception of wailing, which would be totally foreign to Alcedans. Freeman refers to the wake in her Castilian village and notes its apparent difference (1970: 91) to its counterpart in north-western Spain. Kenny (1961: 186) observes that in Castile 'wakes were *de rigueur*' at the turn of the century, but that the 'feeling of obligation' to participate had since 'weakened': a sharp contrast to Alcedans where the wake, more than any other social function, is absolutely *de rigueur*. Thomas (1971: 65) refers to late sixteenth century English Protestant views on Catholic rites as being 'thinly disguised mutations of early pagan ceremonies'. Included in this category were holy water, Shrove Tuesday Saturnalia, and wakes which were, in their view, Bacchanalia. Contemporary Aberdonian Protestants, while visiting Highland compatriots (Celts or Gaels), 'noted the peculiarity of the wake, [and] were shocked by the heavy consumption of whisky [at the wake]' (Williams 1990: 127).

Glossary

aldeano member of settled community

bable the central Asturian dialect

barrio sector of village

berza winter cabbage

bichos small animals, insects

brujería witchcraft

buey ox

bula religious dispensation for which a charge was made

capilla chapel

carnecero butcher

casa house or family

centeno rye

chato flat-backed male calf

chorizo type of sausage made from inferior quality beef and pig meat

colono type of cattle bred for beef

comadrona trained midwife

contestar lit. to answer; hold refrain contests

contrarios Republicans

corro circular stone enclosure for chestnuts; circle for traditional dance and repartee

cuadrilla work team

cuadro includes area below the granary where animals are killed

cuñado brother-in-law

curandero, curandera healer

curioso, curiosa healer

decima tithe

derecho Nationalist

empanada a kind of meat pie

escanda spelt wheat (*Triticum spelta L.*)

en casa inheriting the family house

envidia envy

fascistas Nationalists

fila gathering where women spin and knit

fresno ash tree

foros taxes paid to the manors

fuerza force

gaita bagpipe

gorros Republicans

granero granary

hijo/hija en casa son or daughter who inherits the family house

hual dowry or trousseau

jegua semi-wild horse

madrina de boda godmother who assists at a wedding

madrina de pila baptismal godmother

maleficio witchcraft

manda official legal document

matador man expert in killing animals

matanza winter killing of animals for meat

merienda picnic

mohan stone marker used to mark the end of a strip field

monte countryside beyond the village

morcillo type of sausage made from pigmeat, beef and pig's blood

moriscos migratory pastoralists of supposed southern Mediterranean or Moorish descent; *vaqueiros*

mozo, moza young unmarried man or woman

mujer en casa woman who inherits her family house

multa fine

naturaleza nature, the old beliefs

nicho recess or niche for coffin in cemetery

nogal walnut tree

novio, novia boyfriend, girlfriend

padrino de boda godfather who assists at a wedding

padrino de pila baptismal godfather

palacio manor

parroquia parish

pasquinero 'place of satire and lampooning' to the north of Alcedo

perito person skilled in division of properties

prado meadow

refrán traditional refrain

regero irrigated valley bottom meadow

regidor locally elected village official

romería festival

salchicha type of sausage made from prime pork and beef

tambor drum

ternero calf (male or female)

tierra strip field

tontería stupidity

vaqueiro migratory pastoralist

vara unit of measurement shorter than a metre

vigilante village official appointed by local authorities

xaldo member of settled community

Bibliography

Aduengo Caso, J. 1977. *La Religión de los Asturianos*. Gijón: Imprenta-Offset.

Attwater, D. 1965. *The Penguin Book of Saints*. London: Penguin.

Braudel, F. 1992 (1949). *The Mediterranean and the Mediterranean World in the Age of Philip II*. London: Harper Collins.

Beamish, H.V. 1958. *The Hills of Alentejo*. London: Geoffrey Bles.

Borrow, G. 1959 (1843). *The Bible in Spain*. London: Macdonald.

Brenan, G. 1990 (1943). *The Spanish Labyrinth: an Account of the Social and Political Background of the Civil War*. Cambridge: Cambridge University Press.

Campbell, J.K. 1964. *Honour, Family and Patronage*. Oxford: Oxford University Press.

Castañon, L. 1977. *Refranero Asturiano*. Oviedo: Instituto de Estudios Asturianos.

Cátedra Tomás, M. 1992. *This World, Other Worlds*. Chicago: University of Chicago Press.

Censo de la Población de España de 1970. 1973. Tomo IV, 33. Madrid.

Christian, W.A. 1972. *Person and God in a Spanish Valley*. New York: Seminar Press.

Davis, J. 1976. *People of the Mediterranean: an Essay in Comparative Social Anthropology*. London: Routlege & Kegan Paul.

Douglass, W.A. 1969. *Death in Murelaga: Funerary Ritual in a Spanish Basque Village*. Seattle: University of Washington Press.

Estadismo de la Diocesis de Oviedo. 1894. Oviedo.

Fernandez, J.W. 1976. 'La poesía en moción: siendo desplazado por diversiónes, por burlas y por la muerte en el país asturiano'. In C. Lisón Tolosana (ed). *Temas de Antropología Española*. Madrid: Akal.

_____1998. 'Trees of knowledge of self and other in culture: on models for the moral imagination'. In L. Rival (ed). *The Social Life of Trees: Anthropological Perspectives on Tree Symbolism*. Oxford: Berg.

Floriano, A.C. 1960. *Colección Diplomática del Monasterio de Belmonte*. Oviedo.

Freeman, S.T. 1970. *Neighbours: The Social Contract in a Castilian Hamlet*. Chicago: University of Chicago Press.

_____1979. *The Pasiegos: Spaniards in No Man's Land*. Chicago: University of Chicago Press.

Hardy, T. 1985 (1896). *Jude the Obscure*. London: Penguin.

Iturra, R. 1977. 'Strategies in social recruitment: a case of mutual help in rural Galicia.' In M. Stuchlik (ed). *Goals and Behaviour*. Vol. 2. Belfast: The Queen's University Papers in Social Anthropology.

Kenny, M. 1961a. *A Spanish Tapestry: Town and Country in Castile*. London: Cohen & West.

_____1961b. 'Twentieth century Spanish expatriates in Cuba: a sub-culture.' *Anthropological Quarterly* 34.

Lawrence, D.L. 1988. 'Menstrual politics: women and pigs in rural Portugal'. In T. Buckley & A. Gottlieb (eds). *Blood Magic: The Anthropology of Menstruation*. Berkeley: University of California Press.

Lisón Tolosana, C. 1976. 'The ethics of inheritance.' In J.G. Peristiany (ed). *Mediterranean Family Structures*. Cambridge: Cambridge University Press.

_____1979. *Brujería, Estructura Social y Simbolismo en Galicia*. Madrid: Akal.

Loizos, P. 1992. 'User-friendly ethnography?' In J. de Pina-Cabral & J. Campbell (eds). *Europe Observed*. London: Macmillan Press.

MacMaster, N. 1990. *Spanish Fighters: an Oral History of Civil War and Exile*. London: Macmillan.

Madoz, P. 1849. *Diccionario-Geográfico-Estadístico-Histórico de España*. Tomo XIII. Madrid.

Muñiz, O. 1982. *Asturias en la Guerra Civil*. Gijón: Ayalga Ediciones.

Pina-Cabral, J. de. 1986. *Sons of Adam, Daughters of Eve: The Peasant Worldview of Alto Minho*. Oxford: Clarendon Press.

Pitt-Rivers, J. 1976. 'Ritual kinship in the Mediterranean: Spain and the Balkans.' In J.G. Peristiany (ed). *Mediterranean Family Structures*. Cambridge: Cambridge University Press.

Reynolds, P.J. 1979. *Iron Age Farm*. London: British Museum.

Rico-Avello, P.J. 1964. *El Bable y la Medicina*. Oviedo: Instituto de Estudios Asturianos.

Southern, R. 1970. *Medieval Humanism and Other Studies*. Oxford: Basil Blackwell.

Thomas, K. 1971. *Religion and the Decline of Magic*. London: Weidenfeld & Nicholson.

Tumbo de Monasterio de Belmonte. 1604. Oviedo.

Uría Riu, J. 1976. *Los Vaqueiros de Alzada y Otros Estudios (de Casa y Etnografía)*. Oviedo: Biblioteca Popular Asturiana.

Williams, R. 1990. *A Protestant Legacy: Attitudes to Death and Illness Among Older Aberdonians*. Oxford: Clarendon Press.

Index